Maps and Mapping in Children's Literature

Children's Literature, Culture, and Cognition (CLCC)

ISSN 2212-9006

The overarching aim of the CLCC series is to promote new theoretical approaches in the realm of children's literature research on the one hand, and to emphasize a non-Anglo-American focus, bringing in exciting research from other areas, on the other hand. In addition, the new book series will present research from many linguistic areas to an international audience, reinforce interaction between research conducted in many different languages and present high standard research on the basis of secondary sources in a number of languages and based in a variety of research traditions. Basically the series should encourage a cross- and interdisciplinary approach on the basis of literary studies, media studies, comparative studies, reception studies, literacy studies, cognitive studies, and linguistics. The series includes monographs and essay collections which are international in scope and intend to stimulate innovative research with a focus on children's literature (including other media), children's culture and cognition, thus encouraging interdisciplinary and multidisciplinary research in this expanding field.

For an overview of all books published in this series, please see *http://benjamins.com/catalog/clcc*

Volume 7

Maps and Mapping in Children's Literature. Landscapes, seascapes and cityscapes
Edited by Nina Goga and Bettina Kümmerling-Meibauer

Maps and Mapping in Children's Literature

Landscapes, seascapes and cityscapes

Edited by

Nina Goga
Western Norway University of Applied Sciences

Bettina Kümmerling-Meibauer
University of Tübingen

John Benjamins Publishing Company

Amsterdam / Philadelphia

The paper used in this publication meets the minimum requirements of the American National Standard for Information Sciences – Permanence of Paper for Printed Library Materials, ANSI Z39.48-1984.

DOI 10.1075/clcc.7

Cataloging-in-Publication Data available from Library of Congress.

ISBN 978 90 272 0161 4 (HB)
ISBN 978 90 272 6546 3 (E-BOOK)

John Benjamins Publishing Company · https://benjamins.com

Table of contents

Table of figures

Chapter 1

Chapter 2

Chapter 4

Chapter 5

Chapter 7

Chapter 8

Chapter 9

Chapter 10

Chapter 11

Chapter 12

Chapter 13

INTRODUCTION

Maps and mapping in children's literature

Nina Goga and Bettina Kümmerling-Meibauer

Introduction

More than one childhood memory has revolved around the fascination of maps and maps' imaginative power. Hours have been spent turning globes or piecing together puzzles of unknown countries, alone or in the company of friends and family members. More than a few board games, mapping the whole or part of the world, have passed from one generation to another. The original Finnish game *Afrikan tähti* (The Star of Africa, 1951) made Africa known to generations of Nordic boys and girls. Something similar may happen to children's increasing knowledge about the USA, Europe, or Asia when they play board games such as the German award-winning *Zug um Zug* (Ticket to Ride, 2004). One may wonder why this link between children and maps is so tight. John Locke's educational thoughts might be part of the explanation. In *Some Thoughts Concerning Education* (1693), Locke claims that geography is an exercise for both the eyes and the memory (2000: 235). Without geography skills, history would "[…] be very ill retained, and very little useful; but be only a jumble of Matters of Fact, confusedly heaped together without Order or Instruction" (237). Thus maps may be a didactic tool to structure or anchor what happens at different times within a specific field, area, or piece of land. Another explanation of the strong bond between children and maps can be sought in the imaginative power of maps, their invitation to depart without risk to foreign places with strange names. In front of a map children can develop their own thoughts, metaphorically flying away to unknown territories and inventing new stories about them.

No wonder that the history of children's literature is packed with children's books that contain maps displaying where the story takes place. The range of book types and genres is astounding, ranging from picturebooks, children's books, young adult novels and nonfiction books to adventure stories, animal stories, school stories, fantasy novels, detective stories, and travelogues. The maps, which depict itineraries, conquests, landmarks, and changes in cityscapes and landscapes, are narrative in character and prepare the reader for the ensuing story. Maps may

DOI 10.1075/clcc.7.01gog

also intensify a story's suspense or establish an image of an idyll, a crime scene, or a fantasy world. Besides maps that are included as illustrations, there are also children's books where the maps are part of the textual level only. In these books, maps are often described in full detail and propel the story as they are closely connected with the narrative.

A well-known and often cited example is the map in Robert Louis Stevenson's *Treasure Island* (1883), which appears both on the visual and the textual level. The hand-drawn map that is printed on the half-title page gives an overview of the island to which the protagonist and other treasure hunters sail in order to discover the mysterious treasure chest buried by a pirate. On closer inspection, this map only displays the information which is relevant for the treasure hunt, while other cartographic symbols and marks which are typical for islands cannot be found. By skipping back and forth, the reader is able to follow the protagonist's as well as his antagonists' routes on the island, thus spotting where the events take place. Moreover, the text refers to the map several times, describing its appearance as well as showing its impact on the different owners, who are constantly fighting to get hold of the map as it is the most important device revealing clues about the exact place of the hidden treasure.

Considering the significant role of the map in Stevenson's novel, one might assume that maps that visualize the places in a story also exert a great impact on young readers' ability to organize and orient their reading experience. In this regard, maps may even influence children's own experiences of place and space, contributing to their ability to develop mental maps of their real surroundings in general and of fictional places as they are described in literary texts in particular. However, maps cannot be fully understood without acknowledging the cognitive capacity of mapping, that is, the ability to construct a mental picture of a setting, whether it refers to a real or a fictional place (Tally 2013). Moreover, the understanding of maps requires knowledge of geographical and cartographic features. Studies in the realm of geography literacy in general, and map literacy in particular, have shown that this knowledge is not innate but is mainly acquired during the preschool and primary school years in a basic sense (see, for instance, Downs & Liben 1987; Liben & Yekel 1996; Liben & Myers 2007). Moreover, since maps are a specific kind of illustration, they presuppose the ability to discern and interpret the visual signs and cartographic symbols on maps in order to transfer this knowledge to real or fictional places.

All these and other issues have been addressed in such diverse fields as geography studies, developmental psychology, literacy studies, art history, and cultural studies. The interest in investigating the impact of the environment on people's lives initiated a spatial turn, whose roots can be traced in the benchmark studies *Die Großstädte und das Geistesleben* (The Metropolis and Mental Life, 1903/2006) by German sociologist Georg Simmel, 'The Arcades Project' (written 1927–1940, published posthumously in 1999) by Walter Benjamin, and *The City in History* (1961) by American historian Lewis Mumford. While these studies called attention to the interdependencies of the changing cityscapes of the nineteenth and twentieth centuries and the likewise altering cultural and social conditions of their inhabitants, Michel Foucault (1984) and Henri Lefevbre (1974; Engl. 1991) discussed the close connection with ideological matters by emphasizing the triad of knowledge, power, and space. These reflections paved the way for human geography, a specific branch of the social sciences, which examines human interactions with space and place (Tuan 1974, 1977; Massey 2005; Gregory et al. 2009).

Since the breakthrough of the so-called 'New Geography' in the 1980s and 1990s, attention has been increasingly drawn to the fact that maps are not objective, one-to-one descriptions of the physical world but discursive constructs which are subject to historical, political, and social changes (Harley 1988, 2001; Thrower 1996; Pickles 2004). At the same time, scholars highlight the phenomenon of 'mapping' as a mental activity of orientation. The concept of (cognitive) mapping is not particularly new, but was explicitly developed by geographers in the 1970s and was also implicit in the edifice of ideas of sociologists and psychologists at that time. In their benchmark study *Maps in Mind* (1977), Roger Downs and David Stea define basic cognitive mapping as "an abstraction covering those cognitive or mental abilities that enable us to collect, organize, store, recall, and manipulate information about the spatial environment" (6). Downs and Stea emphasize that cognitive mapping requires an active process, where the outcome results from the individual's cognitive capacities. On the same line, Marie-Laure Ryan argues that a cognitive map is "a mental model of *spatial* relations" (2003: 215, emphasis in text). This mental model can represent individual experiences of factually existent land- and cityscapes or imagined land- and cityscapes. Moreover, Ryan avers that cognitive mapping is essential for the depiction of space in narratives. This mapping of space, especially in relation to the narrative representation of place, is also the object of inquiry of literary studies in general and children's literature research in particular. In literary texts, cognitive mapping may function as a geographical substitute for mental, emotional, moral, and physical transformations of fictional characters, as they are positioned in a specific place which impacts on their feelings, thoughts, and behavior.

As for the analysis of maps numerous monographs and articles have sketched the history of maps and cartography in general, with a particular interest in antique maps and the initial stages of modern mapping (Moreland & Bannister 2004) or specific thematic aspects such as cartographic details (Reinhartz 2012). The particular features of fictional maps, characterized as 'maps of the imagination,' are the main emphasis of the studies by Harmon (2004), Turchi (2004), and

Ekman (2013). Another issue tackled in map research is the design of maps, which has changed over the course of the centuries due to the development of cartography and the societal and ideological contexts of maps (Schneider 2004; Jacob 2006; Cosgrove 2008; Wood 2012). Other studies, in turn, have focused on different types of maps, such as propaganda maps (Bar-Gal 2003), humorous maps (Caquard & Dormann 2008), and pictorial maps (Holmes 1992), or the impact of maps on specific genres, such as crime novels (Knight 2012). Several books inspired by geography literacy and cognitive studies explain how maps work (Downs & Stea 1977; MacEachren 1995), while other studies trace new frontiers in cartography theory (Dodge, Kitchin & Perkins 2009) and the impact of maps on philosophical thinking (Camp 2007) and the idea of nation building (Brückner 2006). The study of Monmonier (1996) calls the reader's attention to the possible unreliability of maps, as they do not give a one-to-one representation of the settings described in texts. This is particularly evident in those cases where maps are tightly connected with political and ideological issues (Harley 1992; Wood 1992; Stockhammer 2007; Norcia 2009). Finally, recent studies argue that maps are an important issue in spatial humanities by focusing on the differences between texts and maps as well as discussing the specific properties of maps seen from intermedia studies (Eide 2015).

All these issues could be transferred to the investigation of maps in children's literature, whether it concerns the historical changes in the depiction of maps in children's books from the Enlightenment until the present, the distinction between different types of maps, the cognitive abilities required by the child reader in order to fully grasp the meaning of maps, the multifarious functions of maps in different genres, or the close connection between maps, ideology, and power relations.

This survey indicates that the investigation of maps and mapping in children's literature is a promising topic at the interfaces of children's literature research, picturebook studies, geography literacy, and cognitive studies. However, while the number of general studies on maps and cartography is overwhelming, the number of studies on maps in children's literature is quite modest. The examination of maps in children's books would certainly benefit from the academic investigations of maps and mapping undertaken during the last decades. Therefore, a closer look at these studies gives an idea of the broad range of topics discussed so far and how they might inspire future studies in children's literature research.

Research on maps and mapping in children's literature

Children's literature may depict settings, whether landscapes, cityscapes, or seascapes, without providing a map. Space and place have been thoroughly discussed in general literature studies during the last decades, but only few have fully embarked on the investigation of space and place in children's literature. The important studies by Massey (2005), Carroll (2012), Cutter-Mackenzie, Payne & Reid (2011), Doughty & Thompson (2011), and Cecire et al. (2015) have demonstrated that the representation of places as settings plays a crucial role in children's books. They essentially influence the protagonists' sense of place, which forges their identity and imagination. As a result, several studies focus on the descriptions of the young protagonists' way of moving in space, particularly in cities, which prompt child readers to develop a mental picture of a specific cityscape (Tribunella 2010; Freeman & Tranter 2011; Mallan 2012). In contrast, it is interesting to note that research on children's own reading and writing highlights that these activities may influence their sense of place and foster place-related identities (Charlton et al. 2014; Spring 2016).

Hence, it is evident that the analysis of maps and mapping in children's literature is a promising topic in children's literature research. Not only do maps in children's books offer visual support to verbal descriptions of various places, they may also invite the reader to follow the narrative route of the story, or to imagine passages to unreal worlds. Some maps and some acts of mapping even challenge fixed ways of thinking and engage readers in creative, imaginative, and metaphorical thinking or stimulate them to develop these capacities. Investigating these issues provides new insights into the historical as well as theoretical impact of maps in children's literature. Moreover, by integrating findings from different disciplines, such as children's literature research, picturebook studies, cognitive studies, and geography literacy, the investigation of maps and mapping in children's literature takes an interdisciplinary approach. Although some scholars have already emphasized the significance of maps in children's books, for example Baker (2006), Charlton et al. (2014), Druker (2006, 2012), Goga (2014, 2015), Kümmerling-Meibauer & Meibauer (2013, 2015), Pavlik (2010), and Sundmark (2014a, 2014b), this field is still in its fledgling state.

The most well-explored field when it comes to maps for children and to how children map and understand both maps and their own surroundings is studies in geography literacy and childhood geography (Holloway 2014). Several studies discuss when and how children develop their geography skills and how teachers and books can stimulate this development (Downs & Liben 1987; Lloyd 2000; Wiegand 2006; Rogers 2008; Liben 2009). Other studies are more concerned with the relation between mapping, cognition, and memory (Downs & Stea 1977; Kulhavy et al. 1993; Kitchin & Freundschuh 2000). Related to these issues are those studies that analyze people's individual childhood geographies, where crucial places, such as woods, gardens, and the wilderness, are particularly attractive (Tuan 1974; Nabhan & Trimble 1994; Holloway & Valentine 2000; Honeyman 2001). Along these lines runs another potential strand, namely the desire to discover secret and unknown places. This wish is aligned with the child's craving for independence, which is expressed in the longing to have a place of one's own as well as the aspiration to autonomously conquer the rural and urban space (O'Brien et al. 2000; Uttal & Tan 2000; Ryan 2003). It is only a short step from knowledge about real maps and mapmakers to fictional maps and literary cartographers. Hence, a fourth line of inquiry puts an emphasis on research on literary cartographies and theories about how imaginary worlds are constructed (Mitchell 2011; Wolf 2013; Rossetto 2014; Tally 2011, 2014).

Since maps are a specific kind of illustration, their analysis is closely connected with picture theory and picturebook research. The study of picturebooks has a long and rich tradition within the field of children's literature research (see, for instance, Nodelman, 1988; Lewis 2001; Nikolajeva & Scott 2001; Painter, Martin & Unsworth 2013). Although these studies do not deal explicitly with maps, their findings are relevant to the investigation of maps in children's books. Since maps are often printed in the endpapers, before the start of the main story, the studies of paratextual elements in picturebooks are especially worth mentioning. Moreover, maps present a particular kind of visual narration, a topic often discussed by picturebook scholars (for an overview, see Kümmerling-Meibauer 2014). Another important research field that overlaps with the investigation of maps is studies on fantasy, since fantasy novels are often provided with maps (Mendlesohn 2008; Immel & Briggs 2009). These studies might enhance the investigation of maps, since they shed light on the specific demands of fantasy and how this genre affects the understanding of maps that depict a fantasy world. As already mentioned, the depiction and use of maps may also be related to questions of national and ideological power; hence studies on ideological (including gender issues) and national topics in children's literature are relevant when analyzing maps in children's literature (Phillips 1997; Charlton et al. 2014).

So far we do not have any detailed studies on the history and development of maps in children's books. Most of what is available is spread out in journal articles and book chapters. Three particular tendencies can be distinguished. First, scholars pay tribute to authors who have made extensive use of maps, for instance, Robert Louis Stevenson (Phillips 1997), Tove Jansson (Druker 2006; Sundmark 2014b), and J. R. R. Tolkien (Sundmark 2014a). Second, and related to the first tendency, researchers have paid special attention to specific genres which often include maps, in particular fantasy (Baker 2006; Immel & Briggs 2009) and crime stories for children (Goga 2014, 2015). Finally, another tendency is recognizable in studies dealing with the possible cognitive and aesthetic functions and purposes of maps in children's books (Pavlik 2010; Druker 2012; Kümmerling-Meibauer & Meibauer 2013, 2015).

Aims and structure of the present volume

In view of these considerations, the cognitive, cultural, and ideological shifts that have governed the changes in and significance of maps and mapping in children's literature since the end of the eighteenth century are a major concern of the various contributions to the present volume. With this essay collection, the editors intend to embed children's literature in a broader field of literary and cultural studies, thus situating children's literature research within a general context of literary theory. Moreover, the chapters in this volume pursue a comparative approach as they represent, within and across the different sections, a wide spectrum of diverse genres and national children's literatures, whose investigation draws on different theoretical frameworks as well. The theoretical and methodological approaches range from geography and developmental psychology, maps and geography literacy, ecocriticism, historical contextualizations with both new historicist and political-historical leanings, and intermediality with an emphasis on sound, to materialist cartographies, social anthropology and cultural studies, island studies, genre studies, and nonsense geography. The contributions also engage with a variety of literary materials, both fictional and nonfictional, from a broad spectrum of languages and eras. Hence, the chapters not only deal with British and American children's literature, but also introduce Canadian, Danish, German, Italian, Norwegian, and Russian children's literature. With this selection the editors hope to inspire an international and interdisciplinary academic discussion on the importance of maps and mapping in children's literature, which has thus far been considerably underestimated. It is therefore one of the aims of this volume to partially close this research gap.

This volume is structured in three sections. The first section explores, with an emphasis on cognition, how maps and mapping in children's literature contribute to children's growing capacity to orient themselves in different places. The second section focuses on the depiction of real cityscapes, such as Berlin, Milan, New York, and Prague, in picturebooks and children's novels. The third section sheds light on maps that depict fictional seascapes and landscapes in children's literature, and highlights two essential seminal aspects: the impact of genre and the significance of underlying ideological issues on the understanding of maps and related spaces.

Looking from a cognitive-development perspective, Lynn Liben considers how children's cognitive concepts and skills influence the ways children interpret and learn from and about maps in children's literature. Liben also sets forth suggestions for empirical research on how maps in children's literature are used and how they influence cognitive development in general and map literacy in particular.

Nikola von Merveldt looks at the place and meaning of maps in the late eighteenth-century German pedagogic reform movement of philanthropism, in particular those found in Joachim Heinrich Campe's geographical writings. Taking their cue from John Locke and advocating a realist reform of the humanist schooling tradition, philanthropists declared geography to be the foundational elementary science upon which all other knowledge should be built. More importantly, geography was understood as the referential framework to educate children to become active citizens in the "real world" instead of absent-minded scholars living in their own worlds.

Janet Grafton presents an ecocritical examination of how personal geography and physical geography are intertwined and informed by each other. A thorough investigation of two early twentieth century novels, Dorothy Canfield Fisher's *Understood Betsy* (1919) and Lucy Maud Montgomery's *Jane of Lantern Hill* (1937), reveals how the old-fashioned worlds depicted in these works convey a strong sense of place that roots the characters with an intrinsic cartography and helps them to develop their geographic literacy.

The cognitive and narrative functions of metaphorical maps in picturebooks are discussed in Bettina Kümmerling-Meibauer and Jörg Meibauer's chapter. In contrast to maps that present real or fictional city- and landscapes, metaphorical maps are used to visualize abstract concepts. By a thorough analysis of metaphorical maps in several picturebooks, the authors investigate the cognitive and narrative impact of this specific map category on the understanding of the picturebook story.

Since the appearance of Erich Kästner's detective story *Emil and the Detectives* (1929), the city of Berlin has been set as an urban topos in which children navigate in an independent and self-confident way. Starting from this observation, Corina Löwe focuses on Andreas Steinhöfel's *Rico, Oskar und die Tieferschatten* (The Spaghetti Detectives, 2008), which intertextually refers to Kästner's novel. Although the novel does not provide a map – similar to Kästner's model – readers are able to follow the protagonist's route. In this regard, Steinhöfel's book can be interpreted as a general representation of children's growing mapping capacities, which are mirrored in the main protagonist's increasing abilities to independently move in an urban space.

In the juxtaposition of two young adult novels, *Nick and Norah's Infinite Playlist* (2006) and *Dash and Lily's Book of Dares* (2010), co-written by Rachel Cohn and David Levithan, Anna Katrina Gutierrez analyzes the visual and verbal maps of New York City. The two novels evoke an abundance of scripts and schemas related to adolescent romance, adventure, and coming-of-age. In these books New York is a storyworld enriched by intertextual links with music, poetry, and literature, grounded on a map that exists outside of the narrative but is built from the blend of disparate New York schemas: those called upon by the focalizing characters and those held in the mind of the reader.

Anna Juan Cantavella elaborates on the importance given to travel and its role in the construction of personal identity in the picturebooks of Peter Sís. Her chapter shows that Sís' two picturebooks, *The Three Golden Keys* (1994) and *Madlenka* (2002), can be characterized as fragments of Sís' personal cartography. What both picturebooks have in common is the predominance of the act of walking, which is crucial for the arrangement and understanding of the maps displayed throughout the picturebook stories.

Based on a close reading of Bruno Munari's *Nella nebbia di Milano* (The Circus in the Mist, 1968), Marnie Campagnaro examines how this picturebook pays special attention to children's capacity to organize their reading experience by focusing on visual as well as textual clues. Campagnaro shows that Munari appeals to the child's senses and activity by combining visual impressions with tactile experiences on the one hand, and by stimulating the child's visual mapping on the other.

Olga Holownia explores the ways in which geography functions (or fails to function) in nonsense verse, prose, and illustration, and more specifically, in the representations of seascapes. The key purpose of maps, which conventionally help the readers envision and navigate a fictional world, tends not to be fulfilled in literary nonsense, even when maps or detailed descriptions are provided. This chapter outlines selected common features of nonsense geography and shows how the nonsense game has since been followed in our own time, using Walter Moers' *The 13 ½ Lives of Captain Bluebear* (2001) as a popular example drawn from contemporary literature.

Maria Nikolajeva and Liz Taylor discuss three children's novels set on islands: *Kensuke's Kingdom* (1999) by Michael Morpurgo, *Gullstruck Island* (2009) by Frances Hardinge, and *Midwinterblood* (2011) by Marcus Sedgwick, all of which operate within ambiguous fictional worlds and use ambiguous narrative perspective. The two authors argue that rather than being an embellishment appearing outside the narrative, the maps are incorporated into it in a subtle way, which also creates a fascinating tension between the visual map and its verbal ekphrasis.

Olga Mikhaylova investigates the artistic functions of the visual and verbal depiction of the fantasy world invented by the child protagonists in Lev Kassil's novel *Schwambrania* (1933) against the background of the Soviet state's interest in geography and cartography. The author demonstrates that the increasing complexity of the two maps parallels the main protagonists' emotional and cognitive development on the one hand, and the changing political situation in the Soviet Union on the other. By considering the graphic and linguistic components of these maps and their description in the text, this chapter is able to reconstruct the political and cultural context relevant to Kassil's book.

Björn Sundmark argues that there is widespread critical consensus that fantasy as a genre rather than as a mode of writing is largely the result of Tolkien's work, and that his maps are part and parcel of this generic construction. Tolkien's Middle Earth is a fully realized and believable secondary world, and the published maps in *The Hobbit* and *The Lord of the Rings* contribute to this effect in significant ways. Consequently, Sundmark investigates the tight connection between the different maps of Middle Earth and the novels' descriptions of places and characters. The concluding section of this chapter discusses the changing role of the Tolkienian fantasy map as it is moved from the printed page to the screen, by looking at examples from *The Lord of the Rings* films (2001–2003) and the use of maps in the TV-series *Game of Thrones* (2011ff.).

The final chapter, by Nina Goga, investigates the connection between the maps and the protagonist's formative growth in the Norwegian fantasy novel *Landet under isen* (The Land beneath the Ice, 2009) by Lars Mæhle. The novel consists of a mix of fantasy and crime story and this mix is particularly explicit in the two maps presented on the endpapers of the book: a city map and a larger secondary world map. Goga argues that the maps not only serve as a reference guide to the storyline and place, but also as visual expressions of the faith and doubt-directed identity development of the protagonist. The chapter explores how the maps in *The Land beneath the Ice* reflect and strengthen the bodily perception as well as the personal, inner struggles of the protagonist.

With the present volume the editors hope to offer the reader a broad range of new approaches to and new perspectives into the study of maps and mapping in children's literature. The diverse issues touched upon in the deliberate selection of chapters allow glimpses at literary traditions and the intricate relationships between maps and children's books that are very often overlooked. In this regard, the chapters in this volume aim to show that the investigation of maps and cognitive mapping is a subject which merits consideration among scholars working in the fields of children's literature, cognitive studies, and (geography) literacy.

References

Baker, Deirdre F. 2006. What we found on our journey through fantasy land. *Children's Literature in Education* 3: 237–251. doi: 10.1007/s10583-006-9009-1

Bar-Gal, Yoram. 2003. The blue box and JNF propaganda maps, 1930–1947. *Israel Studies* 8.1: 1–19. doi: 10.2979/ISR.2003.8.1.1

Benjamin, Walter. 1999. *The Arcades Project*, ed. by Rolf Tiedemann, transl. by Howard Eiland & Kevin McLaughlin. Cambridge MA: Belknap Press of Harvard University Press (written 1927–1940, posthumously published).

Brückner, Martin. 2006. *The Geographic Revolution in Early America. Maps, Literacy, and National Identity*. Chapel Hill NC: University of North Carolina Press.

Camp, Elizabeth. 2007. Thinking with maps. *Philosophical Perspectives* 21: 145–182. doi: 10.1111/j.1520-8583.2007.00124.x

Caquard, Sébastian & Dormann, Claire. 2008. Humorous maps: Exploration of an alternative cartography. *Cartography & Geographic Information Science* 35.1: 51–64. doi: 10.1559/152304008783475670

Carroll, Jane S. 2012. *Landscape in Children's Literature*. New York NY: Routledge.

Cecire, Maria Sachiko, Field, Hannah, Finn, Kavita Mudan & Roy, Malini (eds). 2015. *Space and Place in Children's Literature, 1789 to the Present*. Farnham, Surrey: Ashgate.

Charlton, Emma, Hodges, Cliff, Pointin, Pam, Nikolajeva, Maria, Spring, Erin, Taylor, Liz & Wyse, Dominic. 2014. My Place: Exploring Children's Place-Related Identities through Reading and Writing. *International Journal of Primary, Elementary and Early Years Education* 42: 154–170.

Cosgrove, Denis. 2008. *Geography and Vision. Seeing, Imagining, and Representing the World*. London: Tauris.

Cutter-Mackenzie, Amy, Payne, Philip G. & Reid, Alan (eds). 2011. *Experiencing Environment and Place through Children's Literature*. New York NY: Routledge.

Dodge, Martin, Kitchin, Rob & Perkins, Chris. 2009. *Rethinking Maps: New Frontiers in Cartographic Theory*. New York NY: Routledge.

Doughty, Teri & Thompson, Dawn. 2011. *Knowing Their Place? Identity and Space in Children's Literature*. Newcastle-upon-Tyne: Cambridge Scholars.

Downs, Roger M. & Liben, Lynn S. 1987. Children's understanding of maps. In *Cognitive Processes and Spatial Orientation in Animal and Man*, Vol. 2: *Neurophysiology and Developmental Aspects*, Paul Ellen & Catherine Thinus-Blanc (eds), 202–219. Dordrecht: Martinus Nijhoff.

Downs, Roger M. & Stea, David. 1977. *Maps in Mind*. New York NY: Harper & Row.

Druker, Elina. 2006. Picture book as conceptual space: Spatial transformation in Tove Jansson's book about Moomin, Mymble and Little My. In *From Colonialism to the Contemporary: Intertextual Transformation in World Children's and Youth Literature*, Lance Weldy (ed), 114–125. Newcastle-upon-Tyne: Cambridge Scholars.

Druker, Elina. 2012. Mapping absence: Maps as meta-artistic discourse in literature. In *Visualizing Law and Authority: Essays on Legal Aesthetics*, Leif Dahlberg (ed.), 114–125. New York NY: De Gruyter. doi: 10.1515/9783110285444.114

Eide, Øyvind. 2015. *Media Boundaries and Conceptual Modelling: Between Texts and Maps*. Basingstoke: Palgrave Macmillan.

Ekman, Stefan. 2013. *Here Be Dragons: Exploring Fantasy Maps and Settings*. Middletown CT: Wesleyan.

Foucault, Michel. 1984. Space, knowledge, and power. In *The Foucault Reader*, Paul Rabinow (ed.), 239–255. New York NY: Pantheon.

Freeman, Claire & Tranter, Paul. 2011. *Children and Their Urban Environment: Changing Worlds*. London: Earthscan.

Goga, Nina. 2014. Kart og krim. Litterære kart og steders betydning i krimserier for barn. *Tidskrift för Litteraturvetenskap* 2: 69–82.

Goga, Nina. 2015. *Kart i barnelitteraturen*. Kristiansand: Portal Akademisk.

Gregory, Derek, Johnston, Ron, Pratt, Geraldine, Watts, Michael & Whatmore, Sarah (eds). 2009. *The Dictionary of Human Geography*, 5th edn. Oxford: Wiley-Blackwell.

Harley, John Brian. 1988. Maps, knowledge, and power. In *Iconography of Landscape: Essays on the Symbolic Representation, Design and Use of Past Environments*, Denis Cosgrove & Stephen Daniels (eds), 277–312. Cambridge: CUP.

Harley, John Brian. 1992. Deconstructing the map. Reprinted in *Writing Worlds: Discourse, Text and Metaphor in the Representation of Landscape*, Trevor Barnes & James Duncan (eds), 231–247. London: Routledge (first published 1989).

Harley, John Brian. 2001. *The New Nature of Maps*. Baltimore MD: The Johns Hopkins University Press.

Harmon, Katherine. 2004. *You Are Here. Personal Geographies and Other Maps of the Imagination*. New York NY: Princeton Architectural Press.

Holloway, Sarah. 2014. Changing children's geographies. *Children's Geographies* 12.4: 377–392. doi: 10.1080/14733285.2014.930414

Holloway, Sarah L. & Valentine, Gill (eds) 2000. *Children's Geographies. Playing, Living, Learning*. London: Routledge.

Holmes, Nigel. 1992. *Pictorial Maps*. London: The Herbert Press.

Honeyman, Susan. 2001. Childhood bound: In gardens, maps, and pictures. *Mosaic: A Journal for the Interdisciplinary Study of Literature* 34(2): [117]–132.

Immel, Andrea, Knoepflmacher, U.C. & Briggs, Julia. 2009. Fantasy's alternative geography for children. In *The Cambridge Companion to Children's Literature*, Matthew O. Grenby & Andrea Immel (eds), 226–241. Cambridge: CUP. doi: 10.1017/CCOL9780521868198.014

Jacob, Christian. 2006. *The Sovereign Map. Theoretical Approaches in Cartography throughout History*. Chicago IL: University of Chicago Press.

Kitchin, Rob, & Freundschuh, Scott. 2000. Cognitive mapping. In *Cognitive Mapping. Past, Present and Future*, Rob Kitchin & Scott Freundschuh (eds), 1–8. New York NY: Routledge.

Knight, Stephen. 2012. *The Mysteries of the Cities. Urban Crime Fiction in the Nineteenth Century*. Jefferson NC: McFarland.

Kulhavy, Raymond, Stock, William A., Verdi, Michael P., Rittschof, Kent A. & Savenye, Wilhelmina. 1993. Why maps improve memory for text: The influence of structural information on working memory operations. *European Journal of Cognitive Psychology* 5: 375–292. doi: 10.1080/09541449308520126

Kümmerling-Meibauer, Bettina 2014. Picturebooks between representation and narration. In *Picturebooks. Representation and Narration*, Bettina Kümmerling-Meibauer (ed.), 1–15. New York NY: Routledge.

Kümmerling-Meibauer, Bettina & Meibauer, Jörg. 2013. Towards a cognitive theory of picturebooks. *International Research in Children's Literature* 6: 143–160. doi: 10.3366/ircl.2013.0095

Kümmerling-Meibauer, Bettina & Meibauer, Jörg. 2015. Maps in picturebooks: Cognitive status and narrative functions. *Nordic Journal of ChildLit Aesthetics* 6. Retrieved from doi: 10.3402/blft.v6.26970

Lefevbre, Heni. 1991. *The Production of Space*. Oxford: Blackwell (first French publ. in 1974).

Lewis, David. 2001. *Reading Contemporary Picturebooks. Picturing Text*. London: RoutledgeFalmer.

Liben, Lynn S. 2009. The road to understanding maps. *Current Directions in PsychologicalScience* 18: 310–315. doi: 10.1111/j.1467-8721.2009.01658.x

Liben, Lynn S. & Myers, Lauren J. 2007. Developmental changes in children's understanding of maps. What, when, and how? In *The Emerging Spatial Mind*, Jodie M. Plumert & Spencer, John P. (eds), 193–218. Oxford: OUP. doi: 10.1093/acprof:oso/9780195189223.003.0009

Liben, Lynn S. & Yekel, Candice A. 1996. Preschoolers' understanding of plan and oblique maps: The role of geometric and representational correspondence. *Child Development* 67: 2780–296. doi: 10.2307/1131752

Lloyd, Robert. 2000. Understanding and learning maps. In *Cognitive Mapping*, Rob Kitchin & Scott Freundschuh (eds), 84–107. New York NY: Routledge.

Locke, John 2000. *Some Thoughts Concerning Education*. Oxford: Clarendon (first published 1693).

MacEachren, Alan. 1995. *How Maps Work. Representation, Visualization, and Design*. New York NY: Guildford Press.

* Mallan, Kerry. 2012. Strolling through the (post)modern city: Modes of being a flâneur in picture books. *The Lion and the Unicorn* 36: 56–74. doi: 10.1353/uni.2012.0002

Massey, Doreen. 2005. *For Space*. London: Sage.

Mendlesohn, Farah. 2008. *Rhetorics of Fantasy*. Middletown CT: Wesleyan.

Mitchell, Peta. 2011. *Cartographic Strategies of Postmodernity. The Figure of the Map in Contemporary Theory and Fiction*. New York NY: Routledge.

Monmonier, Mark. 1996. *How to Lie with Maps*. Chicago IL: University of Chicago Press. doi: 10.7208/chicago/9780226029009.001.0001

Moreland, Carl & Bannister, David. 2004. *Antique Maps*. London: Phaidon.

Mumford, Lewis. 1961. *The City in History*. New York NY: Harcourt, Brace & World.

Nabhan, Gary & Trimble, Stephen (eds). 1994. *The Geography of Childhood*. Boston MA: Beacon.

Nikolajeva, Maria & Scott, Carole. 2001. *How Picturebooks Work*. New York NY: Garland.

Nodelman, Perry. 1988. *Words about Pictures*. Athens GA: University of Georgia Press.

Norcia, Megan A. 2009. Puzzling empire: Early puzzles and dissected maps as imperial heuristics. *Children's Literature* 37: 1–32. doi: 10.1353/chl.0.0807

O'Brien, Margaret, Jones, Deborah, Sloan, David & Rustin, Michael. 2000. Children's independent spatial mobility in the urban public realm. *Childhood: A Global Journal of Child Research* 7(3): 257–277. doi: 10.1177/0907568200007003002

Painter, Clare, Martin, J. R. & Unsworth, Len. 2013. *Reading Visual Narratives. Image Analysis of Children's Picture Books*. Sheffield: Equinox.

Pavlik, Anthony. 2010. A special kind of reading game: Maps in children's literature. *International Research in Children's Literature* 3(1): 28–43. doi: 10.3366/ircl.2010.0004

Phillips, Richard. 1997. *Mapping Men & Empire. A Geography of Adventure*. London: Routledge.

Pickles, John. 2004. *A History of Spaces. Cartographic Reason, Mapping and the Geo-Coded World*. London: Routledge.

Reinhartz, Dennis. 2012. *The Art of the Map*. New York NY: Sterling.

Rogers, Linda K. 2008. *Shaped by the Standards. Geographic Literacy through Children's Literature*. Westport CT: Teacher Ideas Press.

Rossetto, Tania. 2014. Theorizing maps with literature. *Progress in Human Geography* 38(4): 513–530. doi: 10.1177/0309132513510587

Ryan, Marie-Laure. 2003. Cognitive maps and the construction of narrative space. In *Narrative Theory and the Cognitive Sciences*, David Herman (ed.), 214–241. Stanford CA: CSLI.

Schneider, Ute. 2004. *Die Macht der Karten. Eine Geschichte der Kartographie vom Mittelalter bis heute*. Darmstadt: Primus.

Simmel, Georg. 2006. *Die Großstädte und das Geistesleben*. Frankfurt: Suhrkamp (first published 1903).

Spring, Erin. 2016. Place and identity in young adult fiction. In *Identities and Subjectivities*, Vol. 4: *Geographies of Children and Young People*, Nancy Worth, Claire Dwyer & Tracy Skelton (eds), 1–23. Singapore: Springer.

Stockhammer, Rudolf. 2007. *Die Kartierung der Erde: Macht und Lust in Karten und Literatur*. Munich: W. Fink.

Sundmark, Björn. 2014a. 'Dragons be here': Teaching children's literature and creative writing with the help of maps. In *Thinking through Children's Literature in the Classroom*, Agustín Reyes-Torres, Luis S. Villacañas-de-Castro & Betlem Soler-Pardo (eds), 64–78. Newcastle-upon-Tyne: Cambridge Scholars.

Sundmark, Björn. 2014b. "A serious game": Mapping Moominland. *The Lion and the Unicorn* 38: 162–181. doi: 10.1353/uni.2014.0022

Tally, Robert T. Jr. 2011. *Geocritical Explorations: Space, Place, and Mapping in Literary and Cultural Studies*. Basingstoke: Palgrave Macmillan. doi: 10.1057/9780230337930

Tally, Robert T., Jr. 2013. *Spatiality: The New Critical Idiom*. New York NY: Routledge.

Tally, Robert T., Jr. (ed). 2014. *Literary Cartographies: Spatiality, Representation, and Narrative*. Basingstoke: Palgrave Macmillan.

Thrower, Norman J.W. 1996. *Maps and Civilization. Cartography in Culture and Society*. Chicago IL: University of Chicago Press.

Tribunella, Eric L. 2010. Children's Literature and the Child *Flâneur*. *Children's Literature* (38): 64–91.

Tuan, Yi-Fu. 1974. *Topophilia. A Study of Environmental Perception, Attitudes, and Values*. Upper Saddle River NJ: Prentice-Hall.

Tuan, Yi-Fu. 1977. *Space and Place: The Perspective of Experience*. Minneapolis MN: University of Minnesota Press.

Turchi, Peter. 2004. *Maps of the Imagination: The Writer as Cartographer*. San Antonio TX: Trinity University Press.

Uttal, David & Tan, Lisa. 2000. Cognitive mapping in childhood. In *Cognitive Mapping. Past, Present and Future*, Rob Kitchin & Scott Freundschuh (eds), 147–165. New York NY: Routledge.

Wiegand, Patrick. 2006. *Learning and Teaching with Maps*. New York NY: Routledge. doi: 10.4324/9780203477793

Wolf, Mark J. P. 2013. *Building Imaginary Worlds: The Theory and History of Subcreation*. New York NY: Routledge.

Wood, Denis. 1992. *The Power of Maps*. New York NY: Guildford.

Wood, Denis. 2012. The anthropology of cartography. In *Mapping Cultures*, Les Roberts (ed.), 280–303. Basingstoke: Palgrave Macmillan. doi: 10.1057/9781137025050.0022

PART 1

About mapping

Learning to orientate oneself

CHAPTER 1

A cognitive-developmental perspective on maps in children's literature

Lynn S. Liben

Maps in children's literature vary in many ways, for example, by representing real or imagined places; employing abstract or pictorial symbols; and depicting spaces at differing scales, orientations, and viewing angles. Although authors and illustrators may presume that children readily "see through" such maps to understand their underlying meaning, cognitive-developmental research suggests otherwise. This chapter reviews children's developing representational and spatial concepts and their relevance for map understanding; contrasts perspectives of geography, literature, and cognitive development; and urges that future researchers study explicitly how maps are used during reading, and how these varied uses influence the cognitive and emotional consequences of the reading experience.

The topic of this volume – maps in children's literature – may be approached from many different perspectives. A cartographer might focus on how the impact of such maps varies with differing map qualities such as scale and symbol abstraction. An expert in children's literature might focus on ways that these maps clarify, embellish, or contextualize the narrative. A scholar approaching the topic from the disciplinary tradition of developmental psychology – my scholarly heritage – might focus on the children who encounter these maps. This, indeed, is my tack. The thesis I develop is that children's own cognitive qualities have a critical impact on what children take from their encounters with maps.

In developing this thesis, I draw most heavily from two strands of my prior work. The first is already implied by my having labeled my scholarly heritage as developmental psychology. From this field I draw from work in cognitive development in general and from specialized work on children's developing understanding of spatial concepts and representations in particular (see Liben 1981, 1982, 1999, 2003). The second strand is situated within the discipline of geography. My expertise in geography grew initially via collaborative research on children's map understanding with geographer Roger Downs (for example, Downs & Liben 1987,

DOI 10.1075/clcc.7.02lib

1991; Liben & Downs 1989, 1993) and then by engagement with the discipline more generally (e.g., course work in cartography; participation in geography conferences and organizations).

In the context of discussing expertise, is also important to acknowledge that although I have conducted some research on children's understanding of picture-books (see Szechter & Liben 2004), I am not an expert in children's literature *per se*. Thus, the illustrations I later draw from this domain are intended to offer examples of work in this field rather than to offer characterizations of how maps are used in children's literature as a whole. A more overarching review may be found in the introduction to this volume and to the sources cited within it.

This chapter is organized into three sections. In *Foundations of map understanding* I identify key qualities of maps, highlight childhood progressions in foundational representational and spatial concepts, and review empirical work linking these progressions to map understanding. In *Map foci across perspectives* I illustrate ways that maps in children's books have been conceptualized within geography and children's literature, and consider how these relate to empirical work conducted by developmental psychologists. In *A cognitive-developmental perspective: Where next?* I briefly note contributions of past cognitive-developmental research and then offer suggestions for future interdisciplinary empirical work.

Foundations of map understanding

Developmental psychologists vary with respect to where they look for explanations of cognitive outcomes. Some scholars focus on biological variables such as genetic endowments; others focus on environmental variables such as educational resources in homes or schools. My 'constructivist' approach encompasses both environmental and child variables insofar as I hold that "what a child experiences, understands, and uses from the environment is as much determined by the child's active, self-directive processing as it is by what is 'in' the environment itself" (Liben 2014: 275). Applying this approach to children's understanding of maps requires addressing both what is contained in maps and what children bring to those maps. Thus, in this section I define maps, highlight key cartographic processes, describe progressions in children's relevant underlying representational and spatial concepts, and sample past empirical work linking these concepts to children's understanding (or misunderstanding) of maps.

Geography: Cartographic foundations

Although perhaps hackneyed, a useful way to clarify any topic is to consult a dictionary. The definition of "map" in my 1997 print copy of the *Unabridged Random House Dictionary* reads: "a representation, usually on a flat surface, as of the features of an area of the earth or a portion of the heavens, showing them in their respective forms, sizes, and relationships according to some convention of representation" (Flexner & Hauck 1997: 1173). A contemporary online search for "map definition" returns the identical definition from *Dictionary.com* and similar ones. Almost all contain the concept of representation, name at least one illustrative place, and mention spatial properties such as location.

A second helpful way to clarify a construct is to establish what it is not. Maps are *not* re-presentations of physical spaces (where "re-presentation" is used in the sense of presenting again). Instructive is a passage from Lewis Carroll's *Sylvie and Bruno Concluded* (1893):

> 'What do you consider the *largest* map that would be really useful?'
> 'About six inches to the mile.'
> 'Only *six inches!*' exclaimed Mein Herr. 'We very soon got to six *yards* to the mile. Then we tried a *hundred* yards to the mile. And then came the grandest idea of all! We actually made a map of the country on the scale of *a mile to the mile*!'
> 'Have you used it much?' I enquired.
> 'It has never been spread out, yet,' said Mein Herr: 'the farmers objected; they said it would cover the whole country and shut out the sunlight! So now we use the country itself as its own map, and I assure you it does nearly as well.'
> (Carroll 1939: 169)

The exchange makes obvious the impossibility and, indeed, the vacuity of attempting to produce a map that mimics the cognitively undigested physical world. Maps are valuable precisely because even as they offer information about the world, they also offer something different from what is provided by the world as is.

As discussed in more detail elsewhere (see Dodge, Kitchin & Perkins 2011; Downs 1981, 1985; Down & Liben 1988; Liben 2001; Liben & Downs 1989), cartographers use symbolic and spatial tools to serve particular communicative or rhetorical purposes: "On the one hand, [maps] are powerful instruments for preserving and recording old truths: They are data stores par excellence. On the other hand, maps are a device for the invention or discovery of new truths" (Downs 1981: 158). The "new truths" may be discovered and intentionally communicated by the cartographer or they may be independently generated by the map reader. But they are neither identical to old truths, nor are they "inaccurate" simply because they do not reproduce (or replicate) the experiences and inferences that emerge from direct interactions with the referent space. "Above all else [...] a map is a shared exercise in communication" (326).

Designing a map invariably involves first, selecting representational content and form – the substance that is mapped (for instance, airports, enemy encampments, vineyards, roads, mountains) and the manner in which it is symbolized (with abstract or pictorial symbols); and second, selecting spatial qualities – the way that the referent space is shown on the two-dimensional surface (thereby creating the "base map" on which the content is displayed). More specifically, each map requires decisions about the three spatial qualities depicted in Figure 1.

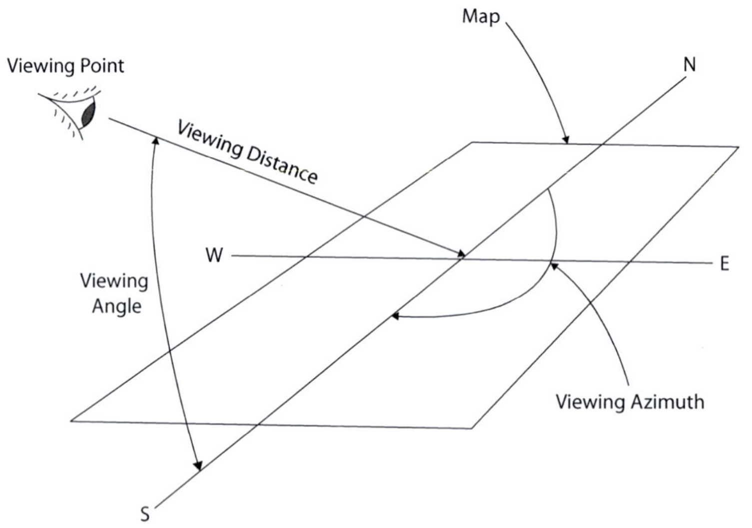

Figure 1. Three elements of the cartographic vantage point from Downs (1981) and reproduced with permission

The first, viewing distance, establishes scale: looking at an environment from far away allows one to see a large area but in little detail (a small-scale map); zooming in reveals detail, but covers only a small area (a large-scale map). One cannot create a very large-scale map of a very large environment unless – as in the Lewis Carroll passage quoted earlier – one is willing to replace a pocket-size map with a country-sized map. The second, viewing azimuth, refers to the direction from which the referent space is viewed. The contemporary default places north at the top, but conventions vary over time and place. During the Middle Ages, for example, European cartographers commonly oriented maps of the Mediterranean region so that east and therefore Jerusalem were at the top of the page. The third, viewing angle, refers to the vertical dimension from which the referent space is depicted. A 90° angle is straight-down, producing plan-view (orthogonal, vertical, or nadir) maps. A 30° angle is tilted down, creating oblique-perspective maps

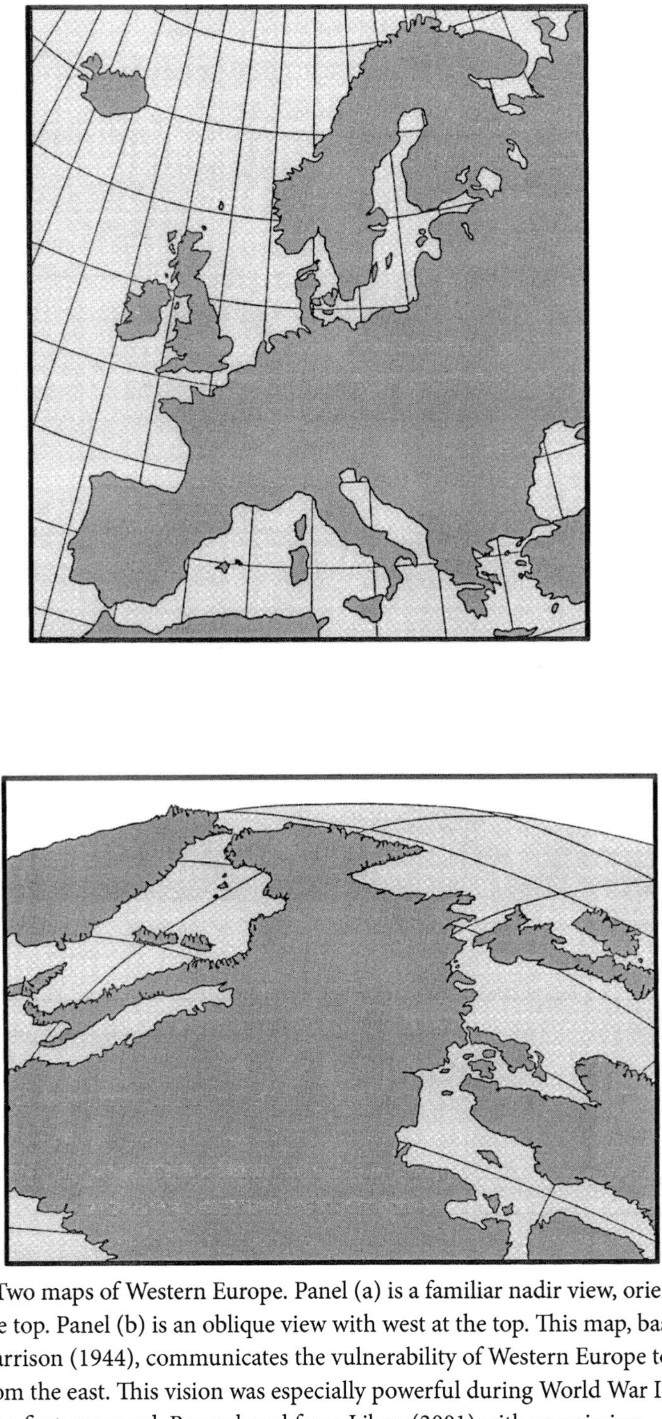

Figure 2. Two maps of Western Europe. Panel (a) is a familiar nadir view, oriented with north at the top. Panel (b) is an oblique view with west at the top. This map, based on Richard Harrison (1944), communicates the vulnerability of Western Europe to armies arriving from the east. This vision was especially powerful during World War II when the original map first appeared. Reproduced from Liben (2001) with permission.

like those often found in city tourist maps depicting landmarks with perspective drawings. Figure 2 illustrates the impact of varying these spatial qualities in small-scale maps.

In short, a map is not simply a convenient, portable, flattened and singular miniaturization of some portion of real or imagined space, any more than a book is a convenient, portable, linguistic, and singular rendition of some portion of lived or imagined experience. Maps are representations that – like prose – can communicate the creator's (cartographer's or author's) visions, and that – again, like prose – can provoke readers to see new visions, ask new questions, and expand or change previously held beliefs. Importantly, just as one must have some facility with English to understand and extrapolate from English prose, so too one must have some facility with cartography to understand and extrapolate from maps. Children may be limited in what they gain from encountering a map in a book not only because they have not yet accumulated previous experience with maps in particular, but also because they have not yet mastered foundational cognitive concepts and skills in general.

Cognitive development: Representational foundations

In this and the following section I discuss early shortcomings and later progressions in two cognitive-developmental domains relevant to maps – representation and space. Before beginning, however, it is important to state explicitly that the arguments and evidence I present are not intended to imply that young children are unable to understand anything at all about any kind of map, nor are they meant to suggest that children are entirely devoid of foundational concepts needed for map understanding. I sound this cautionary note because earlier writings on children's map understanding have sometimes been falsely dichotomized into "late and difficult" or "early and easy" camps. For example, early writings in which we (Liben & Downs 1989) discussed confusions in three- to six-year-old children's map understanding were mistakenly taken to be arguments for postponing early map exposure and education (Blaut 1997a, 1997b; see Downs & Liben 1997). At the other extreme, very young children's successes on spatial and mapping tasks (for example, toddlers' recognition of metric locations in small, simple spaces, see Newcombe & Huttenlocher 2000) have sometimes been taken to mean that reading maps is well within three-year-olds' behavioral repertoires (Pavlik 2010: 39, endnote 30). I intend to imply neither of these extremes. Instead, my position is that relevant cognitive-developmental progressions during childhood are non-trivial and gradual, and that it is therefore critical to consider these progressions when addressing children's responses to maps in literature (or anywhere else).

One relevant domain is symbolic representation. This domain is central to human cognition: Without representation, one's ability to retain, manipulate, or communicate ideas would be severely constrained. Humans have invented many kinds of representations, including words that have no inherent link to their referents (that is, they are arbitrary rather than motivated symbols), icons or drawings that are motivated by (that is, in some way resemble) their referents (as when a picture of a suitcase is used to represent luggage storage), and formal notational systems that may be linked physically or metaphorically to referential qualities (as when marks drawn increasingly higher on a music stave denote increasingly higher-pitched sounds).

Infants' and toddlers' spontaneous behaviors suggest that they do not necessarily interpret graphic representations as distinct from actual objects. For example, there are anecdotal reports of infants trying to lift pictures from books (Ninio & Bruner 1978), and systematic studies showing that nine-month-olds grasp at photographs with hand positions like those needed to grasp the depicted objects (DeLoache et al. 1998).

Judith DeLoache (1987) reported that it is even later that children understand that one thing can stand for another. To study this idea, she first created a scale model of a life-sized room and its contents. Children were shown that the little room was just like the big room and told that Little and Big Snoopy (toy dogs) did exactly the same things. After watching Little Snoopy being hidden in the model room (for example, under the little pillow on the little couch), the child was asked to go next door to the big room and find Big Snoopy, and then to return to the model to retrieve Little Snoopy. Whereas three-year-olds went directly to the analogous hiding place and effortlessly retrieved Big Snoopy, two-and a half-year-olds routinely failed, searching randomly in the big room as if the model had provided no information whatsoever. Failures could not be attributed to faulty memory: Children found Little Snoopy immediately upon returning to the model. They simply seemed oblivious to the model as a representation of the real room.

Children also only gradually develop the understanding that meaning may be assigned to symbols intentionally, that these assignments can be changed, and that interlocutors must be explicitly informed about newly-assigned meaning. Illustratively, in the domain of language, preschool children believe that a symbol's meaning is inherent and immutable. Asked if the word ink could be used for a cow and cow for ink, preschoolers responded negatively because "ink is used for writing, and the cow gives milk" (Vygotsky 1962: 129). Young children may also believe that words necessarily resemble their referents. Ellen Bialystok and Michelle Martin (2003), for example, found that preschool children assumed that small objects would be labeled with short words and large objects would be labeled with long ones.

Similar confusions arise in non-linguistic representations. In the photographic medium, Harry Beilin and Elise Pearlman (1991) found that some three- to five-year-olds displayed iconic realism – the belief that representations share physical qualities with their referents. For example, when asked: "if you touched this picture [of an ice cream cone] here, how would the picture feel?" some children answered "cold." When asked to test their prediction by touching the image, older

Table 1. Progressive competencies in understanding external spatial representations such as maps. Reproduced from Liben (1999) with permission

I.	**Referential Content.** The viewer begins to identify the referential meaning of the representation, with varying ease depending upon the physical similarity of representation and referent. Thus, the viewer "understands" the representation in the sense of identifying the denoted referent, but appears to confuse them (as in trying to pick up a depicted object)
II.	**Global Differentiation.** The viewer identifies the denotative meaning of the representation, distinguishes the representation and referent, and responds to each differentially. The viewer does not, however, reflect upon the correspondence between the two. The "stand for" relation is implicit in identification, but not generally subject to intentional manipulation.
III.	**Representational Insight.** The viewer distinguishes between representation and referent, and intentionally interprets or assigns "stand for" meaning to the representation. Representational insight occurs first for objects that are inherently representational (as a photograph) and only later for objects that do not normally function as representations, but rather are most salient as objects in their own right (as a scale model).
IV.	**Attribute Differentiation.** The viewer comes to appreciate that some, but not all attributes of the representation are motivated by attributes of the referent, and that some, but not all attributes of the referent motivate graphic attributes of the representation. Until doing so, the viewer inappropriately expects that attributes of the representation necessarily mimic attributes of the referent (as in inferring that a red line means a red road) and that attributes of the referent will necessarily be mimicked by attributes of the representation (as in expecting that a large building will appear large in the representation).
V.	**Correspondence Mastery.** The viewer extends the prior understanding of attribute differentiation to develop understanding of the formal representational and geometric correspondences between representation and referent. The former allows the viewer to understand the referential content of symbols; the latter allows the viewer to understand the referential meaning of graphic space.
VI.	**Meta-representation.** The viewer is able to reflect upon the mechanisms by which, and the purposes for which, graphic representations are created, including understanding that different correspondence rules and conventions are used in different media (as in maps versus graphs), different traditions (as in Western versus Asian art), and different renditions (as in a world map in a Mercator versus a Peters projection). As a result, the viewer is able to understand representations not simply as convenient substitutions for referents, but rather as cognitive tools that enrich understanding of the referent, and to select among them appropriately for particular purposes.

preschoolers recognized their error, but some younger ones maintained that the picture was indeed cold. More generally, and as summarized in Table 1 (reproduced from, and explained more fully in Liben, 1999), children only gradually develop competencies needed to understand representations' symbolic meaning, components, conventions, and, ultimately, their power:

Empirical findings on children's map understanding parallel the gradual emergence of general representational understanding discussed above. Consistent with the observation that children begin to understand the basic stand-for function of representations by about three years (DeLoache 1987), it is at this age that maps' place meaning emerges. For example, of three- to six-year-old children who were asked what maps were (Liben & Yekel 1996), about half named location-archiving or wayfinding functions (for example, "Something that shows the whole world around you. [It] shows where aunts and uncles live and I can see where my aunt lives" and "Something to look at to show you where to go"). Similarly, when asked what a Pennsylvania road map showed (Liben & Downs 1989), most preschoolers named a place (e.g., "states and stuff"), albeit not necessarily the correct one (for example, "California, Canada, the West, and the North Coast"). Likewise, preschoolers routinely identified an aerial photograph of Chicago as a place (for instance, "a city" and "buildings and roads") but erred in identifying its scope (for example, "the whole world" or "the United States").

Consistent with the observation that coming to differentiate qualities of symbols and referents is a protracted process, children often assume that all features of map symbols carry referential meaning by resemblance (Liben & Downs 1989). Sometimes this assumption leads to correct interpretations, as when preschoolers shown the Pennsylvania road map correctly identified the Susquehanna River as a river "because it's blue." Sometimes, however, this assumption leads to misinterpretations, as when preschoolers who had correctly interpreted a red line as a road symbol then incorrectly concluded that the road itself was red. Younger preschoolers also interpret individual symbols untethered by general referential context. For example, even having just interpreted the Pennsylvania map as a place, the map's compass rose was identified by one child as "feathers" and by another as "a basketball stadium" and the irregularly-shaped yellow areas (symbolizing high-population regions) were interpreted by one child as "eggs" and by another as "firecrackers."

Other mapping research has explicitly addressed children's understanding of the role of intentional assignment of meaning to symbols. In one study (Myers & Liben 2008), five- to six-year-old children watched as two adults drew dots on maps of the room. By words and actions, one adult made clear that she was drawing green dots to record where someone was hiding objects; the other made clear that she was drawing red dots to make her paper colorful. When children were asked what each adult had been doing, they answered accurately. However, when asked which map they would use to help them find hidden firetrucks, most incorrectly selected the red-dot map based on resemblance (for example, "the dots are red like the firetrucks"). In a second study with children aged five to six, seven to eight, and nine to ten, data showed that erroneous choices decreased – but did not disappear – across age (100%, 42%, and 17%, respectively). Apparently the pull of symbol-referent resemblance continues well into childhood.

In summary, research has shown that young children (three- to six-years) have particular difficulty distinguishing which qualities of map symbols do and do not carry referential meaning, and understanding the intentional assignment of meaning to symbols. Findings also show that these difficulties continue beyond six years. As discussed next, the developmental trajectory for developing foundational spatial concepts is likewise protracted.

Cognitive development: Spatial foundations

Just as representational thinking is central for human thought, so too is spatial thinking. A rich literature documents the importance of, and developmental progressions in, spatial cognition (see Eliot 1987; Liben, Patterson & Newcombe 1981; Newcombe & Huttenlocher 2000; Piaget & Inhelder 1956; Plumert & Spencer 2007). I focus here on the characterization of spatial development offered by Jean Piaget and Bärbel Inhelder, because the concepts they propose are far-reaching and highly relevant to the spatial challenges of maps.

Specifically, Piaget and Inhelder (1956) identified three major conceptual systems – topological, projective, and Euclidean. Topological concepts were said to emerge during the preschool years. These concern spatial qualities and relationships that are defined by neighborhoods but not by distance or other metrics. Thus, someone who understands only topological concepts can understand spatial concepts such as "open," "closed," "next to," "in," and "on" but not specific lengths or angles. Projective and Euclidean concepts were said to emerge, together, during middle childhood. Projective concepts involve coding objects' relations to one another along straight (projected) lines, enabling understanding of how visual appearance differs from different viewing points. Euclidean concepts involve the representation of locations or distances in relation to a homogeneous spatial frame of reference, allowing measurement and conservation of distances and angles across locations. Figure 3 shows sample assessments for each concept.

Given the relatively late emergence of Euclidean concepts, mapping tasks that draw on metrics such as scale, proportionality, and distance would be expected to be especially challenging to young children. Consistent with this expectation are results of interview studies mentioned earlier (Liben & Downs 1989) in which

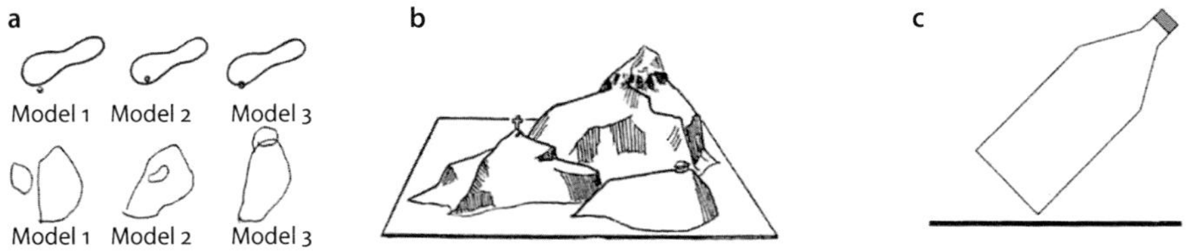

Figure 3. Sample assessments for (a) topological, (b) projective, and (c) Euclidean spatial concepts. In the copy task (a) the child is asked to reproduce model figures in top row. The sample responses in the bottom row show the preservation of topological features (individual figures are closed; one figure is "next to," "inside," and "on the border of" the other) but not Euclidean ones (e.g., absolute and relative sizes are distorted). In the three-mountains task (b) the child, seated at the front the array, is asked how the array looks to an observer seated across the table. Projective concepts are needed for the child to understand that the small mountain he sees is entirely obscured to the facing observer, and that the mid-sized mountain he sees to his left will appear to the observer's right. In the water-level task (c) the child is asked to draw a line to show how the tipped bottle would look if about half full. To draw a correct (horizontal) line requires the child to use a Cartesian coordinate system, a task made especially difficult because of the immediately surrounding non-orthogonal lines of the container. Figure reproduced from Liben (2009) with permission.

children were asked what maps show. Responses revealed misinterpretations related to scale as when one child denied that a line on the road map could be a road "because it's not fat enough for two cars to go on." Comparable errors occurred with a 1:12,000 aerial photograph of Chicago in which, for example, boats on Lake Michigan were identified as "fish" and a baseball field was interpreted as "an eye." At that scale, of course, neither fish nor eyes would be visible.

Additional evidence comes from tasks in which children are asked to mark maps to show locations of something observed in physical spaces or indicated on another kind of environmental representation. Children perform best on locations defined by topological concepts alone; accuracy falls on locations that call on projective or Euclidean concepts. Figure 4 illustrates these comparative success patterns using data from a study in which children were asked to place stickers on a map to show the locations of eight flags found on a university campus (Kastens & Liben 2007). As seen in the figure, almost all children were accurate on the black flag, a location that could be pinpointed by topological concepts alone ("on the [only] statue"). Far fewer children gave correct orange-flag responses which required not only topological concepts ("on a building's corner") but also projective concepts needed for the child to pick out the correct building and the correct corner of that building. Even fewer were correct on the red flag, a location that again required not only topological concepts ("on the road") but also Euclidean concepts needed to identify precisely how far along the road the flag was located.

Similar contrasts in accuracy across items were evident on a task in which children were asked to mark a city map to show locations circled on an aerial photograph of

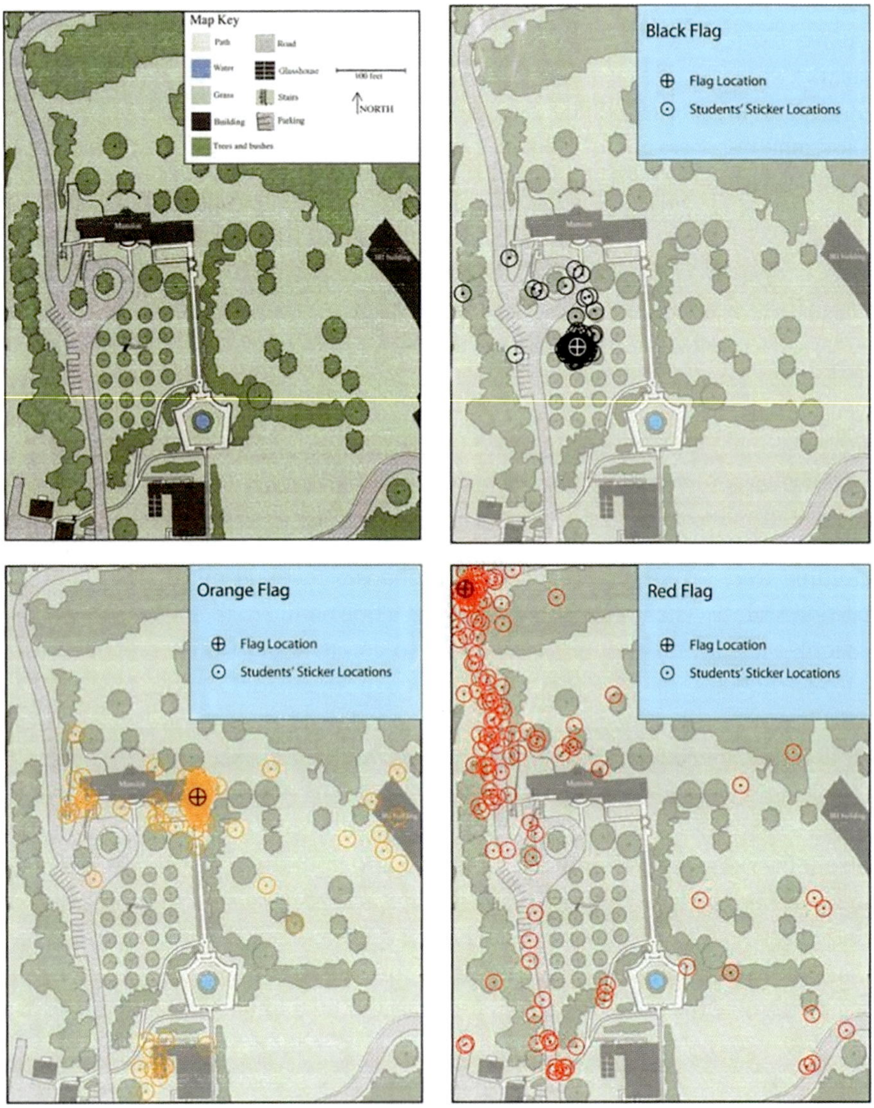

Figure 4. Performance on a mapping task in which children were asked to place stickers on a campus map (upper left) to show locations of 8 colored flags they encountered on the campus. Remaining figures show sticker placements for 3 flags made by 141 children from baseline condition of Kastens & Liben (2007) plus unpublished data collected by Kastens (personal communication). See text for discussion of error patterns by flag. Figure courtesy of Kastens, reproduced from Liben (2009) with permission.

that city and on a task in which children were asked to place stickers on a contour map to show locations of flags on a three-dimensional model of the local terrain (Liben & Downs 1989).

Research has also shown that children find it difficult to identify which of multiple symbols stands for a *particular* referent when the task of distinguishing correctly among the multiple symbols requires Euclidean concepts. This point is illustrated by a study in which preschoolers were asked to point to objects in their classroom and then mark those objects' locations on a plan-view classroom map (Liben & Yekel 1996). Given multiple pieces of rectangular furniture (e.g., desks, bookcases, tables) and thus multiple rectangular symbols, children needed to use Euclidean concepts (relative size, side-end ratios) to identify correct symbols. Performance on such locations was very low.

Indeed, many preschoolers in this study showed great difficulty using the plan-view map at all (for example, many failed to distinguish between floor and furniture locations). This difficulty may well reflect underdeveloped projective concepts needed to interpret overhead views that differ so dramatically from everyday eye-level experience. Support for this hypothesis comes from the finding that preschoolers performed significantly better when given an oblique (rather than a plan-view) map of their classroom (Liben & Yekel 1996). Additional support comes from spontaneous misinterpretations of individual map symbols that suggest confusion about viewing angle. Illustrative are errors in which preschoolers interpreted the two abutting rectangles symbolizing the double sink as a "door." Such an interpretation is plausible if one imagines that the symbol depicts a "straight ahead" view in which the rectangles might be understood as door panels. Also suggesting the impact of underdeveloped projective concepts are findings that young children's mapping performance drops precipitously when maps are misaligned with the spaces they represent. Young children often appear to be oblivious to the direction from which either a space or a map is being viewed, and their mapping performance suffers accordingly (see Liben 2006, 2008; Liben & Downs 1993).

Summary

The material presented in this section addressed, first, the purpose and diversity of maps. Only if one appreciates that maps are not singular re-presentations of the referent world and only if one appreciates the diversity of symbolic and spatial qualities of maps can one appreciate the cognitive demands that maps present to users. I offered evidence that meeting these demands is a challenging task for children given that map-relevant representational and spatial concepts develop only gradually over the course of childhood. Additionally, I sampled from empirical research to show that age-linked differences in patterns of mapping performance parallel age-linked progressions in symbolic and spatial development more generally. Before concluding that this work is relevant to challenges posed by maps in children's literature, however, it is important to consider the links between the qualities of the maps found in children's books and those found in developmental research.

Map foci across perspectives

The question motivating this section is whether the qualities and kinds of maps and mapping tasks presented by children's literature are also the qualities and kinds of maps and mapping tasks studied by developmental psychologists. To address this question, I first sample ways that maps in children's literature have been characterized by scholars and practitioners in the disciplines of geography and children's literature, and then consider how these connect to the foci of empirical research within developmental psychology.

The perspective of geography

One systematic study of maps in children's literature was prepared jointly by a geographer and map librarian (Patton & Ryckman 1990) who drew their book corpus from a U.S. city's public library collection of about 10,000 children's fiction books. They selected every tenth book on the shelves of two existing divisions, one labeled as easy, thus targeted to pre- and beginning readers, and the other labeled for third- to sixth-graders (G3–6; about 9 to 12 years), thus targeted to more established readers. Additionally, they compiled all books receiving Caldecott or Newbery awards.

All illustrations in these books were examined to find "maps," a step that proved difficult because sometimes one or the other coder judged contenders to be only "maplike." Given that earlier research had also revealed disagreements among people asked to judge whether various place representations were or were not maps (Downs & Liben 1987), Jeffrey Patton and Nancy Ryckman established the explicit rule that to be coded as a map, the illustration had to be judged as "specifically intended to show spatial location" (1990: 4). As an example, they included a perspective drawing from *Fly High, Fly Low* (1957) by Don Freeman that had been excluded from the map category "even though it could be used to understand the spatial relationships of the San Francisco Bay Area. If the Golden Gate Bridge, Alcatraz Island, or other sites had been labeled, we would have counted the illustration as a map" (4). Using this particular and strict definition, about 8% of the

898 books examined had one or more maps. Percentages were lower in easy than in G3–6 books (5% vs. 10%) and in standard than in award books (7% vs. 12%).

Each map was then coded for "type" along dimensions of scale, environmental reality, and symbol type. Overall, large-scale maps were more common than small-scale maps (with the difference being greater in G3–6 and in award-winning books than in easy or standard books); real and fantasy environments were represented about equally (similarly so across book samples); and mimetic (pictorial) symbols were more common than abstract ones (again, similarly so across samples).

Maps were also categorized for "purpose" along a complexity dimension. In low-level uses, maps served merely as props (for example, a wall map to convey a classroom setting); in mid-level uses, maps provided only basic location information (for example, where a story event occurred), and in high-level uses, maps provided complex spatial information (for example, displaying multiple locations that supported understanding of routes or spatial relations among story events). Tallies revealed differing patterns across samples: in easy books the three levels of purposes occurred about evenly whereas in G3–6 books, low-level purposes were relatively less common and high-level purposes were relatively more common. The same contrast held in the comparison of general versus award books. Patton and Ryckman identified one additional purpose: books with maps that were explicitly designed to promote children's understanding of, or skill in using maps. They found only a single such book in their entire corpus, thus precluding comparisons across the three book samples.

The review just described was published in a journal dedicated to cartographic scholarship. In contrast, a review by another map librarian, Marianne McKee, was prepared for a map society, with the stated practical goal of disseminating information about books that could "stimulate another generation to enjoy and appreciate maps" (2011: 8). Thus, rather than starting from a sample of books in a public library and characterizing frequencies and ways that maps were used in those library books, McKee explicitly hunted for books that contained maps (for example, by surveying members of the Washington Map Society, visiting local book fairs, and exploring local and national book stores). Not surprisingly, the annotated bibliography she compiled included far more books explicitly designed to teach children about maps and map skills than did the random sample of books examined by Patton and Rykman (1990).

Geography educators have also assembled lists of children's books that include maps. Illustrative is a paper entitled "Mapping Skills and Activities with Children's Literature" (2006) by Kay Gandy that lists 18 books addressed to one or more U.S. National Geography Standards and one or more map skills (Geography Education Standards Project 1994). Of these eighteen books, seventeen included graphic environmental representations, thirteen of them maps. The maps were rated by a geographer for "usability" although criteria are not explained. This review and others by geography educators identify many books designed to promote mapping skills, thus again contrasting to the review by Patton and Ryckman (1990) that unearthed only a single such book. The contrast is an excellent reminder that any picture that is painted about the frequencies, types, and uses of maps in children's literature will depend on not only on one's definition of "maps" but also on one's definition (and sampling) of "children's literature."

The perspective of children's literature

Those working from the perspective of children's literature understandably place more emphasis on how maps affect literary experiences rather than on how they affect geographic knowledge and map skills. In a paper addressed to school librarians, for example, Clare Ranson suggests that maps are illustrations that "add another visual level to the text" (1995: 164). Likening maps in chapter books to illustrations in picturebooks, she suggests that maps set books' tones, train children's artistic eyes, and aid story comprehension, especially useful for stories about large or foreign countries. Ranson categorizes maps according to the reality of the referent spaces – real places, fantasy places, and real-fantasy combinations – and then contrasts the categories with respect to map styles (for instance, framing, artistic flourishes, detail, scale, viewing angle). Her emphasis is on how different styles elicit different aesthetic visions, moods, and book uses (for example, to learn facts or to fantasize).

An example of a paper targeted to researchers of children's literature is one written by Anthony Pavlik (2010) who focuses on endpaper maps in children's novels. He argues that their placement away from text communicates that they are not intended to illustrate specific passages. He also argues that it is unlikely that endpaper maps are used primarily to set tone which can readily be established in other ways (for example, by cover illustrations). Looking elsewhere for their purpose, Pavlik ultimately hones in on their cartographic essence: "since they do depict places and spaces, they might also be considered as instances of cartography" (29). He notes that endpaper maps depict both real and imaginary places and then – consistent with earlier discussions of cartographic visions (see *Cartographic Foundations*) and other writings by cartographers – makes the case that maps are always subjective representations of some kind.

Once having made the case for maps as rhetorical, subjective entities, Pavlik discusses the non-confining, non-prescriptive, non-singular ways that literary maps can be understood and used. He notes that maps offer many places to enter and many routes to follow, thereby allowing readers to imagine routes that differ from those described in the text. Interestingly, he observes that few maps in children's literature provide "rules of transformation between representation and represented" (33). For example, Pavlik observes that specification of scale is rare, and that scale is often inconsistent within maps so that "objects [...] contradict or subvert notions of Cartesian spatial certitude" (36). Likewise, he notes that it is common to find – within a single map – referents viewed from directly overhead as well as those viewed from an oblique angle.

However, rather than viewing the absence of transformation rules or spatial inconsistencies as shortcomings, Pavlik argues that these features encourage readers' flexible thought and imagination. For example, he suggests that fluidity of scale may convey affect rather than merely mathematical size (for example,, exaggerating the size of emotionally important places). He suggests that shifts between overhead and oblique views "mean that the eye is always moving, and the landscape is never fixed, controlled or delimited" and that map qualities like these encourage readers' personal involvement, facilitating "the active, participatory role that is required when viewing/reading maps" (35). Pavlik expands this point in the closing pages of his paper in a way that is reminiscent of the constructivist approach in developmental psychology described earlier in this chapter. He proposes that active readers "re-map the territory, creating new connections and understandings" (38) as they "performatively explore [maps] [...] in an endless map-reading game" (40).

Another illustrative article, written by Bettina Kümmerling-Meibauer and Jörg Meibauer (2015), is focused on maps in picturebooks. At the same time that this paper addresses issues central to scholarship in children's literature, it draws from work in geography and cognitive development to suggest ways that maps may challenge young children. The authors identify ten types of map uses in picturebooks. Some are uses in fiction like those described earlier; some are uses in nonfiction books including the use of maps for teaching about history, children's daily lives in different countries, and maps themselves. They also comment on map styles, observing that picturebook maps favor pictorial over abstract symbols, perspective (oblique) over plan views, and large- over small-scale depictions. Like Pavlik, they also note that scale is often uneven within a single map. They end with detailed case studies of three different types of picturebooks, emphasizing ways that these maps support the books' narratives.

Relevant materials written from the perspective of children's literature are also available online. Illustrative is a website entitled *Maps in Literature for Youth*, prepared by educators and educational media experts Lamb and Johnson (2014). The web pages they have assembled provide lists of relevant books, discussions of the way maps are used in books about real and imagined places, suggestions for instructional activities, and citations to scholarly and other resources. Although these materials acknowledge the role maps play in promoting children's mapping skills and geographic knowledge, much of the focus is on ways that maps can serve to "excite and assist readers" and "help youth better understand the setting of the book."

Comparing perspectives

A systematic comparison of the way maps are viewed in children's literature and the ways maps are studied in empirical cognitive-developmental research is beyond the scope of this chapter, but I offer some brief comments about similarities and differences suggested by the material reviewed above.

There is consensus among all three approaches (geography, children's literature research, and developmental psychology) that an important variation across maps is symbol type, specifically whether symbols are pictorial, mimetic, or motivated versus abstract or arbitrary. Similarly, all three perspectives identify as important the spatial properties of map scale (and metrics more generally) and of viewing angle (for example, distinctions between vertical and oblique views). Interestingly, although the developmental research community has also identified viewing azimuth or map orientation as important, there is little attention to this in discussions of maps in children's literature. One likely reason for this difference is that when using a map to understand locations and configurational relationships within the narrative space, map orientation is generally less critical than it is when using a map to orient oneself to the environment (as in map-based navigation). The latter requires understanding self-space-map relations, thus making it important to account for map orientation by either physically or mentally aligning the symbolized environment with the real environment (see Liben & Downs 1993).

Two map qualities discussed in reviews of maps in children's literature have not played a central role in developmental mapping research. One concerns stylistic qualities of maps, for example, how map colors or line widths may project particular tones or moods (e.g., foreboding or powerful), how fonts may suggest different historical periods, and how decorative flourishes may affect a map's aesthetic appeal. The second concerns the reality of the referent space. That is, discussions of maps in children's literature commonly categorize maps according to whether they depict real versus fantasy environments (or a hybrid of the two), a distinction that has elicited little attention in empirical developmental research. However, as discussed elsewhere (Liben 1997, 2001), the cognitive-developmental research community has been concerned with other kinds of distinctions related to the referent space. For example, is the child currently in the environment that is depicted on the map so that it is currently visible? Is it a known environment but currently beyond view or is it an entirely unfamiliar environment? If the latter, it may be of little importance whether its unfamiliarity stems from the fact that the environment does not exist (that is, is a fantasy environment) or stems from the fact that the depicted environment is unknown to a particular child. Furthermore, what may be assumed to be a fantasy environment may in fact have a real environmental referent (for example, the area mapped on the inside covers of *Winnie-the-Pooh* is a rough representation of Cotchford Farm in East Sussex, UK, see Milne 2007).

Collectively these points are a reminder that when trying to understand what maps contribute to children's reading experiences, it is essential to consider qualities of children as well as qualities of the maps. This point harks back to the earlier constructivist arguments for the "child's active, self-directive" role in processing environmental input (Liben 2014) and of the children's "active, participatory role" in viewing or reading maps (Pavlik 2010). Likewise, this point foreshadows the message of the final section which argues for the importance of examining the active ways that maps are actually used during independent or shared reading.

A cognitive-developmental perspective: Where next?

The material reviewed in this chapter demonstrates that a cognitive-developmental perspective provides useful insights into how children approach and learn from the maps that they encounter in literature. There is a wide range of empirical research showing that children's understandings and misunderstandings of maps are linked to normative progressions in children's representational and spatial concepts. However, not yet tackled within this research tradition are two interesting and important questions.

The first question asks how maps available in children's literature are actually used during the reading process. For example, do children pause before beginning a book proper to examine maps appearing inside book covers? Do they look back at these maps regularly as they read? When adults (parents, teachers, or librarians) read books to or with children, do they point back to the maps along the way? Do adults show signs of trying to engage children in understanding connections among locations mentioned in the prose or try to puzzle out how locational information contained in the prose connects to locational information contained in the map? Do adults spontaneously use maps in children's literature as opportunities to focus children's attention on maps and map skills *per se*? How does this use vary in relation to whether or not the book is patently "about" maps? Do behaviors of these kinds (in children or adults) differ in relation to the cartographic variables identified earlier, for example, with respect to the kinds of symbols that are used or with respect to spatial scale, viewing angle, or other map qualities? To understand the effects of maps it is necessary to look beyond what appears on the surface of the paper.

The second major question asks whether the availability of embedded maps, their qualities, or the ways they are used have measurable effects on what children take from their reading experiences in either cognitive or emotional domains. For example, do children show better understanding of the narrative or greater liking of the book if they had a map inside the book's cover? Do they show better understanding of the narrative or can they remember the sequence of events better if they looked back at the map repeatedly, either because they did so spontaneously or because an adult guided them to do so? Do maps that use spatial transformation rules (e.g., concerning scale) inconsistently rather than systematically elicit greater reader involvement (as suggested by Pavlik 2010) or do such maps confuse children's spatial understanding? This is only a small sample of the kinds of questions that emerge from the material reviewed earlier.

Methods already exist to study moment-by-moment processes in shared book reading (for example, Kümmerling-Meibauer et al. 2015; Szechter & Liben 2004), but before they can be adopted here, it will be critical to identify outcomes of interest. These might include cognitive outcomes in geography (for instance, understanding and using maps), literature (for example, depth of understanding the plot and context; creativity in extending the narrative), or cognitive development more generally (for example, basic spatial concepts like those assessed by the tasks shown in Figure 3); they might address motivation for activities such as reading or interest in map-rich domains such as geography or history.

As implied by even this small sample of potential research topics, the goal of understanding how children use and profit from maps in children's literature is an important and far-reaching one. There have already been valuable contributions from the disciplines of geography, children's literature, and – if I may be allowed some shameless promotion of my own disciplinary heritage – developmental psychology. The road to advancing our collective understanding is paved with interdisciplinary work that involves scholars from these fields and the professionals (for instance, educators, librarians, authors, illustrators, cartographers) who develop and disseminate the books and maps we study.

References

Primary sources

Carroll, Lewis. 1939. *Sylvie and Bruno concluded* (1893). In *The Complete Works of Lewis Carroll*, by Charles Dodgson. London: Nonesuch Press.

Freeman, Don. 1957. *Fly High, Fly Low*. New York NY: Viking.

Secondary sources

Beilin, Harry & Pearlman, Elise G. 1991. Children's iconic realism: Object versus property realism. In *Advances in Child Development and Behavior*, Vol. 23, Hayne W. Reese (ed.), 73–111. New York NY: Academic Press.

Bialystok, Ellen & Martin, Michelle M. 2003. Notation to symbol: Development in children's understanding of print. *Journal of Experimental Child Psychology* 86: 223–243. doi: 10.1016/S0022-0965(03)00138-3

Blaut, James Morris. 1997a. Children can. *Annals of the Association of American Geographers* 87: 152–158. doi: 10.1111/0004-5608.00045

Blaut, James Morris. 1997b. Piagetian pessimism and the mapping abilities of young children: A rejoinder to Liben and Downs. *Annals of the Association of American Geographers* 87: 168–177. doi: 10.1111/0004-5608.00047

DeLoache, Judith S. 1987. Rapid change in the symbolic functioning of very young children. *Science* 238: 1556–1557. doi: 10.1126/science.2446392

DeLoache, Judith S., Pierroutsakos, Sophia L., Uttal, David H., Rosengren, Karl S. & Gottlieb, Alma. 1998. Grasping the nature of pictures. *Psychological Science* 9: 205–210. doi: 10.1111/1467-9280.00039

Dodge, Martin, Kitchin, Rob & Perkins, Chris (eds). 2011. *The Map Reader*. Oxford: Wiley-Blackwell. doi: 10.1002/9780470979587

Downs, Roger M. 1981. Maps and mappings as metaphors for spatial representation. In *Spatial Representation and Behavior across the Life Span*, Lynn S. Liben, Arthur H. Patterson & Nora Newcombe (eds), 143–166. New York NY: Academic Press.

Downs, Roger M. 1985. The representation of space: Its development in children and in cartography. In *The Development of Spatial Cognition*, Robert Cohen (ed.), 323–345. Hillsdale NJ: Lawrence Erlbaum Associates.

Downs, Roger M. & Liben, Lynn S. 1987. Children's understanding of maps. In *Cognitive Processes and Spatial Orientation in Animal and Man*, Vol. 1: *Neurophysiology of Spatial Knowledge and Developmental Aspects*, Paul Ellen & Catherine Thinus-Blanc (eds), 202–219. Dordrecht: Martinius Nijhoff. doi: 10.1007/978-94-009-3533-4_18

Downs, Roger M. & Liben, Lynn S. 1988. Through a map darkly: Understanding maps as representations. *Genetic Epistemologist* 16: 11–18.

Downs, Roger M. & Liben, Lynn S. 1991. The development of expertise in geography: A cognitive-developmental approach to geographic education. *Annals of the Association of American Geographers* 81: 304–327. doi: 10.1111/j.1467-8306.1991.tb01692.x

Downs, Roger M. & Liben, Lynn S. 1997. The final summation: The defense rests. *Annals of the Association of American Geographers* 87: 178–180. doi: 10.1111/0004-5608.00048

Eliot, John. 1987. *Models of Psychological Space: Psychometric, Developmental, and Experimental Approaches*. New York NY: Springer. doi: 10.1007/978-1-4612-4788-3

Flexner, Stuart Berg & Hauck, Leonore C. (eds). 1997. *Random House Unabridged Dictionary*. New York NY: Random House.

Gandy, S. Kay. 2006. Mapping skills and activities with children's literature. *Journal of Geography* 105: 267–271. doi: 10.1080/00221340608978696

Geography Education Standards Project. 1994. *Geography for Life: National Geography Standards 1994*. Washington DC: National Geographic Research & Exploration.

Harrison, Richard Edes. 1944. *Look at the World: The Fortune Atlas for World Strategy*. New York NY: Knopf.

Kastens, Kim A. & Liben, Lynn S. 2007. Eliciting self-explanations improves children's performance on a field-based map skills task. *Cognition and Instruction* 25: 45–74. doi: 10.1080/07370000709336702

Kümmerling-Meibauer, Bettina & Meibauer, Jörg. 2015. Maps in picturebooks: Cognitive status and narrative functions. *Nordic Journal of ChildLit Aesthetics* 6. doi: 10.3402/blft.v6.26970

Kümmerling-Meibauer, Bettina, Meibauer, Jörg, Nachtigäller, Kerstin & Rohlfing, Katharina (eds). 2015. *Learning from Picturebooks. Perspectives from Child Development and Literacy Studies*. New York NY: Routledge.

Lamb, A. & Johnson, L. 2014. *Maps in Literature for Youth*. Retrieved from <http://eduscapes.com/sessions/maps/index.htm>

Liben, Lynn S. 1981. Spatial representation and behavior: Multiple perspectives. In *Spatial Representation and Behavior across the Life Span*, Lynn S. Liben, Arthur H. Patterson & Nora Newcombe (eds), 3–36. New York NY: Academic Press.

Liben, Lynn S. 1982. Children's large scale spatial cognition: Is the measure the message? In *New Directions in Child Development: Children's Conceptions of their Spatial Environments*, Robert Cohen (ed.), 51–64. San Francisco CA: Jossey Bass.

Liben, Lynn S. 1997. Children's understanding of spatial representations of place: Mapping the methodological landscape. In *A Handbook of Spatial Research Paradigms and Methodologies*, Nigel Foreman & Raphael Gillett (eds), 41–83. Hove: Psychology Press.

Liben, Lynn S. 1999. Developing an understanding of external spatial representations. In *Development of Mental Representation*, Irving E. Sigel (ed.), 297–321. Mahwah NJ: Lawrence Erlbaum Associates.

Liben, Lynn S. 2001. Thinking through maps. In *Spatial Schemas and Abstract Thought*, Merideth Gattis (ed.), 44–77. Cambridge MA: The MIT Press.

Liben, Lynn S. 2003. Beyond point and shoot: Children's developing understanding of photographs as spatial and expressive representations. In *Advances in Child Development and Behavior*, Vol. 31, Robert V. Kail (ed.), 1–42. San Diego CA: Elsevier.

Liben, Lynn S. 2006. Education for spatial thinking. In *Handbook of Child Psychology*, 6th edn, Vol. 4, K. Ann Renninger & Irving E. Sigel (eds), 197–247. Hoboken NJ: Wiley and Sons.

Liben, Lynn S. 2009. The road to understanding maps. *Current Directions in Psychological Science* 18: 310–315. doi: 10.1111/j.1467-8721.2009.01658.x

Liben, Lynn S. 2008. Embodiment and children's understanding of the real and represented world. In *Developmental Perspectives on Embodiment and Consciousness*, Willis F. Overton, Ulrich Mueller & Judith L. Newman (eds), 191–224. New York NY: Lawrence Erlbaum Associates.

Liben, Lynn S. 2014. The individual ↔ context nexus in Developmental Intergroup Theory: Within and beyond the ivory tower. *Research in Human Development* 11: 273–290. doi: 10.1080/15427609.2014.967048

Liben, Lynn S. & Downs, Roger M. 1989. Understanding maps as symbols: The development of map concepts in children. In *Advances in Child Development and Behavior*, Vol. 22, Hayne W. Reese (ed.), 145–201. New York NY: Academic Press.

Liben, Lynn S. & Downs, Roger M. 1993. Understanding person-space-map relations: Cartographic and developmental perspectives. *Developmental Psychology* 29: 739–752. doi: 10.1037/0012-1649.29.4.739

Liben, Lynn S. & Downs, Roger M. 1997. Can-ism and can'tianism: A straw child. *Annals of the Association of American Geographers* 87: 159–167. doi: 10.1111/0004-5608.00046

Liben, Lynn S., Patterson, Arthur H. & Newcombe, Nora (eds). 1981. *Spatial Representation and Behavior across the Life Span*. New York NY: Academic Press.

Liben, Lynn S., & Yekel, Candice A. 1996. Preschoolers' understanding of plan and oblique maps: The role of geometric and representational correspondence. *Child Development* 67: 2780–2796. doi: 10.2307/1131752

McKee, Marianne. 2011. Expanding a child's world: Map books for children and young readers. *Journal of the Washington Map Society* 81: 8–14.

Milne, James. 2007. Cotchford Farm and the Surrounding Area. <http://www.pooh-corner.org/map.shtml> (16 April 2016).

Myers, Lauren J. & Liben, Lynn S. 2008. The role of intentionality and iconicity in children's developing comprehension and production of cartographic symbols. *Child Development* 79: 668–684. doi: 10.1111/j.1467-8624.2008.01150.x

Newcombe, Nora & Huttenlocher, Janellen. 2000. *Making Space*. Cambridge MA: The MIT Press.

Ninio, Anait & Bruner, Jerome. 1978. The achievements and antecedents of labeling. *Journal of Child Language* 5: 1–15. doi: 10.1017/S0305000900001896

Patton, Jeffrey C. & Ryckman, Nancy B. 1990. Maps in children's literature. *Cartographic Perspectives* 6: 3–12. doi: 10.14714/CP06.1110

Pavlik, Anthony. 2010. A special kind of reading game: Maps in children's literature. *International Research in Children's Literature* 3: 28–43. doi: 10.3366/ircl.2010.0004

Piaget, Jean & Inhelder, Bärbel. 1956. *The Child's Conception of Space*. New York NY: Norton (original work published 1948).

Plumert, Jodie & Spencer, John (eds). 2007. *The Emerging Spatial Mind*. Oxford: OUP. doi: 10.1093/acprof:oso/9780195189223.001.0001

Ranson, Clare. 1995. Cartography in children's literature. *Sustaining the Vision. Selected Papers from the Annual Conference of the International Association of School Librarianship Worcester, England*. <http://eric.ed.gov/?id=ED400859> (16 April 2016).

Szechter, Lisa E. & Liben, Lynn S. 2004. Parental guidance in preschoolers' understanding of spatial-graphic representations. *Child Development* 75: 869–885. doi: 10.1111/j.1467-8624.2004.00711.x

Vygotsky, Lev S. 1962. *Thought and Language*. Cambridge MA: The MIT Press (original work published 1934). doi: 10.1037/11193-000

CHAPTER 2

Mapping the new citizen – Pedagogy of cartophobia

Philanthropic geographies in the late Enlightenment

Nikola von Merveldt

This chapter looks at the place of maps in the late eighteenth-century German pedagogic reform movement of philanthropism. Advocating a realist reform of the humanist schooling tradition, philanthropists declared geography to be the foundational elementary science. More importantly, geography was understood as the referential framework to educate children to become active citizens in the "real world." Focusing on Joachim Heinrich Campe's geographical writings, this chapter explores the historically specific version of geographic literacy that the philanthropists embraced. Far more than mere mappings of geographic realities, philanthropic maps were ideological projections of a new kind of citizen who took his bearings from a new vision of his place within the world.

"I remember seeing a geography somewhere," writes Jean-Jacques Rousseau in his *Emile*, "which began with [the question]: 'What is the world?' – [Answer:] 'A sphere of cardboard.' That is the child's geography." And he continues his lament: "You think you are teaching him what the *world* is like; he is only learning the *map*; he is taught the *names* of towns, countries, rivers, which have no existence for him except on the *paper* before him" (2010, II: 183; italics mine). This quote betrays what Stockhammer has aptly called "a pedagogy of cartophobia" (2007: 59) – a pedagogy deeply suspicious of maps and their semiotic potential. Yet despite this distrust, maps – both literal and metaphorical – play an important part in eighteenth-century children's literature.

A world of cardboard and symbols on paper – that is what not only traditional geography, but schooling in general had taught children: empty signifiers, abstract symbols, and hollow words filled the heads of children instead of knowledge of the world and of objects around them. Rousseau's disenchantment with traditional learning resonated deeply with a group of progressive German pedagogues and writers who called themselves "Philanthropen," or "Philanthropists." In the name

DOI 10.1075/clcc.7.03von

of the love of humankind, they set out to reform the "cardboard" education system in the last third of the eighteenth century and to teach children about the real world in ways that would be true, relevant, and meaningful – with the ultimate goal of turning children into a new kind of citizen. They did so by founding model reform schools, rethinking the formats and functions of books for children, and by engaging enlightened thinkers across Europe in a public dialogue discussing the status, purpose, and methods of education in civic society. They put the child on the map of Enlightenment discourse, earning the eighteenth century the title of the "century of pedagogy" (Wild 2008: 49).

The philanthropic reform of the educational system, which marked a realist and spatial turn in pedagogic thinking and practice (cf. Schmitt 2007: 195–206, 228), concerned all areas of the curriculum. But for the purpose of this chapter, I will focus on the subject of geography in general and on maps in the geographical writings of Joachim Heinrich Campe more specifically. In fact, geography provided the basic cognitive matrix and foundational grid for all learning according to philanthropic pedagogy. Johann Christoph Friedrich GutsMuths, teacher of physical education and geography at Schnepfenthal, one of the famous philanthropic reform schools, contended that all knowledge was essentially spatial in nature and that all facts had to be anchored in geographic space: "Everything that History tells us, that Natural History proclaims, begs the question of where" (1835: 11, translation by the author). Unless children were able to assign knowledge its rightful place – not within an abstract scientific or symbolic system or within a mnemonic structure but within the real world – they were wandering in cognitive darkness. Knowledge of their surroundings – beginning with their home and gradually extending into the gardens and beyond – and their specific physical features, their proportions, and relationships to one another was absolutely essential to literally ground the facts. In other words: philanthropists considered geographic literacy a key cultural technique and an indispensable prerequisite for all learning. They thus developed a variety of pedagogic media, methods, and practices to engrain in their pupils what could be called a "topographical consciousness" (von Merveldt 2014).

Printed maps in books, it is important to note, were only one element in a complex combination of media and a variety of cultural practices which constitute this topographical mindset. Others included printed maps circulating separately, hand-drawn maps, educational media such as globes and spheres or copper engravings of cities and landscapes, or pedagogical practices such as mapping or surveying the immediate surroundings, walks, and field trips. Maps in eighteenth-century books for children are part of what Martin Brückner has called "geographic texts" (2006; see also Brückner 1999). Instead of reading maps as tools of oppression, which has been the standard interpretation of post-colonial criticism, he shows how "various forms of geographical writing (like maps and textbooks) profoundly informed early American literary documents – such as poems and natural histories, diaries and novels – because their conception and production were deeply linked to the cognitive, pedagogic, and material practices derived from the study of geography" (Brückner 2006: 4). He reveals this broader ensemble of textual forms as functioning as "narratives of selfhood," aiming to define a nascent national identity for American citizens and "providing many ordinary people with a vehicle for describing and defining their personal place in both the local and global community" (7). Following Brückner's lead, I will read the "geographic texts" of Joachim Heinrich Campe as tools of the self-fashioning of a new kind of citizen – teaching children to adopt the mindset of the "Bürger," an active and productive member of German civil society. I will argue that within the specific context of late Enlightenment Germany, maps functioned first and foremost as a moral compass to an emerging social class eager to find its place in the world.

Pedagogy of cartophobia

Before embarking on the voyage of discovery exploring maps in the geographic writings of Campe, a brief return to Rousseau and his pedagogy of cartophobia is useful. Robert Stockhammer's interpretation of Rousseau's apprehension is based on a semiotic reading of maps. Building on Charles Peirce's semiotic triad of icon, index, and symbol, Stockhammer defines maps as complex networks of signs (2007: 12–19). This definition allows him to analyze different kinds of maps within changing historical and literary contexts (2001, 2007). Reading maps as interacting networks of signs thus provides a useful analytical tool to describe and understand how maps function in general, and within the specific historical context of philanthropic children's books and pedagogy. On the most basic level, maps create *iconic illusions*. Signs, such as curves, for example, *resemble* the topography of a coastline. They are based on a correlation of resemblance. Most signs on maps, however, are *symbolic* in nature, meaning they are using a standardized code that has no correlation whatsoever to the real world (letters, numbers, lines, names, etc.). Finally, both icons and symbols function as *indexical signs*, pointing towards places, based on a correlation in space in time. The deictic phrase "here is" is the basic indexical gesture inscribed into each map.

The danger of maps, according to Rousseau, resides in their iconic illusion, in the fact that most signs on maps are symbols rather than icons, but create the illusion of being icons: younger children looking at the circles and figures of an armillary sphere, Rousseau warns, will be "confused" and "not know what [they] see" if they are told that these circles, which they see before their eyes, are, in fact, only imaginary (2010: 99–100). And indeed, this is precisely what happens to little

Frederic, one of the younger children listening to his sibling's explanation of longitude and latitude in *Columbus, or The Discovery of America* (Campe 1799a: 49): "But is there in reality such a line upon our globe?" is his question when Henry, the eldest of the children, traces the equator with his finger on "a little map of the world" (46; see Figure 1), which the father provided for better illustration. But despite the fact that Henry uses his index finger to point to the equator, the sign is not indexical: "No, my dear Frederic," Henry corrects the iconic illusion his younger brother has fallen prey to, "our learned men have only imagined such a line to extend round the earth" (49). The black line of the equator corresponds to imaginations of the learned, which escape the realist and iconic world view of those who are still learning.

Given that young children, in Rousseau's pedagogy, can only comprehend what they can see or have seen with their own eyes, icons are the only kinds of

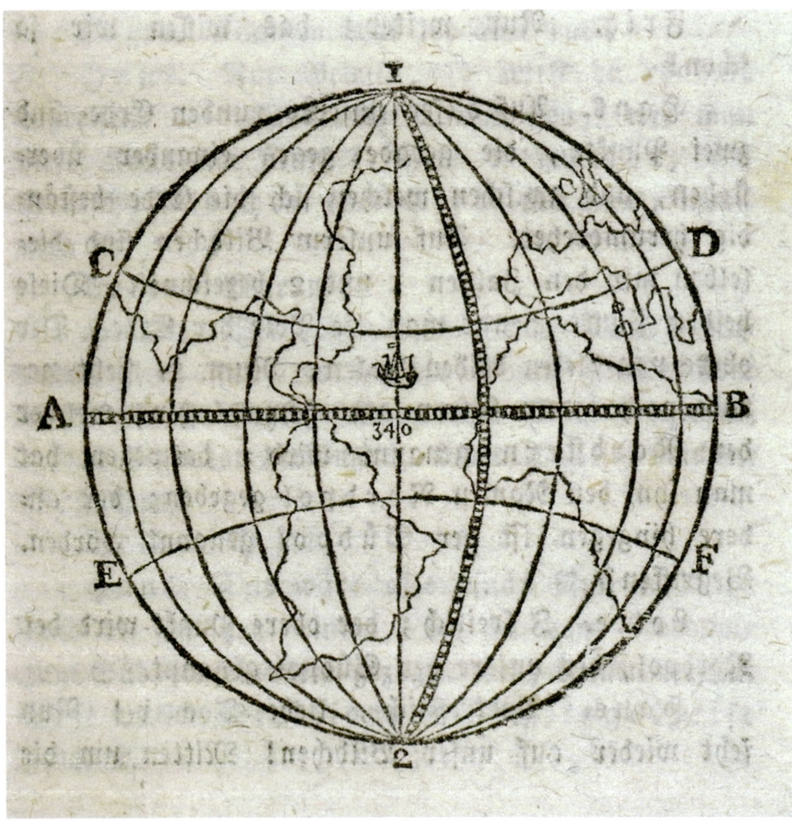

Figure 1. Illustration explaining longitude and latitude, in Campe 1799a: 49. © Pictura Paedagogica Online. Bibliothek für Bildungsgeschichtliche Forschung des Deutschen Instituts für Internationale Pädagogische Forschung, Berlin

signs accessible to them. Unable to understand the complex nature of signs, they will misread symbols as icons, resulting in a cardboard view of the world. "In general, never substitute the sign for the thing," Rousseau summarizes his reflection on geography and cosmology, "except when it is impossible for you to show the latter, for the sign absorbs the child's attention and makes him forget the thing represented" (2010: 99). Rousseau's cartophopia, then, Stockhammer argues, is part of his general phobia of symbolic representation, which relies on arbitrary and ultimately uncontrollable combinations of sign and meaning.

This pedagogic cartophobia, shared by the philanthropists, is grounded in the cognitive and pedagogic theories of the time. In his treatise *Versuch über die anschauende Erkenntnis* (Essay on Sensory Cognition, 1782), Philipp Julius Lieberkühn takes a close look at the cognitive development of children and distinguishes between two types of cognition: "anschauende Erkenntnis" (sensory cognition) and "symbolische Erkenntnis" (symbolic cognition). While younger children naturally acquire knowledge via their senses – seeing, touching, smelling, tasting, hearing the world immediately surrounding them – symbolic cognition involves the mind's higher faculties of rational thinking and thus is not accessible to them before they reach the age of reason, between eight and ten years of age. Symbolic cognition relies on the arbitrary nature of symbolic signs and involves "nonsensory objects of study," privileged by the scholarly canon of learning: dead languages like Latin or Hebrew, theology, and philosophy (Heesen 2002: 80). "Anschauung," sensory cognition, on the other hand, literally stays in touch with the children's world and builds the foundation of their knowledge. Once children are old enough to use their mind to reason, symbolic cognition can build on this foundation, provided it is solid enough and built up from the ground. "Anschauung" thus becomes the magic wand of philanthropic pedagogy and publishing strategies, and so-called "Anschauungsbücher," literally "books of sensory cognition," become the medium of choice if immersion in or immediate contact with the objects of study is not possible. These picturebooks range from collections of plate engravings over pictionaries to lavishly illustrated books. Johann Bernhard Basedow's *Elementarbuch* (Primer, 1774), accompanied by one hundred copper plate engravings in the second edition of 1774, most of them designed by one of the finest artists of the time, Daniel Chodowiecki, or Friedrich Justin Bertuch's later *Bilderbuch für Kinder* (Picturebook for Children, 1790–1830) are prime examples of this pedagogic impulse.

The Rousseauian and philanthropic view of maps is deeply informed by this pedagogy of "Anschauung." This is why the only appropriate maps for younger children are those *reproducing* – rather than *representing* – their immediate surroundings: "[Emile's] geography will begin with the town he lives in and his father's country house, then the places between them, the rivers near them [...]"

(Rousseau 2010: 270). Just like the rest of learning, the acquisition of geographic knowledge is to follow the natural order of things, progressing from the elementary to the more complex, staying close to home before progressively extending the child's horizon. Printed maps representing foreign places are doomed to remain paper objects with empty signs. Instead, the best maps are those drawn by the child himself: "Let him make his own map," Rousseau encourages the educators, "a very simple map, at first containing only two places; others may be added from time to time, as he is able to estimate their distance and position" (2010: III, 270–271). And indeed, that is what "the German reformers" made children do in the philanthropic model schools. In his geographic textbook, GutsMuths recommends that six- to eight-year-olds should begin their initiation into maps by drawing maps of their immediate surroundings: the classroom, the school building, eventually the courtyard, reproducing their environment to which they could relate and of which they knew the scale (1835: 36–38). "Making his eye his compass" – this is the wording used by Rousseau (2010: III, 271) – is the true key to pedagogically valuable maps and mapping skills.

Finally, the pedagogic mapping principle of "making his eyes his compass" radically reduces the scale of maps, since they only reproduce the child's surroundings and do not extend further than the child can walk or see. This has important implications for the *indexical function* of these pedagogical maps: the pointing phrase "here is" of the paper map sign coincides with the real-world "here" of the child instead of referring to far-away and unknown places. The indexical time-space correlation remains within the child's bounds.

To sum up this semiotic excursus: Rousseau – and the German philanthropists following his lead – resented the symbolic nature and iconic illusion of maps. True to the ideal of "Anschauung," that is, sensory cognition, signs in maps should be true icons, pointing toward the true "here and now" familiar to the child. However, on an ideological level, the location of the "here" differed radically between Rousseau and the German reformers.

From topos to topography: Campe's geographical writings

The philanthropists took their intellectual bearings from Locke and Rousseau. The *Allgemeine Revision* (General Revision), the most important professional pedagogical journal of the time, edited by Campe, impressively documents how intensely the reformers engaged with their two icons. Issues 12–15 reprinted Rousseau's entire *Emile*, offering a new German translation and adding, as the subtitle specifies, "explanatory, specifying and corrective annotations" (Campe 1785–1792, vol. 12, title-page; see also Austermann 2010: 267–271). Coincidentally, the

German pedagogues were attempting to revolutionize the German schooling system while the French Revolution, of which Campe was a fervent admirer, was raging in France.

While the philanthropists tended to enthusiastically endorse most of what Rousseau had to say, they differed in one important respect: the result of all their pedagogic efforts. Rousseau declared that – if faced with the choice between raising his child to become either a Man (*homme*) or a citizen (*citoyen*) – he would opt for Man, the human being (Rousseau 2010: I, 84). Philanthropists, on the contrary, emphatically agreed that children had to be raised first and foremost to become citizens – that is, active members of civil society (Campe 1785–1792:, vol. 12: 48–49). Metaphorically then, philanthropists abandoned the utopian island on which model student Emile was raised far removed from society's evil influences, and programmatically situated child-rearing and education in the midst of civil society. Thus, they transported the utopian topos of the Rousseauian pedagogic island (Liebs 1977) into realist topography. In doing so, they radically redefined the indexical "here" of maps. In fact, amplifying and controlling the indexical function of maps became an important controlling device in philanthropic books for children. The geographical writings of Campe convincingly illustrate this ideological indexicalization of maps.

Joachim Heinrich Campe (1746–1818) was the most prolific writer and successful publisher of the philanthropic movement. His geographical writings, most of which were quickly translated into English, include

his famous international bestseller, *Robinson der Jüngere* (1779/1780) – Engl. *Robinson the Younger*, 1789,
his less well-known trilogy *Die Entdekkung von Amerika: ein angenehmes und nüzliches Lesebuch für Kinder und junge Leute* (1781/82) – Engl.: *The Discovery of America*, which critically retells the New World conquests of Columbus (Engl. 1799a), Cortez (Engl. 1799b) and Pizarro (Engl. 1799c),
his *Sammlung interessanter und durchgängig zweckmäßig abgefaßter Reisebeschreibungen für die Jugend* (published in various editions beginning in 1785) – Engl.: *Collection of Interesting and Instructive Travel Accounts for the Young*, not translated, a pedagogically revised compilation of the latest travelogues totaling twelve volumes,
and finally his *Geographisches Kartenspiel* (Geographic Card Game, 1784) – a geographic card game featuring a map of Germany.

These geographical writings are part of Campe's *Kinderbibliothek* (Children's Library), a complete series of "age-appropriate, graduated works for children" (Apgar 2008: 86), accompanying future citizens from childhood into adulthood, and supporting their cognitive progression from sensory perception to rational reasoning and symbolic representation. The story of Robinson, told in dialogue form, is designed for children between six and ten, the *Discovery of America*, still in dialogue form, but much less so, for those between eight and ten, and the collection of travel accounts, mainly third-person accounts, takes children from the age of ten into adulthood. Together, these texts take the growing readers around the globe. "By retelling narratives that feature 'real' places," Richard Apgar remarks, Campe "seeks to curb the use of the imagination. Rather than transporting the reader/listener to an imaginary world, Campe provides specific, if not entirely genuine, geographies […]" (2008: 107).

Geography in the guise of adventure and discovery narratives, then, is the literature philanthropic children are to grow on. Indeed, the geographic writings represent the very core of the *Kinderbibliothek*, and their volume of more than 6000 pages materially supports Campe's claim that travel literature, both amusing and instructive, is the only appropriate kind of literature for emerging citizens because it tells about real places instead of fictional ones, "not only furnishing the minds of my pupils with useful and agreeable knowledge," as he explains in his preface to *Columbus*,

> but inflaming them with an ardent zeal for their religion, and a love of the social virtues, arming them betimes with a courage that will render them proof against adversity, and inspiring them with a lively desire of signalizing themselves by acts of humanity and public utility. (Campe 1799a: xvii–xviii)

The geographic card game: Useful play

Destined to become virtuous and useful members of civil society contributing to the public good, children nevertheless enjoyed the privilege of play while they were young. Up until the age of eight, they were to learn through play because it was best suited to capturing and holding their attention. Inspired by Rousseau's ideological dictum that children were categorically different from rational adults and informed by Locke's methodology of playful learning, philanthropists developed a pedagogy of play, programmatically making the Horacian motto "instruct and delight" their own.

Campe was also an extremely successful publisher, whose *Schulbuchhandlung* (School Bookshop) provided the educational market of his time with an impressive selection of books as well as educational games and toys. In 1784, he designed a card game to initiate children, eight years and older, into the reading of maps and to playfully inculcate geographic and statistical knowledge that would later on prove useful to the enterprising citizen. His *Geographisches Kartenspiel* (Geographic Card Game), marketed as the ideal Christmas present for children of bourgeois families, included a large-scale map of what was then the German Empire and 300 game cards with the names of cities and facts such as population, industry, landmarks, or agriculture. The map presents no detail, merely the black outlines delimiting the political and geographical borders of Germany (Figure 2). Black dots on the map invited children to find the right location for the city names printed on the little cards. Once the city cards were in place, children were to add the information on population size, main industry, and main sights to each city name, reciting the data and sharing related anecdotes or adding explanations if they remembered them from previous lessons.

While statistical information on German towns and cities may seem far removed from the horizon and concerns of young children, the material nature of the printed map, which served as game board and would have been mounted on cardboard for greater durability, brought it back home and literally into the grasp

Figure 2. Illustration from Joachim Heinrich Campe: *Geographisches Kartenspiel: ein Weihnachtsgeschenk für Kinder und junge Leute, nebst 300 geogr. Spielkärtchen u. e. geogr. Umrißkarte von Deutschland*. Hamburg: Carl Ernst Bohn, 1784. Germanisches Nationalmuseum Nürnberg

of children. They could manipulate the cards, place them on the map, move them around, develop a sense for relative distance and scale, engage in conversations with their play partners or teachers and thus playfully combine the instructive with the amusing. Most importantly, the large scale of the printed map and the handy game cards allowed for interaction with the map, making abstract information tactile and transforming learning into sensory experience and play. Every time they put down a card, aligninged a card with a dot, this action was combined with the indexical gesture of "here is." By placing a card on a specific spot on the map, children made the connection between the abstract "there" of a remote geographic location and the concrete "here" of the card game itself. Black outlines and dots on the printed map provide a zone of interaction for curious children, inviting them not only to interact with the map and geographic and statistical knowledge connected to it but also with their peers, engaging in communal learning, playfully rehearsing rules of civic interaction (Kühme 1997: 223). The geographic card game thus served to engrain lessons learned in geography but, first and foremost, it helped shape the future citizen.

"Here is" – Bringing the world back home

Maps, whether only mentioned in the text, visually integrated into the text page, printed separately and bound into the book as fold-outs, or circulating entirely separately, play an important role in evoking the reference to the real world – and especially in teaching children how to relate to this world rationalized by cartographers and domesticated by well-meaning educators who share the philanthropic cartophobia.

Apgar's insightful dissertation (2008) on Campe's travel narratives helps contextualize the maps in Campe's writing. Apgar shows how Campe employs a wide array of narrative and didactic devices to shape the dynamic relationship between the domestic and the foreign, ultimately aiming at the domestification of the exotic and adventurous to serve the creation of citizens. The paratextual element of the maps joins in this effort and helps amplify some of the narrative strategies employed by Campe.

The maps printed or bound into the books function as visual paratexts, guiding the readers in their use and understanding of the text. While *Robinson* features no separate map illustrations at all, most editions of the *Discovery of America* include one copper engraving fold-out map per volume (Pohlmann 1996: 140–144): *Columbus* showing the Gulf of Mexico, *Cortez* Mexico from coast to coast, and *Pizarro* all of South America. *Columbus* also includes the woodcut figure illustrating latitude and longitude mentioned above (Figure 1), which is printed directly into the text of the fictional dialogue. For the *Sammlung*, which was a long-term publishing project appearing in many different editions, a map was bound into the back only in two of the twelve volumes, one tracing the English voyages of discovery of the South Seas (including Commodore Byron and Captain Cook), the other one Mr. Lesseps's journey through Siberia.

Even though there is no separate illustration showing a map in Campe's *Robinson*, a little map can be seen in the frontispiece – and maps feature very

Figure 3. Frontispiece of Joachim Heinrich Campe: *Robinson der Jüngere*. Vol 1. Hamburg: Carl Ernst Bohn, 1779. © Pictura Paedagogica Online, Universität Hildesheim, http://www.bbf.dipf.de/cgi-opac/bil.pl?t_direct=x&f_IDN=b0006461hild

prominently in the narrative setting (Figure 3). Campe transforms Defoe's first-person narrative in his *Robinson the Younger* into a moral tale told and controlled by the father, alias Campe himself. This narrative frame, written in dialogue form, allows him to bring the adventurous and potentially infectious story of the seafaring Robinson back home to Hamburg, firmly grounding the foreign and exotic in the domestic and familiar – in the "here and now" of his storytelling (cf. Apgar 2008: 68–84; Erlin 2006; O'Malley 2006, 2009 and 2012: 23–47). It is no coincidence therefore that the map of the alluring Caribbean appears only in miniature format in the background of the full-page frontispiece, which foregrounds the controlled storytelling setting. The imaginary potential of the map is visually contained through this didactic use of ekphrasis, just as Robinson's adventures are reduced to a story within a story. The domestic setting thus metaphorically maps out the correct behavior children are to emulate, while the map within this moral mapping frames, contains, and tames the adventurous plot set on the remote island.

In fact, Campe insists in his preface that the fictive story of Robinson is only a byproduct, a necessary tool to convey the ample instructive and useful factual knowledge – mainly geographic in nature – found in the story of Robinson. This geographic mindset is visualized by the map hanging on the tree above the father. The map allows the children to trace the adventures of the anti-hero while remaining firmly grounded in their domestic environment. Their vantage point remains the home, their point of reference the family. While their eyes gaze into the distance, their hands are busy sewing, shelling peas, or performing other useful activities a *Bürger* should busy himself or herself with.

The map pinned to the apple tree as well as a little atlas one of the children has incidentally brought along to one of the storytelling evenings (Campe 1789: 39, 45) are explicitly mentioned in the text and presented as useful didactic tools: "Lookee [sic], Children," the father introduces the second storytelling evening, "I have brought a large map with me, on this you can see more distinctly than upon a little one, what way the ship was to take, and whither she was driven by contrary winds" (Campe 1789: 47–48). So while the material book itself offers no separate geographical map to its readers, the narrative frame recommends and models the correct use of maps. It does so by stressing the indexical function of these maps. Again and again throughout the text, the father or children interrupt the narrative to point towards the map and locate the narrative: "They wanted to steer down all along *this way*," or "this coast here," or "look, *this is* where…." By pointing to the map only present in the narrative frame and pronouncing the "here," they invariably convert the "Carribean *there*" to a "Hamburg *here*," bringing the story of Robinson back home, domesticating the exotic, pinning it down, so to say, on paper.

The same holds true for the three volumes of the *Discovery of America*, which include very precise maps of Middle and South America. These paratextual maps also feature prominently in the narrative text itself. Just before the arrival of Columbus in the New World, the storytelling father advises his children to bring along a map of America, so that they may understand more of what they see than poor Columbus, for whom it was yet uncharted territory. "Here is the map, my dear father, which you desired me to bring yesterday," exclaims little John, and the father invites the children to a lesson in map-reading: "Well then, draw near, all of you, and observe" (1799a: 76). He guides their gaze by pointing out sites relevant to the narrative, identifying them by name and placing them within their specific geographic and narrative context: "These isles (*pointing to them on the map*) are in general called the *Lucayos* or *Bahama Isles* [...]" (1799a: 76–77). Rather than inviting the solitary reader to explore exotic places and dream up adventures, philanthropic maps function as focal points for intergenerational and interactive learning, anchoring the narrative in the real world and defining geographic, social, commercial, and moral relationships. As Apgar has shown, "[t]hese maps are often 'exact' reproductions of maps that the Father uses in the narrative, which serve to draw the reading child into the circle of the listening children, or permit a storyteller to more effectively play the role of the Father" (2008: 107). The map as printed object in the book thus becomes the physical point of intersection between the extratextual world of child readers and the intratextual world of the narrative frame. By pointing towards the Bahama Isles, for example, extratextual readers repeat the pedagogic gesture of the storytelling father rather than pointing into the exotic distance, thus transforming stories of adventurous discovery into tales of moral reflection and enlightening self-discovery.

For the voyages of discovery compiled and retold in the *Sammlung*, Campe no longer added a narrative frame, convinced that adolescent readers had internalized proper reading habits by the time they reached this last part of the *Kinderbibliothek*. The two maps found here, then, take a different approach: they guide and discipline the gaze of the map-reading adolescent by visually marking the voyages of discovery of English explorers through the South Seas and the travels of Mr. Lesseps through Siberia with lines. These lines do not map coastlines or islands, but travel routes; they map time onto space, resulting in visual travel narratives. The moral message of these travel narratives is one of curiosity, active engagement with the world, integrity, and perseverance. The stories of Byron, Cooke, and Lesseps are not told as stories of men leaving home to go on adventures, but as tales of exemplary men who go out into the world only to come back home to share their discoveries and new-found knowledge, which then, in turn, can be mapped.

Performing the map

To conclude, I would like to stress what one could call the "domestification" of the indexical function of maps. Pointing to foreign places and trying to bring them home by doing so is a gesture I consider to be characteristic of the philanthropic use of maps. It is a gesture firmly grounded in the material culture of eighteenth-century geography and education.

This domestification of the indexical function of maps is nicely illustrated in the frontispiece of the *Etrennes pour les Enfans* (New Year's Wishes for Children, 1782), a French translation and abridgement of Campe's *Kleine Kinderbibliothek* (Little Children's Library). It shows a family – father, mother, and three sons between the ages of four and ten – in a setting typical for enlightened members of the educated bourgeoisie: shelves full of books to the right, with busts of antique authorities sitting on the top shelf, an engraving (a map?) hanging on the back wall, and a huge globe standing in front of the shelves. The globe is visually framed by the bodies of the bourgeois family – mother in front left, father in the central background, the children to the right. Behind the globe, we see the father, pointing to a spot on the map with his left hand, while raising his right hand in a declamatory gesture underscoring the importance of what he is showing. And while the pictorial composition of the engraving guides the readers' eyes toward the pointing hand, only one of the four listeners, one of the older boys, seems to be paying attention and following the father's indexical gesture (unless he is looking at the ship his little brother is pointing out).

The smallest boy, maybe four years of age, seems incapable of grasping the significance of the many lines apparently resembling coastlines and representing political borders. Instead of looking at the abstract spot his father is pointing to, he points out the only sign he is able to read: the iconic image of a ship sailing across the ocean. The mother, sitting on a chair, apparently holding a large-format book or collection of printed plates, does not follow the father's indexical gesture either. She intently gazes into the face of her husband, less interested in what he is showing than in the act of showing and telling itself. She seems to care little about what exactly he is pointing out on the map; all she is interested in is the fact that her husband is there with her in the study of their bourgeois home, teaching their children. Not the geographical knowledge imparted counts in her eyes, but the performance of family responsibility, the father modeling correct behavior and teaching their children far more than geographical facts – namely how to become a decent man, husband, father, and citizen. The indexical gesture of the father is transformed into a self-referential, performative gesture, pointing toward the act of teaching, educating, and enlightening the future *Bürger*.

Figure 4. Frontispiece of Joachim Heinrich Campe: *Etrennes pour les Enfans*. Hamburg: Carl Ernst Bohn, 1782. © Pictura Paedagogica Online, Bibliothek für Bildungsgeschichtliche Forschung des Deutschen Instituts für Internationale Pädagogische Forschung, Berlin

The geographic writings of Campe reveal that maps in philanthropic children's books were considered paratexts with great didactic and practical potential on the one hand – their capacity to visualize useful information and to speak to the senses – and of great danger on the other because they could confuse and seduce through the power of symbolic representation, inspiring children to follow the flights of their fancy. Most importantly, however, they clearly show that, within the philanthropic context, maps function less as sign systems representing foreign worlds than as spaces of pedagogic performance, reproducing the utilitarian and moral lessons that support the self-fashioning of the enlightened Bürger.

References

Primary sources

Basedow, Johann Bernhard. 1774. *Elementarwerk mit den Kupfertafeln Chodowieckis u.a. Critical edition in three volumes*, Theodor Fritsch (ed.). Leipzig: Wiegandt (reprinted 1909).

Bertuch, Friedrich Justin, and Bertuch, Carl (eds). 1790–1830. *Bilderbuch Für Kinder. Enthaltend eine angenehme Sammlung von Thieren, Pflanzen, Blumen, Früchten, Insecten, Trachten und allerhand andern unterrichtenden Gegenständen aus dem Reiche der Natur, der Künste und Wissenschaften; Alle nach den besten Originalen gewählt, gestochen, und mit einer kurzen wissenschaftlichen, und den Verstandes-Kräften eines Kindes angemessenen Erklärung begleitet*, 12 Vols. Weimar: Expedition des Journals des Luxus und der Moden.

Campe, Joachim Heinrich. 1779/80. *Robinson der Jüngere: Zur angenehmen und nüzlichen Unterhaltung für Kinder*, 2 Vols. Hamburg: Carl Ernst Bohn.

Campe, Joachim Heinrich. 1781/82. *Die Entdekkung von Amerika: ein angenehmes und nüzliches Lesebuch für Kinder und junge Leute.* 3 vols. Hamburg: Carl Ernst Bohn.

Campe, Joachim Heinrich. 1785–1787. *Sammlung interessanter und durchgängig zweckmäßig abgefaßter Reisebeschreibungen für die Jugend*, 3 Vols. Vol 1: Hamburg: Herold. Vol 2: Wolfenbüttel: Schulbuchhandlung. Vol 3: Braunschweig: Schulbuchhandlung.

Campe, Joachim Heinrich. 1789. *Robinson the Younger by Mr. Campe: Illustrated by German notes for the use of those, which are learning the English*, 2 Vols. Frankfurt: Kessler.

Campe, Joachim Heinrich. 1799a. *Columbus: Or, the Discovery of America: As related by a father to his children, and designed for the instruction of youth*, 2 Vols. London: Sampson Low.

Campe, Joachim Heinrich. 1799b. *Cortez: Or, the Conquest of Mexico: As related by a father to his children, and designed for the instruction of youth*, 2 Vols. London: Sampson Low.

Campe, Joachim Heinrich. 1799c. *Pizarro: Or, the Conquest of Peru: As related by a father to his children, and designed for the instruction of youth*, 2 Vols. London: Sampson Low.

Campe, Joachim Heinrich. 1782. *Etrennes pour les Enfans.* Hamburg: Carl Ernst Bohn. Digital version <http://vd18.de/de-sub-vd18/content/titleinfo/10779529> (14 January 2016).

Campe, Joachim Heinrich. 1784. *Geographisches Kartenspiel: Ein Weihnachtsgeschenk für Kinder und junge Leute, nebst 300 geogr. Spielkärtchen u. e. geogr. Umrißkarte von Deutschland.* Hamburg: Carl Ernst Bohn.

Campe, Joachim Heinrich (ed). 1785–1792. *Allgemeine Revision des gesammten Schul- und Erziehungswesens von einer Gesellschaft praktischer Erzieher*, 16 Vols. Wien & Wolfenbüttel: Wolf Gräffer. Available online at: <http://opac.bbf.dipf.de> (14 January 2016).

GutsMuths, Johann Christoph Friedrich. 1835. *Versuch einer Methodik des geographischen Unterrichts*. Weimar: Verlag des geographischen Instituts.

Lieberkühn, Philipp Julius. 1782. *Versuch über die anschauende Erkenntnis: Ein Beytrag zur Theorie des Unterrichts*. Züllichau: Frommann-Holzboog.

Rousseau, Jean-Jacques. 2010. *Emile, or, On Education: Includes Emile and Sophie, or, The Solitaries. Collected Writings of Rousseau*, ed. by Kelly, Christopher; Bloom, Allan David Hanover NH: University Press of New England (first French ed. 1762).

Secondary sources

Apgar, Richard B. 2008. Taming Travel and Disciplining Reason: Enlightenment and Pedagogy in the Work of Joachim Heinrich Campe. PhD dissertation, University of North Carolina at Chapel Hill.

Austermann, Simone. 2010. *Die "Allgemeine Revision": Pädagogische Theorieentwicklung im 18. Jahrhundert*. Bad Heilbrunn: Klinkhardt.

Brückner, Martin. 1999. Lessons in geography: Maps, speller, and other grammars of nationalism in the early republic. *American Quarterly* 51(2): 311–343. doi: 10.1353/aq.1999.0022

Brückner, Martin. 2006. *The geographic revolution in early America: Maps, literacy, and national identity*. Chapel Hill NC: Published for the Omohundro Institute of Early American History and Culture by University of North Carolina Press.

Erlin, Matt. 2006. Book fetish. Joachim Heinrich Campe and the commodification of literature. *Seminar: A Journal of Germanic Studies* 42(4): 355–376.

te Heesen, Anke. 2002. *The World in a Box: The Story of an Eighteenth Century Picture Encyclopedia*, transl. Anne M. Hentschel. Chicago IL: University of Chicago Press.

Kühme, Dorothea. 1997. *Bürger und Spiel Gesellschaftsspiele im deutschen Bürgertum zwischen 1750 und 1850. Historische Studien*. Frankfurt: Campus-Verlag.

Liebs, Elke. 1977. *Die pädagogische Insel: Studien zur Rezeption des "Robinson Crusoe" in deutschen Jugendbearbeitungen*. Stuttgart: Metzler.

von Merveldt, Nikola. 2014. Pädagogische Raumpraktiken: Zur Topographie philanthropischer Anschauungspädagogik. In *Topographien der Kindheit. Literarische, mediale und interdisziplinäre Perspektiven auf Orts- und Raumkonstruktionen*, Caroline Roeder (ed.), 183–198. Bielefeld: transcript-Verlag.

O'Malley, Andrew. 2006. Crusoe at home. Coding domesticity in children's editions of Robinson Crusoe. *Journal for Eighteenth-Century Studies* 29(3): 337–352. doi: 10.1111/j.1754-0208.2006.tb00652.x

O'Malley, Andrew. 2009. Acting out Crusoe. Pedagogy and performance in eighteenth-century children's literature. *The Lion and the Unicorn* 33(2): 131–145. doi: 10.1353/uni.0.0459

O'Malley, Andrew. 2012. *Children's Literature, Popular Culture and Robinson Crusoe*. New York NY: Palgrave Macmillan. doi: 10.1057/9781137027313

Pohlmann, Carola (ed.). 1996. *Erfahrung schrieb's und reicht's der Jugend: Joachim Heinrich Campe als Kinder- und Jugendschriftsteller*. Wiesbaden: Reichert.

Schmitt, Hanno (ed.). 2007. *Vernunft und Menschlichkeit: Studien zur philanthropischen Erziehungsbewegung*. Bad Heilbrunn: Klinkhardt.

Stockhammer, Robert. 2001. "An dieser Stelle": Kartographie und Literatur der Moderne. *Poetica* 33(3–4): 273–306.

Stockhammer, Robert. 2007. *Kartierung der Erde: Macht und Lust in Karten und Literatur*. Munich: Fink.

Wild, Reiner. 2008. Aufklärung. In *Geschichte der deutschen Kinder- und Jugendliteratur*, 3rd edn, Reiner Wild (ed.), 43–95. Stuttgart & Weimar: Metzler.

CHAPTER 3

A subtle cartography

Navigating the past in children's fiction

Janet Grafton

The shift from rural to urban is mapped out in fiction, providing crucial reference points in environmental and cultural history. The old-fashioned worlds depicted in L.M. Montgomery's Jane of Lantern Hill and Dorothy Canfield Fisher's Understood Betsy are mapped not visually but verbally, conveying a strong sense of place that roots the characters with an intrinsic cartography. In this chapter, the author applies ecocriticism to fiction from the past to explore how personal geography and physical geography are entwined and informed by the other. The author analyzes the ways in which substantial and experiential contact with the land helps the protagonists develop their geographic literacy.

Since childhood, landscapes in literature have been as important to me as the literal landscapes I explored on Vancouver Island in Western Canada. And both have contributed to my sense and understanding of place, which I define here as geographic literacy. Connections between places real and fictional, between characters, readers and authors, and between different disciplines, are at the heart of my work, which brings together children's literature and environmental studies. Robert Louis Stevenson touches on this idea of interconnectivity when he writes that all authors need to begin their stories with a map, for in the process, "relations will appear that [the writer] had not thought upon" (1995: 134). In a similar vein, Dava Sobel shares that while she is writing, she must "keep a map of the territory at hand, to help characters find their roots" (2013: 11).

In the two primary texts that I discuss in this chapter, Lucy Maud Montgomery's *Jane of Lantern Hill* and Dorothy Canfield Fisher's *Understood Betsy*, the central movement of the stories pivot on the two protagonists finding their respective roots. There are a number of notable commonalities between the books. Published within twenty years of each other, *Understood Betsy* in 1916 and *Jane of Lantern Hill* in 1937, both stories are set in the early 1900s. The young female protagonists in both novels are relocated against their will to rural places, and both become

DOI 10.1075/clcc.7.04gra

intimately involved with the land and learn to grow things, in particular, food. They are both prepubescent, which is noteworthy in that these girls are granted a freedom to explore that is often denied older girls or women in fiction from this era. Both books promote a harmonious relationship with the natural world, and both very clearly hinge on dialectics of urban versus rural. And finally, both books are set in fictionalized (and arguably romanticized) versions of real places: Prince Edward Island (PEI) in Canada in the early 1920s in *Jane of Lantern Hill* and rural Vermont in New England in the early 1900s in *Understood Betsy*.

The rural worlds depicted in *Jane of Lantern Hill* and *Understood Betsy* are mapped not visually but verbally, conveying along the way a strong sense of place that roots the characters with an intrinsic cartography. The details of country landscapes and farming communities embedded in these stories are unfamiliar to the young protagonists at the beginnings of their stories. Through close engagement with these environments, the girls journey towards a new understanding of themselves and their place in the world. In this chapter, my explorations are twofold: firstly, to discover the ways in which geographic literacy is promoted and achieved in the novels, which are pastoral in nature and considered nostalgic by today's standards; and secondly, to investigate how this nostalgia in literature from prior eras can be mapped, and how such an exercise is vital in fostering geographic literacy in contemporary readers.

Ecocriticism

I begin this investigation by applying ecocriticism to fiction from the past to explore the question of how personal geography and physical geography are entwined and informed by each other. My use of this theory aligns with Cheryl Lousley's belief that ecocritical analysis should be used to explore how characters are positioned as knowing or not knowing the environments they inhabit (2007: 12). At the beginning of their stories, both girls are positioned as not knowing their environments. *Understood Betsy* begins with an emphasis on the insignificance of the story's urban geography. The narrator describes it as "a medium-sized city in a medium-sized state in the middle of this country" (Fisher 1987: 1). *Jane of Lantern Hill* begins in a similar fashion, with a description of a street, dark and dingy in winter (Montgomery 1988: 1).

The limitations imposed by urban geography on these girls are apparent at the beginning of both stories, and the girls are almost entirely denied primary experience in their urban environments. Montgomery's narrator reports that "it was so seldom that Jane was allowed to walk anywhere alone [...] to walk anywhere at all, indeed" (30). Jane craves the chance to move freely, but as the narrator states, "one was almost terrified to walk over the lawn lest one do something to Uncle William's cherished velvet. You had to keep to the flat stepping-stones path. And Jane wanted to *run*" (4). In *Understood Betsy*, Aunt Frances, who is in a state of constant concern for the girl's frail physical state, tells the doctors, "I try to see that Elizabeth Ann has plenty of fresh air. I go out with her for a walk every single day. But we have taken all the walks around here so often that we're rather tired of them" (Fisher 1987: 53). Exercise and movement become structured, mechanical activities in the city. In these novels, the freedom to explore is curbed by the limits of cityscapes, by concerned caregivers, and by fear and restraint. Urban, indoor environments render the girls' lives confined and circumscribed, which limits their inner lives and psychological growth, as well as their physical health (Grafton 2010: 49–50). In pinpointing the moments of the girls' interactions, or lack thereof, with their surroundings, both urban and rural, ecocritical analysis underscores the inherent connections between well-being and environment.

Geographic literacy

The effects of oppressive environments and the subsequent inability of these environments to provide primary experience are central to Edward Reed's belief that there is something wrong with a society that hinders or does not foster firsthand exploration of the world (1996: 3). Virtual knowledge and virtual experience, while useful for introducing places and concepts, can only produce a two-dimensional experience. Just as travelers read maps to achieve a sense of a place before physically exploring it, readers (and in the case of my key novels, the characters) must step away from the map, or the story, or the city streets, into the world represented on the paper, and make connections with the environments that were first established on those pages. For contemporary readers reading books set in bygone times, the only way to access past environments is through secondhand experience. Understanding how the past connects to the present is an integral component of geographic literacy. In reading about characters that develop their own sense of geographic literacy through firsthand experience with the natural world, contemporary readers' own sense of geographic literacy is enhanced. The depictions of rural landscapes in *Understood Betsy* and *Jane of Lantern Hill* are fictionalized, and arguably idealized, but they provide at least a glimpse into ways of life that had their basis in history and that can only be accessed through fiction now. This oftentimes-nostalgic glimpse is vital in promoting for contemporary readers a connection to past landscapes. Later in this chapter, I discuss how nostalgia can be critically reframed in terms of geographic literacy, which must include an understanding of how contemporary landscapes connect to landscapes in history.

The ability to make connections is at the core of geographic literacy; it centers on ecology, which operates on an understanding of living systems and their interconnectedness. Urban environments are not separate from ecological systems, but their relation to the natural world is complex; living systems in these environments are often literally covered up and erased, buried beneath concrete and built structures, or fragmented into the patchwork of parks. The development of a full geographic literacy requires movement beyond the surface; it requires going further and deeper than the screen, paper, or, as in the case of these stories, the street. Stories can introduce ideas about a place, but learning to read the landscape requires that these ideas, this virtual knowledge, must be followed with firsthand primary engagement with the land to achieve a genuine sense of place. In terms of narrative analysis, the protagonists in *Jane of Lantern Hill* and *Understood Betsy* start their lives with knowledge of urban environments, but their familiarity with ecological systems in the natural world is based solely on secondhand experience. The development of their geographic literacy requires a rural relocation.

This valorization of the country over the city, particularly in terms of healthy childhoods, is a common trope in literature from this time. Both protagonists are urban children at the beginning of their stories, and neither girl thrives in her environment. Fisher in particular very clearly aligns fresh air, rural landscapes, and nature with "health, self-sufficiency, happiness, freedom, and independence, obvious and hallowed American traits" (Cummins 2004: 15). And while Montgomery's Jane is not suffering poor health, her lack of confidence and physical awkwardness are her traits that most stand out in her city home. Both Montgomery and Fisher are writing in a long tradition of Romantic notions of childhood that suggest children do best in natural settings (15). And at the time that both novels are set, childhood as a social construction has been fully developed, and the literary tradition they are writing in reflects that modern notions of childhood have been legally, socially, psychologically, and politically established (Hendrick 1997: 35). Jane and Betsy are located squarely in their respective childhoods, free to explore yet obliged to learn the rules of growing up.

Personal cartographies

It is in the respective geographies of the stories that these rules take on their own national flavor. In terms of landscape, Fisher's depiction of landscape is distinctly American and peppered with that country's rural details and values, while Montgomery's writing is unequivocally entrenched in the pastoral, imperial English Romantic tradition that most early Canadians were fluent in. And so it is important to look at how the protagonists' personal geographies are embedded in the larger political geographies of the times in which the authors set their stories. On the first page of his seminal work, *The Country and the* City (1973), Raymond Williams explains the dual definition of country as pertaining both to the land and to the nation. Cummins points to Fisher's alignment with country as nation, and in her paper she illustrates how Betsy's education centers largely on becoming American. And as Squire discusses in her paper on literature, place, and tourism in Prince Edward Island, Montgomery's landscapes transcend the regional; they are "intrinsically linked to Canadian identity and culture" (1992: 139). There are no overt instances of Jane being educated as a Canadian citizen, but her story's regional setting serves as a vehicle for the preservation of conservative, nationalistic values. Jane's father is a veteran of the First World War. His retreat to the country is private, yet pointed. The country, for him, is a healing place, somewhere that allows him to live a deliberately simple life, which could be read as Montgomery's critique of the modern, post-war, industrialized world.

In their respective works, Fisher and Montgomery draw from their own landscapes in ways that are pastoral and personal, idealized and regional. Both novels can be regarded as conservative in that the authors used them as a canvas for the preservation of particular ways of life. Epperly remarks on Montgomery's "ambivalent oscillation between social change and protection of old values," values founded on old Victorian and Presbyterian traditions, and which often include values of traditional domestic femininity (1999: 9). And while it is clear that both Jane and Betsy are engaged in traditional domestic activities within the narrow spheres of their time, there is more going on in these books: in the authors' use of green space, they transcend tradition.

Ecocriticism: Where is nature?

As a cornerstone question of ecocriticism, Cheryll Glotfelty asks, "Where *is* the natural world in the text" (1996: xxiii). In these texts, it is located centrally, and in opposition to urban spaces. It is the green, rural world of cultivation, of forests, fields, farms, and gardens. Ecocriticism, which is essentially environmental literary theory that considers the setting in stories with as much attention and critique as is usually granted plot and characters, focuses on integral setting, which is defined as being "essential to the story, and which influences plot, character, and conflict" (Lukens et al. 2012: 149). And as one ecocritical scholar notes, because ecocriticism approaches literature from a biocentric perspective rather than anthropocentric one, the theory allows for an exploration of the interconnectedness between human and nonhuman nature, rather than regarding nonhuman nature as setting for human activity (Sigler 1994/5: 148). Far from being mere backdrop, the relevance of setting in both of these novels is established from the outset, and both stories use urban environments as deliberate foils to the rural relocations that occur. Ecocriticism pinpoints this relevance by highlighting the myriad ways the landscape is integral to both plot and to the girls' personal growth.

Nature and transformation

The authors' use of green space as central to the plots of the story and to the girls' development in many ways reflects Annis Pratt's theory of nature as an archetypal pattern in the female Bildungsroman. For both Jane and Betsy, the green world serves as a place where they find their solace and their independence, as well as a way to keep them in touch with their selfhood and to help them make their way through the alienation of society (Pratt 1981: 21). As stated above, in Fisher's and Montgomery's works, the green space is, for the most part, a domesticated space, well within view of stables and kitchens and comfortable beds. What truly makes their stories unique is that while both girls grow to become the heroes of their respective stories, they remain children in the narratives, their lives uncomplicated by adult manifestations of female sexuality. And so while the authors maintain the status quo with regard to many elements of the dominant cultures in which they were writing, they are also resistant, and even transcendent, in many ways. At a time when it was fashionable in literature to depict girls as invalids, or as tomboys tamed by the story's end, they instead create girls who simply become sturdy and capable. The authors deliberately relocate the girls from urban or indoor places and release them into active outdoor life. Jane and Betsy begin their stories as typical twentieth-century protagonists but are transformed through the course of their narratives into something entirely new (Grafton 2010: 93).

This unique aspect of their transformations within green spaces is contrasted with the deep aversion the girls initially feel towards these spaces. When the girls first behold the rural spaces that are imposed on them, they regard these environments with incomprehension and dismissal (55). Elizabeth Ann, who is renamed Betsy by her farm relatives, first comes to the country in winter via train, and to her eyes, the landscape is terrifyingly dismal:

> She shrank in her seat, more and more frightened as the end of her journey came nearer, and looked out dismally at the winter landscape, thinking it hideous with its brown bare fields, its brown bare trees, and the quick-running little streams hurrying along, swollen with the January thaw which had taken all the snow from the hills. (Fisher 1987: 21)

And when Jane first learns that her father wishes her to spend the summer with him on PEI, she regards it as "that horrible Prince Edward Island, which looked on the map to be a desolate little fragment in the jaws of Gaspe and Cape Breton" (Montgomery 1988: 46). Jane's journey to her new environment and her impression of it are much the same as Betsy's. When she travels to Prince Edward Island for the first time, she thinks to herself, "So this was P.E. Island [...] this rain-drenched land where the trees cringed before the wind and the heavy clouds seemed almost to touch the fields" (54). Each girl is forced into a foreign, rural environment, each is unwell in body and mind, and each sees the land in terms of her state of being. At this moment in their respective stories, the girls have no sense of the land they have been relocated to. Up to this point, they have had no opportunities in which to develop their geographic literacy.

In the country, the girls are allowed to freely explore their new environments, and these stories reflect a level of freedom that is unusual for girls from this era: Jane roams freely around the PEI countryside, herding cows and, once, even an escaped zoo lion. Betsy navigates her way to school and to the country fair solo. In this way, they begin to know the environments they inhabit. These stories map the girls' journeys towards an understanding of their geography, and the impact this geography has on their development. Jane is amazed by her new landscape, where "outside were free hills and wide, open fields where you could run wherever you liked, none daring to make you afraid, spruce barrens and shadowy sand dunes, instead of an iron fence and locked gate" (83). The fact that "she could go where she liked over the countryside, unhindered, uncriticized, was one of the most delightful things about life at Lantern Hill" (121). Betsy is granted the autonomy and the space to explore, whether she desires it or not. Upon first arriving at the farm, she is sent off to the country school by her cousin, who tells her to, "Run along, child. Straight down the road till the first turn to the left, and there in the crossroads, there you are" (Fisher 1987: 62). Here she is given a verbal map, directions to an unfamiliar place, which provide her with the means to navigate alone, however ill-equipped she believes herself to be, and to discover the physical reality connected to these directives.

The nature of the green places

In these stories, the setting is not merely a backdrop for performance, but a place for the girls to do, to build and test their skills, and to prove their abilities. In his article on children and interactive settings, Mark Francis maintains that when children become involved with their landscapes rather than just observing them, a deeper significance and meaning is established (1995: 8). In both novels, the girls grow at ease in their bodies and in their environments through movement, and through learning to do things. Through engagement with the land, they are transformed into capable, confident children.

Louise Chawla refers to archaic consciousness as a way of being in the world in which people do not feel separate from their surroundings; it is the state of being fully immersed and fully engaged with the sensory experience of the environment (2002: 209). Both Jane and Betsy are deeply rooted to the land, and ecocritical analysis pinpoints the moments of connection that take the girls beneath the surface of their experience, and positions them in a place of knowing their environment. After a summer of working on and eating from the land, and of playing and exploring, Jane's connection to the island is intrinsic, and when she must say goodbye, "She knows the fields and the windy golden shore are a part of her. She believes that she and her Island understand each other." "I belong here," she says (Montgomery 1988: 141). As for Betsy, she takes on the colors of her landscape, and at the end of the novel, she and her dog are described as playing like "wild creatures, careering through the air like bright blown autumn leaves" (Fisher 1987: 201). The girls' personal cartographies, the cartographies of how they experience their environments and geographies, go beneath the surface and become three-dimensional. These girls become part of the land.

A number of passages in both novels illustrate clearly the necessity of reaching higher altitudes in order to gain a view of the landscape. This shift in perspective is key in contributing to the girls' sense of place in both novels. In *Understood Betsy*, Putney Farm is elevated, located midway up Hemlock Mountain. When Betsy and her friend climb to a lookout, "they could see the lights in the farmhouses scattered along the valley road and on the side of the mountain opposite them, like big stars fallen from the multitude above" (143). Betsy is positioned as knowing her environment when she becomes curious about it, and when she recognizes that the view from the top will give her knowledge of place that is unattainable any other way:

> [There was] Hemlock Mountain, high above her there, the snow on it bright golden in the sunlight. Uncle Henry had promised to take her up to the top as soon as the snow went off. She wondered what the top of the mountain would be like. Uncle Henry had said the main thing was that you could see so much of the world at once. He said it was queer the way your own house and big barn and great fields looked like little toy things that weren't of any account. It was because you could see so much more than just the... (113)

Here her thoughts are interrupted. This moment simultaneously underscores the relevance and immediacy of the local, as well as highlights the ineffable value and difficulty in understanding the larger world and one's place in it. The flat city streets could not offer Betsy this chance for comprehension; she needs a more dynamic landscape.

In *Jane of Lantern Hill*, the view from hilltops is also key to Jane's understanding of place. She and her father go for a walk, and "when they reached the top of the hill, there before them lay something greater and bluer that Jane knew must be the gulf" (Montgomery 1988: 71). "This is where the sea begins," she thinks. By the end of her first week on the island, Jane knows the geography and people of Lantern Hill perfectly. "Every hill seemed to belong to somebody...Big Donald's hill...Little Donald's hill, Old Man Cooper's hill. She could pick out Big Donald Martin's farm and little Donald Martin's farm" (91). "I like the pattern of this place" (75), she says. For Jane, the hilltop view provides more than a pretty vista; this view allows her to see how her home land is comprised, and to understand how the patterns of this land connect. At the heart of geographic literacy is interpreting the difference between seeing and knowing.[1] Paul Connerton believes that individual features possess meaning because they are perceived as part of something obviously whole, and interpretations as to the meaning of the whole must be approached as a means of unifying the details (1989: 12). This idea extends to individual features of a landscape. Without the intimacy wrought by firsthand experience, it is difficult to see the patterns. The view from an unfamiliar lookout in unknown lands is formless, nameless, and generic. The places that the girls first see as distasteful and barren become familiar and beloved after seasons spent engaging with the land. The girls' ability to decode the details, to see the patterns, and to read the land becomes more fluent as they are educated to recognize the ways in which the individual features relate to the their home environs.

Ecocritical navigation

Ecocriticism acts as a compass between literature and the physical world. The stories contain the subjects. Ecocriticism allows us to locate these subjects in the physical world, and to connect them. In this sense, Jane receives ecocritical lessons in geography, which are mediated by her father. Through stories and dramatizations, her father "set about making [...] geography come alive for her, and the subject, "which had once meant merely a map of the world, became [...] fascinating" (Montgomery 1988: 113). Places such as Thebes, Babylon, Tyre, Athens, and

1. A comment from Bettina Kümmerling-Meibauer at the International Conference on Maps in Children's Literature in Bergen 2015 on the distinction between seeing and knowing helped me clarify my stance on geographic literacy.

Galilee become “places where real folks lived [...] soon Jane knew all the fair lands far, far away as she knew Lantern Hill” (113).

This new interest in global geography is enhanced and supplemented by the freedom she is given to explore her local surroundings. Jane must return to Toronto after the summer, but she returns the following June: “It was so exciting to recognize all the spots along the road [...] green wood lanes, old beloved farms that held out their arms to her. The single row of spruces was still marching up Little Donald’s hill. The dunes and the fishing boats sailing in [...] and the little blue pond laughing at her [...] and Lantern Hill” (169). Unstructured exploration the previous year has given her an understanding of her geography that life in the city was unable to match. And just as the city never feels like home to her, nor feels like a part of her, the ways in which personal geography and physical geography entwine and inform each other in the country are myriad. Her father tells her, “You may not know it, but the sea is in your blood. You were born beside it, one sweet, haunted April night [...] you lived by it for three years. Once I took you down and dipped you in it [...] that was your real baptism. You are the sea’s child and you have come home” (72).

As for Betsy, during times of distress, she seeks solace in the Vermont farmland that becomes familiar and beloved: After receiving some difficult news, she runs to the hill for comfort and clarity. Up there, she finds the certainty and the strength to do the right thing:

> Something up there had told her – perhaps the quiet blue shadow of Windward Mountain creeping slowly over the pasture towards her, perhaps the silent glory of red and gold tree, perhaps the singing murmur of the little brook – perhaps all of them together had told her that now had come a time when she must do more [...] she must do what she herself knew was right. (Fisher 1987: 190)

Her personal geography is grounded in the physical. She gains her bearings from interactions with the land, and her sense of the land has become intrinsic. The cartography is etched within her, and she draws from it.

Critical nostalgia

The second part of my theoretical analysis moves from the central ecocritical question of where is nature, to critical nostalgia, which asks: What is the nature of these places, and why should we value them? Critical nostalgia is a term coined by Jennifer Ladino, and within its theoretical framework, she reframes nostalgia as “a vehicle through which critique happens” (2012: 15). Often in critical arenas, nostalgia is referenced in disparaging terms, regarded as a useless, fruitless longing for the past (Nodelman 1996: 82). But Ladino reclaims the function of nostalgia in productive and subversive terms. Her work centers on the idea that some authors deploy nostalgia intentionally and critically. While I build on her idea of nostalgia as a critical vehicle for analysis, my work departs from hers: in the two texts I look at here, the authors are not necessarily deploying nostalgia, but their use of it is just as productive and subversive as Ladino's. I argue that embedded in Montgomery's and Fisher's work is the concept of eco-nostalgia, which is nostalgia for natural places, and which centers on the inherent value of fragile places, particularly during times of great change.

In the 1980s and 1990s, critics attacked nostalgia for its tendency to falsely idealize the past, and for its inability to engage with modernity and as well as its inherently conservative politics (Cashman 2006: 139). In their respective narratives, Fisher and Montgomery idealize the landscapes of Vermont and PEI, and the conservative values of their novels – Presbyterian/Victorian in Montgomery and Puritan self-reliance in Fisher – are obvious. But as Christopher Lasch points out, as a concept, nostalgia is "endlessly adaptable" (1984: 65). There is more going on than wistful backwards glances or a dogged desire to preserve and propagate particular political and social values. The conservative nature of these books can be read literally: the authors are conserving the landscape. Ecocriticism pinpoints instances of the natural world that have value for the characters; eco-nostalgia helps pinpoint why these instances are worth preserving.

Nostalgia is often about the longing to return to a time, not necessarily a place (Hutcheon 1998: 3). My definition of eco-nostalgia is place-based, and extends to a longing for a way of life that is close to the land, as well as for the places themselves. As the prefix eco- refers to the concept of home, the eco-nostalgic aspects of my primary stories center on growing familiar with places that become home to the protagonists, and to a longing on the part of the authors as to what the world could have been, a longing that is both spatial and temporal. The places that these stories take place in are the product of creative nonfiction, and aspects of both the real and the ideal intermingle. Critics frequently lambast the fairy tale or fantasy qualities of these pastoral landscapes. And although these places have factual counterparts, some critics feel that the "sheltered, even juvenile landscapes of L.M. Montgomery [...] are situated in a fantasy world devoid of industry" (Norcliffe et al. 1992: 5). Such a summation dismisses the quiet power of Montgomery's work. As Shelagh Squire notes, it is possible to draw parallels between Montgomery's fictional world and autobiography, for many of the places in her stories had factual counterparts, places she reconfigured through imagination (1992: 139). Montgomery freely spoke of this process, and said that often the places of her youth were in her mind when she was writing, though she altered the geography to suit her requirements. I argue that her requirements transcend the merely sentimental. It is largely the long, descriptive passages of nature in *Jane of Lantern Hill* that mark it as eco-nostalgic:

> At sunset Jane and dad went down to the outside shore [...] as they were to do almost every night of that enchanted summer. All along the silvery curving sand ran a silvery curving wave. A dim, white-sailed vessel drifted past the bar of the shadowy dunes. The revolving light across the channel was winking at them. A great headland of gold and purple ran out behind it. At sunset, that cape became a place of mystery to Jane. What lay behind it? 'Magic seas in fairylands forlorn'. (Montgomery 1988: 82)

By marrying fancy with fact, Montgomery creates a fluid geography that underscores its deep personal value to her; her experience with the landscape is both physical and internalized, which speaks to her own geographic literacy. And as Hutcheon notes, nostalgia is rarely about "the past as actually experienced; it is the past as imagined, as idealized through memory and desire" (1998: 3). In summing up why applying ecocriticism to nostalgic texts is particularly illuminating, one ecocritical scholar states that to gain a more complete and accurate understanding of how landscapes are understood and depicted in literature, it is essential to recover the works of earlier writers "who may be overlooked because their understanding of the natural world is predicated upon ideological or aesthetic assumptions different from our own" (Branch 2002: 6). By blending the fictitious with the autobiographical in their depictions of landscapes and ways of life in these places, Fisher and Montgomery animate regions and customs that are likely unfamiliar to contemporary readers; in the process, these writers share the best versions of their now-bygone worlds.

For most contemporary readers, the following passage, in which Betsy is making maple candy, requires a leap of imaginative faith, as both the place and the practice are foreign, inaccessible, or outdated:

> She found a clean white snowbank under a pine tree, and setting her cup down in a safe place, began to pat the snow down hard to make the right bed for the waxing syrup. The sun, very hot for that late March day, brought out strongly the tarry perfume of the big pine tree. Near her the sap dripped musically into a bucket, already half full, hung on a maple tree. (Fisher 1987: 112)

When the candy is made, she "crunched it all together into a big delicious lump and sucked on it dreamily, her eyes on the rim of Hemlock Mountain, high above her there, the snow on it bright golden in the sunlight" (113). Essentially, the preservation of place, and place-based practices at a particular moment in history is at the heart of these pastoral novels. Both stories depict worlds largely unmarred by war. Fisher wrote her novel on the cusp of the First World War, and her story unfolds free of its shadow. Montgomery wrote *Jane of Lantern Hill* after the war, and while there is mention of Jane's father's service, Montgomery situates her characters in a quiet rural life away from conflict and creates a landscape embedded with the "cartographies of nostalgia" (Lerer 2008: 257). Fiction from the past that depicts rural landscapes and cultures provides a network of map systems, a means to traverse times and places when personal and physical geographies were more intimately entwined. Ladino asks, "What if we stopped privileging temporality (that is, placing past, present, and future in hierarchies) and began to *map* nostalgia, to follow its winding courses and plot its particular trajectories" (2012: 7). The societal and cultural shift from rural, agricultural life to urban, industrial culture, a shift that has been called "a vast and terrifying disintegration" of organic life, is mapped out in fiction, providing crucial reference points in environmental and cultural history (Leavis & Thompson 2000: 73). The nostalgic territories in Fisher's and Montgomery's works bring to light a version of this organic life, still intact and preserved.

The idealizing function of nostalgia serves to illuminate that which we value, for things fragile and easily endangered, for things ephemeral that impact us emotionally and live in our memories. On Jane's first morning on Prince Edward Island, she opens her window to a new experience:

> [She] did not know she was looking out on the loveliest thing on earth […] a June morning in Prince Edward Island[…] A wave of fragrance broke in her face from the lilac hedge[…] The poplars in a corner of the lawn were shaking in green laughter. An apple tree stretching out friendly arms. There was a faraway view of daisy-sprinkled fields across the harbour where white gulls were soaring and swooping. The air was moist and sweet after the rain. Aunt Irene's house was on the fringe of the town and a country road ran behind it […] a road almost blood-red in the glistening wetness. Jane had never imagined a road coloured like that. (Montgomery 1988: 60)

Critics of Montgomery have called her work overblown and flowery in her excessive descriptions of nature. But from an ecocritical perspective, this inventory reads like an act of conservation, a means of committing to memory something that could fade (Grafton 2010: 71). These pastoral texts serve as a reference point for the natural world, and attitudes towards it, at a particular moment in history. Nostalgic longing can create resistance to rapid, uncritical change: It creates a pause, time in which social and environmental critique can occur to consider the nature of the progress. Nostalgia "can be essential for evaluating the present through contrast with the past" (Cashman 2006: 137).

Despite the political and ideological problems associated with nostalgia, it has the potential, when framed alongside eco-nostalgia and geographic literacy, to critically and productively address the environmental and cultural disconnect that can arise from not understanding how past landscapes, fictional and otherwise, connect to the present.

Mapping the past

All maps are versions of worlds that have been edited, simplified, and idealized. Lucy Maud Montgomery and Dorothy Canfield Fisher treasured the settings that are central to their stories. In capturing a version of the world they wanted to immortalize, they acted as cartographers of these beloved landscapes that were a blend of fictional and real places. Stories *are* maps; they pinpoint (what to) treasure; they provide coordinates to the past; they are a means of bridging the literary and the literal; and a way of connecting geography and literature.

There is an increasing disconnect between the contemporary world and the worlds depicted in literature from prior eras. From an environmental perspective, it is important these texts survive, as they serve as reference points in our collective and imaginative history for what was, what has been lost, and what has changed; they are a counterpoint to our postnatural world. Contemporary urban and degraded landscapes must be considered in the analysis of contemporary literature, but their precursors need to be understood for readers to recognize what they are responding to.

Mapping the past in literary landscapes involves navigating nostalgic cartographies of a time where engagement with the land, and therefore understanding of the land, was different; these cartographies are vital to our understanding of contemporary landscapes. Montgomery's and Fisher's rural worlds are explored and eventually understood by previously unreceptive protagonists. Mediated through substantial and experiential contact with the land, and through others who act as guides, or simply give the girls the space and freedom to explore, an intrinsic sense of cartography is subtly embedded in these characters. They understand their place, and their place in the world, because of this internalized map-making.

References

Primary sources

Fisher, Dorothy C. 1987. *Understood Betsy*. New York NY: Dell (first published 1916).
Montgomery, Lucy M. 1988. *Jane of Lantern Hill*. Toronto: McLelland (first published 1937).

Secondary sources

Branch, Michael P. 2002. Saving all the pieces: The place of textual editing in ecocriticism. In *The Greening of Literary Scholarship*, Steven Rosendale (ed.), 3–25. Iowa City IA: University of Iowa Press.

Cashman, Ray. 2006. Critical nostalgia and material culture in Northern Ireland. *Journal of American Folklore* 119(427): 137–160. doi: 10.1353/jaf.2006.0016

Chawla, Louise. 2002. Spots of time: Manifold ways of being in nature. In *Children and Nature: Psychological, Sociocultural and Evolutionary Investigations*, Peter Kahn & Stephen Kellert (eds), 199–225. Cambridge MA: The MIT Press.

Connerton, Paul. 1989. *How Societies Remember*. Cambridge: CUP. doi: 10.1017/CBO9780511628061

Cummins, June. 2004. Understood Betsy, Understood Nation: Dorothy Canfield Fisher and Willa Cather Queer America. *Children's Literature* 32: 15–40. doi: 10.1353/chl.2004.0009

Epperly, Elizabeth & Gammel, Irene. 1999. Introduction: L.M. Montgomery and Canadian culture. In *L.M. Montgomery and Canadian Culture*, Elizabeth Epperly & Irene Gammel (eds), 3–14. Toronto: University of Toronto Press.

Francis, Mark. 1995. Childhood's garden: Memory and meaning of gardens. *Children's Environments* 12: 1–16.

Glotfelty, Cheryll. 1996. Introduction: Literary studies in an age of environmental crisis. In *The Ecocriticism Reader*, Cheryll Glotfelty & Harold Fromm (eds), xv–xxxvii. Athens GA: University of Georgia Press.

Grafton, Janet Marie. 2010. *Girls and Green Space: Sickness-to-Health Narratives in Children's Literature*. Master of Arts thesis, University of British Columbia at Vancouver.

Hendrick, Harry. 1997. Constructions and reconstructions of British childhood: An interpretive survey, 1800 to the present. In *Constructing and Reconstructing Childhood: Contemporary Issues in the Sociological Study of Childhood*, Allison James & Alan Prout (eds), 33–62. London: RoutledgeFalmer.

Hutcheon, Linda. 1998. *Irony, Nostalgia, and the Postmodern*. Toronto: University of Toronto Press.

Ladino, Jennifer K. 2012. *Reclaiming Nostalgia: Longing for Nature in American Literature*. Charlottesville VI: University of Virginia Press.

Lasch, Christopher. 1984. The politics of nostalgia. *Harper's* (November 1984): 65–70.

Leavis, Frank R. & Thompson, Denys. 2000. The organic community. In *The Green Studies Reader: From Romanticism to Ecocriticism*, Laurence Coupe (ed.), 73–76. New York NY: Routledge.

Lerer, Seth. 2008. *Children's Literature: A Reader's History from Aesop to Harry Potter*. Chicago IL: University of Chicago Press. doi: 10.7208/chicago/9780226473024.001.0001

Lousley, Cheryl. 2007. Knowledge, power, and place: Environmental politics in the fiction of Matt Cohen and David Adams Richards. *Canadian Literature* 195: 11–32.

Lukens, Rebecca J., Smith, Jacquelin J. & Ciffel, Cynthia M. 2012. *A Critical Handbook of Children's Literature*, 9th edn. London: Pearson.

Nodelman, Perry. 1996. Progressive Utopia: Or, how to grow up without growing up. In *Only Connect: Readings on Children's Literature*, 3rd edn, Sheila Egoff & William Sutton (eds), 74–82. Oxford: OUP.

Norcliffe, Glen & Simpson-Housely, Paul. 1992. No vacant Eden. In *A Few Acres of Snow: Literary and Artistic Images of Canada*, Paul Simpson-Housely & Glen Norcliffe (eds), 1–15. Toronto: Dundurn Press.

Pratt, Annis. 1981. *Archetypal Patterns in Women's Fiction*. Bloomington IN: Indiana University Press.

Reed, Edward. 1996. *The Necessity of Experience*. New Haven CN: Yale University Press.

Sigler, Carolyn. 1994–95. Wonderland to wasteland: Toward historicizing environmental activism in children's literature. *Children's Literature Association Quarterly* 19(4): 148–153. doi: 10.1353/chq.0.1011

Sobel, Dava. 2013. Forword: For the love of maps. In *On the Map: A Mind-Expanding Exploration of the Way the World Looks*, by Simon Garfield, 11–14. New York NY: Gotham.

Squire, Shelagh. J. 1992. Ways of seeing, ways of being: Literature, place, and tourism in L.M. Montgomery's Prince Edward Island. In *A Few Acres of Snow: Literary and Artistic Images of Canada*, Paul Simpson-Housley & Glen Norcliffe (eds), 139–146. Toronto: Dundurn Press.

Stevenson, Robert Louis. 1995. *Essays in the Art of Writing*. London: Chatto & Windus.

Williams, Raymond. 1973. *The Country and the City*. Oxford: OUP.

CHAPTER 4

Metaphorical maps in picturebooks

Bettina Kümmerling-Meibauer and Jörg Meibauer

This chapter focuses on the cognitive and narrative functions of metaphorical maps in picturebooks. In contrast to maps that present real or fictional city- and landscapes, metaphorical maps are used to visualize abstract concepts. In particular, two types of metaphorical maps in picturebooks are distinguished: maps of (existing) cities and countries that are shaped like animals and humans, and entities such as the heart and the brain that are structured like maps. In order to understand this map category, children have to develop a basic knowledge of the symbols and functions of maps in general, and to learn that metaphorical maps are imaginative guides which symbolize specific patterns of thinking.

There are maps of almost everything: we can find maps of travel routes, the world, and fictional landscapes, but also of the galaxies, the brain, and the digestive system. What these maps have in common is that they impose an order onto something, steered by the human intention of making sense of the unknown. Mapping, like speaking, is intimately related to thinking (Camp 2007). While maps of real city- and landscapes (as abstractions of the world) belong to the realm of traditional geography, other maps display a more subjective kind of cartography.

One of the best known examples of a subjective cartography is the famous Gall map, created by the German physician Franz Joseph Gall in 1812. Gall, who is regarded as the originator of phrenology, dissected the human brain in order to locate the sources of mental illness. The Gall map shows an open human cranium in profile, thus visualizing the different sections of the brain and its connection with the spinal cord. Gall's map lists 27 faculties, which are divided into several spheres: intellectual, perceptual, emotional, moral, and so on. Most of these faculties deal with abstract individual and hard-to-track traits such as cautiousness, spirituality, and veneration, while other traits have more modern scientific counterparts, such as affection, self-esteem, and causality. This map marks the beginning of the creation of maps of the human head or body, where each body part has been assigned a specific property or function. While this map type initially had a scientific origin, the Gall map already displays a metaphorical character by ascribing moral values

DOI 10.1075/clcc.7.05kum

and individual aspirations such as marriage, employment, and love for the beauty of nature to different sections of the brain.

Another popular map type emerged in the nineteenth century as well: geographical maps of cities, countries, or continents that have been altered by adapting the outlines of the countries and continents to historical figures and events. An often cited example is the humorous map of Europe and Asia designed by the Japanese artist Kisaburo Ohara in 1904, which highlights the devastating threat of Russia at the beginning of the twentieth century. Russia is depicted as a ravaging octopus whose tentacles strangle different European and Asian countries, while some countries, such as Germany, Turkey, and China, attempt to evade the stranglehold (see the figure in Harmon 2004: 116–117). Nobody really believes that Russia has the shape of an octopus, so the viewer has to understand that these maps symbolically visualize power relations in a specific historical and political context. Moreover, the type of presentation reveals the illustrator's ideological attitude towards the historical situation depicted in the map.

In general, both map types are distinct concerning the representational function of the maps. In the first map type, a given entity, such as diverse parts of the human body like the brain or the heart, is structured like a map (entity > map). The second map type is different, because the maps depict a given country or city that is shaped like a human or an animal. In this case, the original city- or landscape is alienated by adapting its outline to another entity (map > entity).

Usually, these two map types are classified as 'maps of the imagination' (Harmon 2004; Turchi 2004). However, this term refers not only to these map types but also to maps that show a fictional geographic entity – like the famous map of *Treasure Island* (1883), created by Robert Louis Stevenson. Since the majority of maps in the tradition of the Gall map on the one hand, and the tradition of the Ohara map on the other, are based on metaphors, we propose the term 'metaphorical map' in order to differentiate them from those maps that display fictional places as they often appear in literary works.

While 'maps of the imagination' like Stevenson's treasure map are quite common in children's literature, one might initially assume that metaphorical maps are hardly represented in children's books, since this category demands a solid cognizance of map literacy and the functions of metaphors in order to understand its complex structure and meaning. The comprehension of metaphorical maps is additionally hampered by the tendency to change map conventions in an idiosyncratic way. However, this map type already emerges in picturebooks, and hence we may ask what purpose they fulfill and which cognitive and narrative capacities they demand (for a cognitive-narratological approach to picturebooks, see Kümmerling-Meibauer & Meibauer 2013).

What is a metaphorical map?

In order to lay some groundwork for our analysis of metaphorical maps, we briefly explain the notions of map and metaphor, before turning to a definition of the term 'metaphorical map.' Since it is our intention to find out how the child meets the cognitive and narrative challenges of metaphorical maps, we also outline some developmental aspects.

Drawing on Kümmerling-Meibauer and Meibauer (2015), we distinguish between real maps and mental maps. While real maps materially represent parts of the real or a fictional world, mental maps (or cognitive maps) represent salient aspects of one's environment which are stored in the brain (Uttal & Tan 2000). According to Downs and Stea, the ability of cognitive or mental mapping enables people to "collect, organize, store, recall, and manipulate information about the spatial environment" (1977: 6).

Both map categories refer to real land- and cityscapes as well as fictional land- and cityscapes. A real map can depict either a real land- or cityscape, such as a roadmap of Denmark and a map of a city like Berlin, or fictional places, such as the map of the 100-acre-wood in A. A. Milne's *Winnie-the-Pooh* (1926). A mental map may represent one's way from a certain spot to another spot, like the way one has to take from the main station to a museum. However, a mental map may also result from reading a verbal description of a fictional land- or cityscape in a narrative. Moreover, real maps and mental maps are dependent on each other. Real maps support the development of mental maps, while mental maps lay the foundation for the comprehension of real maps. The following schema (Figure 1) visualizes the relationship between these categories:

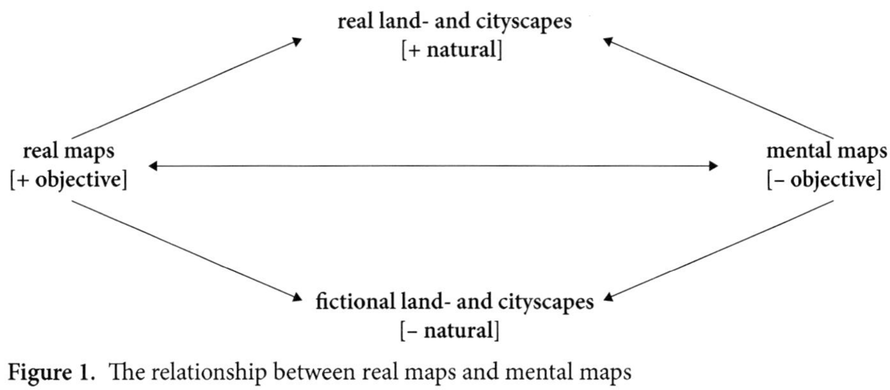

Figure 1. The relationship between real maps and mental maps

A cautionary note is appropriate here: Real maps are objective only in the sense that they are not subjective, as mental maps are. Real maps are objective as they have a material quality aimed at presenting a real (= natural) or fictional (= non-natural)

space. When we speak of real maps we do not assume that there can be a 1:1 mapping from reality to maps. Mental maps, in contrast, exist only in the human brain. Yet it is reasonable to assume that mental maps are the cognitive source of real maps.

Real maps have a symbolic and a spatial character. Maps typically contain map symbols that iconically resemble the entities they represent, but also have a quality of their own, providing important information about the essential landmarks in a given city- or landscape. The comprehension and production of maps require those cognitive skills that are central to the understanding of graphic representation, such as pattern recognition, scale transformation, reduction of information, and comprehension of symbols and notational systems that represent landscapes and cityscapes (Downs & Liben 1987). Concerning the spatial character, maps are highly demanding, since they presuppose the development of cognitive abilities and the comprehension of complex visual codes that touch on viewing distance, viewing angle, and viewing azimuth or direction (see Liben 2009: 311, and the chapter by Liben in this volume). Moreover, mapping of a three-dimensional referent onto a two-dimensional surface causes a loss of information. The understanding of maps also involves the ability to take distinct perspectives, for instance, eye level versus bird's eye view, and to master proportions and map color specification (MacEachran 1995). This list of constants evidently demonstrates that a fully developed interpretation of maps presents a complex cognitive task.

Experimental studies have shown that four- to five-year-olds have map concepts – that is, they have a basic knowledge of what a map is and are able to recognize prototypical maps – although these studies also indicate that preschool children usually have problems with map identification and map utilization. While the first category refers to the identification of map contents, the latter corresponds with the capacity to use maps in a competent manner. In this regard, it has been proved that children, even in the primary school years, are often confused about geometrical relationships, such as scale and perspective (Wiegand 2006). This short survey makes clear that map comprehension has to be learned in the course of children's development.

Considering this, we pose the following questions: What skills can children acquire when they encounter metaphorical maps in picturebooks? Do these maps foster the acquisition of map knowledge and support the child's comprehension of the picturebook story? Before attempting to find some answers to these questions, we have to clarify what a metaphor is and what constitutes a metaphorical map.

In general, metaphors are mappings from source concepts to target concepts. The basic functioning of metaphors is easily demonstrated in a simple sentence like 'Juliet is the sun,' a quote from William Shakespeare's *Romeo and Juliet* (1597). On a literal understanding, this sentence does not make any sense. It shows 'categorial falsity,' that is, it is not possible that a human being is the same as a star.

Yet if we drop some of the semantic components of the word *sun* (such as being a star, and focus on some properties related to its meaning such as 'giving light and warmth,' or 'renders life possible,' we can conclude that this sentence means that Juliet (the topic) resembles the sun (the vehicle) or is in some respects like the sun. The metaphor *sun*, then, is a mapping from the source concept STAR to the target concept LIGHT/WARMTH.

Already this seemingly simple example shows that metaphors are a cognitive mechanism that is not easy to grasp. There are several theories of metaphor on the market, for instance simile theories, interaction theories, Gricean theories, non-cognitivist theories, and conceptual metaphor theory (cf. Gibbs 2008; Reimer & Camp 2006). Without committing to one of these theories, we follow the common practice of pinpointing the metaphorical relation in patterns such as X IS Y.

Early approaches to metaphor acquisition claimed that the comprehension of metaphors is a late process, since it belongs to the realm of metalinguistic awareness. This is the ability to consciously analyze language and to know how language as a system operates, which is necessary in order understand how, for instance, metaphor and irony work (Gombert 1992). Ellen Winner (1988) contends that 'primitive' metaphoric interpretation happens at the age of eight, whereas 'genuine' metaphor interpretation is acquired at the age of ten, with a phase of 'inappropriate' metaphor comprehension in between. Recent research, however, tends to assume a much earlier comprehension of metaphors (Camp 2006). Several observations point in this direction: not all early metaphors produced by children can be dismissed as either overstatements or pretence. Thus, when Max, twenty-one months old, calls the picture of an ice-cream cone a 'pee-pee' (his words for *penis*), Max is 'metaphorical' in the sense that he is aware of not using the conventional word (Bloom 2000). Since it appears that "children understand metaphors before they can successfully explain their understanding," as Winner (1988: 45) puts it, metalinguistic tasks (like the truth value judgment task) seem to demand too much (Pouscoulous 2014: 249). In contrast, acting out tasks or picture matching tasks fare much better. Moreover, conventional or frozen metaphors seem to be acquired earlier than novel metaphors. However, this is not surprising since the comprehension and production of novel metaphors is much more demanding because context information, including the intentions of a communicator, has to be calculated carefully.

Therefore, Nausicaa Pouscoulous concludes that "3-years-olds can be shown to understand metaphors" (250). However, the course of metaphor acquisition is dependent on a number of ingredients, as she convincingly points out: knowledge of the literal word meaning, proficiency of syntactic structure, conceptual knowledge of the domains at stake, understanding of the relevant context, perception of the analogy, and ability to derive pragmatic inferences (250).

These aspects should be kept in mind when it comes to the notion of metaphorical map. While the term metaphor basically relates to language, metaphorical relations have been detected in other cognitive domains as well. Of prime interest for our investigation is the pictorial domain. Thus, the question arises whether there are 'pictorial metaphors.' Pictorial metaphor, as defined by Charles Forceville (2008: 464), is a nonverbal mode of metaphor, in which – like in its verbal counterpart – there is a relation between a target domain and a source domain and a certain mapping from one domain to the other domain.

A typical map that displays a pictorial metaphor is printed in Kaj Munk's picturebook *Danmark* (Denmark, 1946), with illustrations by Herluf Jensenius (Figure 2). A doublespread placed at the end of the book shows a map of Denmark and parts of its surroundings. The different islands that belong to the kingdom of Denmark are presented as family members. The main part of Denmark, Jutland, is the father, who is smoking a pipe and standing on a small hill that represents Germany, the mother is Sjaelland, and the eldest daughter is Fyn. The accompanying verse indicates that the children bathing in the sea represent the smaller islands of Denmark. The mother keeps a watchful eye on her child Bornholm in the south of Sweden.

Figure 2. Illustration by Herluf Jensenius from Kaj Munk: *Danmark*. Copenhagen: Arnold Busck, 1946

This metaphorical map presents the type of 'hybrid metaphor.' In hybrid metaphors, "two objects that are normally distinct entities are physically merged into a single 'gestalt'" (Forceville 2008: 465). Applied to the map in the Danish picturebook, it is evident that maps and humans are normally distinct entities. Hence children might wonder about giving the map of Denmark the shape of several humans that obviously belong to a 'family.' It is not possible that a map of Denmark can simultaneously be a picture of a single man. According to Forceville (2008), who draws on Noel Carroll, hybrid metaphors are instantiated as two phenomena that are "visually represented as occupying the same space in a manner that is physically impossible" (465).

The fundamental metaphor, then, is DENMARK IS A FAMILY. The topic is Denmark, represented by a map, and the vehicle (metaphor) is family. Typical concepts associated with *family*, such as the relations 'father of,' 'mother of,' or 'child of,' do not hold. What matters more is the size of the depicted parts of Denmark. Thus, the father is the biggest part (= Jutland), followed by the mother (= Sjaelland) and the children.

In addition to verbal and pictorial metaphors, there are also 'multimodal metaphors.' In multimodal metaphors, the defining property is that "two phenomena are cued in more than one sign system, sensory mode, or both" (Forceville 2008: 469). Strictly speaking, the map in Munk's picturebook also contains information from the language system, namely the proper names *Sjaelland* and *Fyn* written on the aprons of the mother and the eldest daughter as well as *Danmark* written on the map legend. Hence, in a sense, this map visualizes a multimodal metaphor, because the map (which is a picture of Denmark) is enriched with (Danish) language. However, since a picture-language combination is typical for most maps, we will leave it at the characterization of a metaphorical map indicated above. In sum, then, we can define a metaphorical map as a map that is generally based on a pictorial metaphor. Moreover, metaphorical maps seem to constitute hybrid metaphors, as two distinct entities are physically merged into one shape.

Relating maps and metaphors

Since the concept of family and related emotions plays a significant role in a child's life, it is no wonder that metaphorical maps in picturebooks rely on this domain. In order to flesh out the cognitive and narrative challenges of metaphorical maps in picturebooks, the subsequent sections focus on how the conceptual metaphors X IS FAMILY and X IS WHAT I LOVE are presented in two picturebooks.

The first picturebook is the already mentioned picturebook *Danmark*. On the map, the various parts of Denmark are represented by different family members, whereby the size of the Danish land parts correlates with the size of the individual family members, therefore stressing their importance in descending order. The body proportions, clothes, and facial expressions of the father, the mother, and the children underline their friendliness, thus creating a peaceful and affectionate atmosphere.

The image on the book cover with a signature of the illustrator and the date 1943 indicates that the book project had been developed earlier, during the occupation of Denmark by the Germans. Considering this fact and the patriotic overtone of the verses, the readers are encouraged to identify with their home country. The significant role of the map is emphasized by the book cover, which depicts five children, standing with their backs to the viewer and looking at a map of Denmark, which is in this case depicted like a real map. This map introduces the child readers to the book's topic and mirrors the metaphorical map as it prepares the readers to transfer their knowledge about the cartographic features of Denmark to the altered map that adapts the outlines of the Danish islands to different family members. The didactic purpose of the metaphorical map and its appeal to the audience is additionally stressed by the fact that this map is on a canvas, like an education picture used in a school context. While the verses and the accompanying black and white illustrations introduce the readers to the milestones of Danish history from the Middle Ages up to the present, the map is singled out by its position at the end of the book and the fact that it is printed in full color. The selection of the metaphor DENMARK IS A FAMILY stimulates the child readers to transfer the emotions they have towards their own family to Denmark, in other words, to show feelings of love and affection to their own country. The verses, which appeal for peace after the end of the Second World War, and the final image highlight this emotional attachment. The five children from the book cover are facing each other, jubilantly lifting their hands as if they are supporting the final verse "Long live Denmark!" (38).

The significance of family and the expression of love and emotional intimacy also play an important role in Sarah Fanelli's *My Map Book* (1995). This picturebook contains 'maps' related to the life of a fictive child. The titles of these 'maps' indicate the diverse topics that govern their structure and content. Several maps represent fictional ('treasure map') or real places ('map of my bedroom,' 'map of my neighborhood,' 'map of the seaside'), but there are other entities that are usually not the object of cartographic representation: these are the maps of the family, the day, the tummy, the colors, the heart, the dog, and the face. The general map concept that is introduced here is that of a systematic representation of entities. Most importantly, this systematicity is related to the drawing boundaries, where the spaces constitute something that can be named. A close look at the 'map of my heart' displays the following areas: The contour of a heart is subdivided into nine fields in different sizes. The handwritten words in these fields enumerate people (family members, friends, teachers), pets (dog), and beloved things and events like "books," "sunny days," and "nice surprises." One field mentions "someone special" and another even includes an exclamation mark without further information. While some words are written in capital letters throughout, others are written in lowercase letters. In the case of "chocolate," the implied child creator actually corrects the misspelling by erasing one letter. On the right margin of the doublespread heart there is a 'legend' that enumerates several other entities that the possessor of the heart loves: Aunt Yolanda, holidays, my favorite ice cream, Number 2, my teacher, trips, Milli K., Christmas, maps, Franco Sue. Two words have been crossed out, only one of them, "green," can be deciphered.

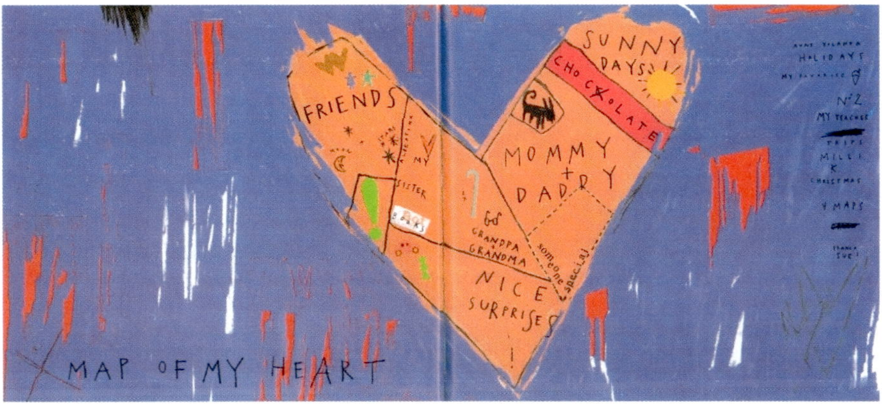

Figure 3. Doublespread "Map of My Heart" by Sara Fanelli from *My Map Book*. New York NY: Harper Collins, 1995. Used by permission of Harper Collins Publisher

The metaphor at work is HEART IS WHAT I LOVE. The major part of the items inserted into the map of the heart is devoted to family members (parents, grandparents, and sister), while other parts concern related persons such as friends and teachers, and beloved things like a favorite food, hobbies, and holidays. Two further aspects may play a role in the comprehension of this map: the space that is covered, for instance "Mommy+Daddy" covers more ground than "my sister," and the size of the letters, for instance "Mommy+Daddy" are written in bigger letters than "Grandpa+Grandma," thus referring to different degrees of emotional attachment. At first glance, Fanelli's map seems to be extraordinary, but it refers to the old tradition of mapping human organs like the Gall map. Especially maps of hearts were very popular in the first half of the twentieth century, such as the "Pictorial Map of Loveland" (1943) by Ernest Dudley Chase. Comparable to the heart map by Chase, Fanelli's map assigns diverse emotions, wishes, and preferences to different sections of the heart. In both cases, the heart is taken metaphorically, as something that is intrinsically associated with affection. In this regard, the 'map of my heart' pictorially provides an idea of how feelings towards other people and personal predilections impact upon one's own emotional state. Moreover, this map also stresses that an emotion like love can be attributed to quite different entities.

The metaphorical maps in the picturebooks by Munk and Fanelli refer to basic conceptual metaphors, but they are distinct concerning the presentation of the map. In Munk's picturebook, the outline of a country is adjusted to the shapes of humans, while Fanelli's picturebook depicts a human organ as a map. Consequently, the metaphorical map in Munk's book stands in the tradition of the map type that metaphorically refers to historical and political events (map > entity). Fanelli's 'map of my heart,' however, is influenced by the Gall map tradition (entity > map).

While the metaphorical maps in picturebooks we have looked at so far belong to either the first or the second type, one picturebook, Emily Gravett's *Little Mouse's Big Book of Fears* (2007), stands out as it combines both map types. Conceived as a fictional diary of a very scared mouse, the mouse's sketchbook is embedded into a framework, which seems to be an academic study about fears. The upper frame on each doublespread lists specific phobias in alleged Old Greek, which are followed by an English translation, such as "Clinophobia (Fear of going to bed)," and complemented by visual symbols. The ripped pages and holes look like as if the mouse has intentionally destroyed the book. These self-referential elements point to the material aspects of the medium itself, thus emphasizing the artistic exploration of the picturebook. The book's climax is emphasized by a map attached to a doublespread that visualizes the "Fear of getting lost," which is convincingly translated to "Whereamiophobia." When folded out, the "Visitor's Map of the Isle of Fright" displays an island shaped like a huge mouse. The legend and the names of villages, mountains, and other landmarks refer to diverse fears as well as to bodily and psychic reactions to fears. The names of these reactions are not randomly distributed on the map, but are assigned to those body parts that primarily show the respective reactions. For instance, on the upper part of the island, which stands for the mouse's head, there are entries like the village of "Great Chatter," the "Wide Eye Lake," the "Twitching Whiskers," and the "Ears Back." The "Dry Throat" runs down to the village "Fastheart," whose headland, which resembles a paw, ends in "Shaking Point." Hence, the different body parts and inner organs of the mouse are clearly indicated on the map, although they are not designated with the correct anatomical terms. Instead, the categories and names on the map refer to the nervous reactions of various body parts, which are evoked by miscellaneous states of anxiety. This description reveals that the map is a hybrid form which connects the first and second map types: the island is shaped like an animal and metaphorically refers to the mouse's emotional condition and her overwhelming fears of everybody and everything.

Metaphorical maps in descriptive picturebooks

Metaphorical maps demand quite complex cognitive skills, since the viewer needs map literacy and an understanding of metaphors in order to comprehend their meaning. What we are especially interested in are the functions of these maps in relation to the accompanying picturebook story and the type of picturebooks that implement metaphorical maps. When browsing through picturebooks with metaphorical maps, one gets the impression that this map category more frequently appears in descriptive than in narrative picturebooks. Descriptive picturebooks bear analogy to nonfiction books as they show a tendency to just describe and enumerate (fictional) events and facts. Moreover, they usually do not have a story climax, although descriptive picturebooks might have narrative sections in which a small story is embedded (Meibauer 2015).

Prototypical descriptive picturebooks with metaphorical maps are Munk's *Danmark*, which introduces children to the history of Denmark, Peter Sís' *The Pilot and the Little Prince* (2014), which presents the life of Antoine de Saint-Exupéry, and *The Wall. Growing up behind the Iron Curtain* (2007) by the same author-illustrator, which focuses on Sís' childhood memories. Fanelli's *My Map Book* is a specific case, as it does not have a continuous narrative at all, but is composed of illustrations and lists of things and names. Nevertheless, the main purpose of Fanelli's picturebook consists in familiarizing children with the idea that entities they encounter in their immediate surroundings, whether spatial constructions or abstract concepts, can be mapped in a systematic, yet playful and creative way. *My Map Book* additionally introduces children to different map concepts, ranging from maps that represent the child's surroundings and maps of fictional places to metaphorical maps, thus covering a broad spectrum of map types.

Like Fanelli's book, Gravett's metafictive picturebook *Little Mouse's Big Book of Fears* does not present a continuous story but consists of short sentences that describe different fears. At first glance, this picturebook looks like a nonfiction book that informs the reader about different phobias, but it soon becomes apparent that it is making fun of medical or psychological terminology. The unusual ad hoc created terms alert the attentive reader that the so-called facts are based on the author's inventions, thus inviting the reader to enjoy a mocking game. The metaphorical map plays a crucial role in this respect, since it visualizes in a funny way that fears are emotions which have bodily and psychic effects. The metaphor at work here seems to be MOUSE IS FEAR, thus highlighting the mouse's emotional condition, which completely dominates her thinking and way of life. However, while the conceptual metaphors that determine the maps in the picturebooks by Munk and Fanelli invite the child to consider the influence of the abstract concepts of 'family' and 'love' on the recognition of one's homeland and one's individual relationships and likings, the conceptual metaphor in Gravett's book fluctuates between a serious meaning (the experience of fear impacts on the individual's behavior and thinking) and a humorous meaning (excessive fear of everything and everyone, even if they are harmless, is a sign of silly behavior).

How fear and threat affect individual life conditions is in the forefront of Peter Sís' autobiographical picturebook *The Wall. Growing up behind the Iron Curtain* (2007), in which the author recalls his childhood memories (on Sís autobiographical picturebooks, see Kümmerling-Meibauer 2010). Having grown up in Czechoslovakia in the 1950s and 1960s, Sís gives an overview of the political and cultural changes in his home country, which culminated in the Prague Spring in 1968. With a collage of drawings, photos, diary entries, maps, and matter-of-fact historical data, Sís skillfully connects historical events and personal reminiscences. Sís shows a preference for maps in his picturebooks. In this regard, the maps in *The Wall* are striking as they provide geographical, historical, and cultural information together with insights into the author's individual feelings. Upon opening the book, the illustration on the endpapers shows a world map onto which the states of the Eastern Bloc as well as Cuba are colored in red, while all other countries and continents are blank. This map gives the reader a rough overview of the political world situation that dominated Sís' childhood and adolescence. In contrast to this geographical map, the two maps inside the book belong to the category of 'metaphorical map.' The first map roughly follows the outline of the Soviet Union. Inside this map, portraits of Soviet leaders such as Stalin, Lenin, Brezhnev, and Khrushchev, a military parade in front of the Kremlin, the armored cruiser "Aurora," lethal weapons, soldiers, rockets, target circles, and a prison camp are discernible. These individual items and figures, the red color, and the phrase "This was the era of brain wash" stress the threatening atmosphere during the Cold War, when the Soviet Union dominated small countries like Czechoslovakia. Here, Sís refers to the Ohara map tradition in order to illustrate the destructive power of the Soviet Union over the neighboring Eastern European states.

The second map shows Europe as seen from the angle of the Eastern Bloc (Figure 4). Europe has a chess board pattern, separated into two parts by a wall with barbed wire on top. New York with the Statue of Liberty is visible at a far distance in the upper right corner. While the lower part representing the countries of the Eastern Bloc is depicted in grey tones, the upper part is colored in yellowish and reddish shades. However, what catches the eye are the inscriptions on the chess board squares, which present human capacities and properties. The fields in the lower part bear exclusively negative characteristics, such as terror, fear, envy, lie, suspicion, and ignorance, whereas the upper part is adorned with positive features, such as hope, justice, freedom, truth, wisdom, happiness, confidence, art, and love. This specific map builds on the contrast between two geographical European

Figure 4. Illustration by Peter Sís from *The Wall. Growing up behind the Iron Curtain.* New York: Farrar, Straus and Giroux, 2007. © 2007, Peter Sís, published by arrangement with Farrar, Straus and Giroux, LLC, New York

areas that are separated by a wall. They are distinguished by the color scheme and their characteristics, which can be interpreted as allegorical allusions to the political situation in Europe. In a general sense, this map emphasizes that Western Europe stands for positive features by representing the human rights of freedom, solidarity, and justice, while Eastern Europe presents negative properties such as suppression and backwardness. The map is connected to the autobiographical text as it visualizes the reasons for the author's flight from Czechoslovakia to the West.

It is not the aim of these maps to convey an accurate image of Europe. Quite the contrary, these maps presuppose the readers' knowledge of how a "real" map of Europe looks in order to comprehend the subliminal meanings of Sís' autobiographical account. By enlivening the maps with historical figures and events or by enriching them with contextual information about the political and cultural situation in the 1950s and 1960s, the author manages to personalize a bygone era. Children, who do not have a concise knowledge about the difficulties people were confronted with in the Eastern Bloc during the Cold War, thus get additional information. Moreover, the two maps give an insight into the narrator's feelings and his overarching wish to leave everything behind in order to find a country where he can live in peace without the fear of being pursued because of his desire for freedom. While the text describes the everyday life of a child that is growing up under difficult conditions, which are aligned with the historical events taking place at the same time, the maps extend the feelings of unease expressed by the narrator. The first map focuses on the conceptual metaphor X IS THREAT (whereby X can be replaced by the Soviet Union). The threat is additionally stressed by the small sad-looking boy – as a self-portrait of the author – in the lower left corner of the illustration. The map hovers like a threatening dark cloud over the boy and seems to be on the verge of crushing him. The red color of the Soviet Union is mirrored in the boy's red pioneer's scarf, thus drawing a line between the boy's forced entry into the pioneer organization and the Communist ideology that symbolically overwhelms the child.

The second map, however, relies on two contrary metaphorical chains: the first one refers to positive issues associated with freedom, justice, and happiness, whereas the second one stresses negative features connected with oppression, fear, and sadness. While the first metaphorical chain is closely connected with Western Europe and the USA, the latter is assigned to Eastern Europe. By including these abstract concepts in a map of Europe, the illustrator provokes the reader into reflecting on the impact of political and historical changes on the narrator's life conditions. Moreover, the arrangement and scale of items on the maps as well as the color scheme serve to evoke the reader's empathy with the narrator's decision to flee to the West. This strategy is additionally emphasized by a tiny figure with wings on a bicycle that is crossing the huge wall. This figure symbolizes the narrator, who dares to overcome all obstacles despite his small size and weakness.

However, one observation still needs an explanation: why is this map type apparently predominant in descriptive picturebooks, while narrative picturebooks primarily show maps of real or fictional city- and landscapes? We contend that this allocation is connected to the narrative structure of the picturebooks. As already indicated, descriptive picturebooks differ from narrative picturebooks as they mainly focus on nonfiction and the mediation of facts, which demands a narrative form that relies on descriptions and a matter-of-fact style. Even those picturebooks whose facts turn out to be the author's and illustrator's inventions, as in *Little Mouse's Big Book of Fears*, are nevertheless significantly influenced by the typical features of descriptive picturebooks.

The metaphorical maps complement the descriptive texts by their humorous and playful character. Humor plays a significant role in children's literature and covers a broad range of genres (Cross 2011). However, how humor influences the understanding of literary texts as well as picture-text-relations is not well investigated, especially in relation to children's cognitive development (McGhee 2013). Nevertheless, one might assume that the humorous effects of mapping the heart or depicting islands as family members support the understanding of the accompanying text. As for the "Isle of Fright" map in Gravett's picturebook, the humorous effect arises from the fact that this map feigns being a scientific map on the one hand, and attributes all pieces of information to just one emotion (fear, fright), on the other. Humorous maps have a long tradition in cartography and are often used to destabilize the scientific character of geographical maps, thus revealing a hybrid character (Caquard & Dormann 2008). This statement also applies to the maps in Sís' picturebook. Although both maps deal with serious issues, they are nevertheless characterized by a humorous and playful note, since it is not a common idea to depict Europe as a chess game or to fill out the contours of a country with historical figures, vehicles, and symbolic items.

By comparison, the metaphorical maps in these picturebooks are surprising because they run against normal expectations about the appearance and functions of maps as conditioned by schoolbooks and nonfiction books. Their unusual appeal invites readers to consider how maps as an entity sui generis can be applied to other entities such as animals, human organs, and even political and ethical issues. Bringing these entities together encourages the child to focus on the shape of a map, and moreover, to consider the meaning of the metaphorical relation. The connection between these entities is mostly astonishing, since they show already known things in an innovative way, thus stimulating children to broaden their restricted world knowledge by acquiring new manners of perception. For instance, the child might ask whether the relations between the Danish family members are exactly of the kind an ideal family should have.

What can children learn from metaphorical maps?

This chapter has shown that metaphorical maps in picturebooks exist and that they belong to a tradition of subjective cartography which was established in the nineteenth century. In this regard, two strands are distinguishable: maps that depict a given entity which is structured like a map (the Gall map tradition) and maps of a given city, country, continent, or the world that are shaped like humans or animals (the Ohara map tradition). While these map types were initially targeted at an adult audience, they also emerged in children's books in the second half of the twentieth century. Both map traditions are observable in picturebooks addressed towards children from age six onwards. The cognitive metaphors in these maps are closely connected to emotions (on the role of emotions in children's literature, see Nikolajeva 2014). The picturebooks we have investigated do not have a story climax and show a tendency to just enumerate facts and events, thus displaying a descriptive character. The metaphorical maps complement the rather descriptive text by their humorous and playful character.

This overview makes it obvious that metaphorical maps are quite complex, since they challenge the reader in different respects. In order to fully comprehend this map type, children have to acquire map literacy as well as an understanding of metaphors, which belong to the realm of metalinguistic awareness. In a next step children must activate a transfer process by building a connection between these two domains. Since studies in map literacy and metaphor acquisition have shown that the processing of map and metaphor present a highly demanding task for children, a profound understanding of metaphorical maps will probably be acquired relatively late, when children are accustomed to the utilization of maps, which starts at the earliest at primary school age. The reference to a school setting in Munk's *Danmark* and the rather complex information given in the picturebooks by Fanelli, Gravett, and Sís support this assumption. Finally, children have to draw a connecting line between the metaphorical maps and the accompanying text. In this regard, the maps are imaginative guides which stimulate new approaches to thinking. By closely looking at the metaphorical maps and reflecting on their meaning for the picturebook narrative, children are initiated in the understanding of abstract concepts, thus broadening their world knowledge as well as their facility for abstraction.

References

Primary sources

Fanelli, Sara. 1995. *My Map Book*. New York NY: Harper Collins.

Gravett, Emily. 2007. *Little Mouse's Big Book of Fears*. London: Macmillan.

Milne, A. A. 1926. *Winnie-the-Pooh*, illus. Ernest H. Shepard. London: Methuen.

Munk, Kaj. 1946. *Danmark*, illus. Herluf Jensenius. Copenhagen: Arnold Busck.

Sís, Peter. 2007. *The Wall. Growing up behind the Iron Curtain*. New York NY: Farrar, Straus and Giroux.

Sís, Peter. 2014. *The Pilot and the Little Prince*. New York NY: Farrar, Straus and Giroux.

Stevenson, Robert Louis. 1883. *Treasure Island*. London: Cassell.

Secondary sources

Bloom, Paul. 2000. *How Children Learn the Meaning of Words*. Cambridge MA: The MIT Press.

Camp, Elizabeth. 2006. Metaphor in the mind: The cognition of metaphor. *Philosophy Compass* 1: 154–170. doi: 10.1111/j.1747-9991.2006.00013.x

Camp, Elizabeth. 2007. Thinking with maps. *Philosophical Perspectives* 21: 145–182. doi: 10.1111/j.1520-8583.2007.00124.x

Caquard, Sébastian & Dormann, Claire. 2008. Humorous maps: Exploration of an alternative cartography. *Cartography & Geographic Information Science* 35(1): 51–64. doi: 10.1559/152304008783475670

Cross, Julie. 2011. *Humor in Contemporary Junior Literature*. New York NY: Routledge.

Downs, Roger M. & Liben, Lynn S. 1987. Children's understanding of maps. In *Cognitive Processes and Spatial Orientation in Animal and Man*, Vol. 2: *Neurophysiology and Developmental Aspects*, Paul Ellen & Catherine Thinus-Blanc (eds), 202–219. Dordrecht: Martinus Nijhoff.

Downs, Roger M. & Stea, David. 1977. *Maps in Mind*. New York NY: Harper & Row.

Forceville, Charles. 2008. Metaphor in pictures and multimodal representations. In *The Cambridge Handbook of Metaphor and Thought*, Raymond W. Gibbs Jr. (ed.), 462–282. Cambridge: CUP. doi: 10.1017/CBO9780511816802.028

Gibbs, Raymond W., Jr. (ed.). 2008. *The Cambridge Handbook of Metaphor and Thought*. Cambridge: CUP. doi: 10.1017/CBO9780511816802

Gombert, Jean. 1992. *Metalinguistic Development*. Chicago IL: University of Chicago Press.

Harmon, Katherine. 2004. *Personal Geographies and Other Maps of the Imagination*. New York NY: Princeton Architectural Press.

Kümmerling-Meibauer, Bettina. 2010. Remembering the past in words and pictures: How autobiographical stories become picturebooks. In *New Directions in Picturebook Research*, Teresa Colomer, Bettina Kümmerling-Meibauer & Cecilia Silva-Díaz (eds), 205–215. New York NY: Routledge.

Kümmerling-Meibauer, Bettina & Meibauer, Jörg. 2013. Towards a cognitive theory of picturebooks. *International Research in Children's Literature* 6(2): 143–160. doi: 10.3366/ircl.2013.0095

Kümmerling-Meibauer, Bettina & Meibauer, Jörg. 2015. Maps in picturebooks. Cognitive status and narrative function. *BLFT – Nordic Journal of ChildLit Aesthetics* 6. doi: 10.3402/blft.v6.26970

Liben, Lynn S. 2009. The road to understanding maps. *Current Directions in Psychological Science* 18: 310–315. doi: 10.1111/j.1467-8721.2009.01658.x

MacEachren, Alan. 1995. *How Maps Work. Representation, Visualization, and Design*. New York NY: Guildford.

McGhee, Paul E. 2013. *Humor and Children's Development*. New York NY: Routledge.

Meibauer, Jörg. 2015. What a child can learn from simple descriptive picturebooks: An inquiry into *Lastwagen/Trucks* by Paul Stickland. In *Learning from Picturebooks. Perspectives from Child Development and Literacy Studies*, Bettina Kümmerling-Meibauer, Jörg Meibauer, Kerstin Nachtigäller & Katharina Rohlfing (eds), 51–70. New York NY: Routledge.

Nikolajeva, Maria. 2014. *Reading for Learning. Cognitive Approaches to Children's Literature* [Children's Literature, Culture, and Cognition 3]. Amsterdam: John Benjamins. doi: 10.1075/clcc.3

Pouscoulous, Nausicaa. 2014. "The elevator's buttocks": Metaphorical abilities in children. In *Pragmatic Development in First Language Acquisition* [Trends in Language Acquisition Research 10], Danielle Matthews (ed.), 239–260. Amsterdam: John Benjamins.

Reimer, Marga & Camp, Elizabeth. 2006. Metaphor. In *The Oxford Handbook of Philosophy of Language*, Ernie Lepore & Barry Smith (eds), 845–863. Oxford: OUP.

Turchi, Peter. 2004. *Maps of the Imagination: The Writer as Cartographer*. San Antonio TX: Trinity University Press.

Uttal, David H. & Tan, Lisa S. 2000. Cognitive mapping in childhood. In *Cognitive Mapping*, Rob Kitchin & Scott Freundschuh (eds), 147–165. New York NY: Routledge.

Wiegand, Patrick. 2006. *Learning and Teaching with Maps*. New York NY: Routledge. doi: 10.4324/9780203477793

Winner, Ellen. 1988. *The Point of Words: Children's Understanding of Metaphor and Irony*. Cambridge MA: The MIT Press.

PART 2

Literary shaping of real cityscapes

CHAPTER 5

Mapping a city – Berlin in a contemporary detective novel

Corina Löwe

In the novel *Emil and the Detectives* by Erich Kästner, published in 1929, the contemporary city of Berlin is set as an urban *topos* in which children navigate in an independent and self-confident way. Also more recent detective novels choose Berlin as the scene and make use of its cultural and geographical diversity. This chapter focuses on Andreas Steinhöfel's *Rico, Oskar und die Tieferschatten* (2008) and examines which urban spaces in Berlin are presented, how the protagonist orients himself in the city, and what function the mapping has. The analysis focuses on how the psychological learning process of orientation in a city can be supported by children's literature.

Introduction

Maps provide knowledge. In everyday use we expect a city map to help with orientation. We assume that the existing territory corresponds with its cartographic representation. According to Sybille Krämer, a map functions as an ambassador "who mediates between the territory and the user or between the knowledge of the map producer and the user's lack of knowledge" (2015: 192). However, the premise here is that the user is already able to read and to understand a map and has developed certain knowledge in mapping that can be instantly applied. Because this knowledge is not congenital, children must first acquire it.

This chapter argues that mapping is a learning process that involves cognitive strategies. Furthermore, mapping is a precondition for orienting oneself in a city and for understanding maps. I believe that books for children which explicitly address these mapping processes can help the young reader to be more aware of what mapping means.

To discuss my ideas, I have chosen the detective novel *Rico, Oscar und die Tieferschatten* (2008), in English *The Spaghetti Detectives* (2011b), written by the

DOI 10.1075/clcc.7.06low

well-known German author Andreas Steinhöfel.[1] Rico, the main protagonist of the novel, is a child with learning disabilities. Rico's reflections on everything he comes into contact with are described in great detail, which lets the reader follow how the protagonist is acquiring his orientational skills in Berlin. Not only Rico's orientation problems are mentioned in detail, but also different steps to overcome these problems can be traced in the text. One can assume that the young readers, when they are at Rico's age, are way ahead in their mapping abilities, but probably never thought about the stepwise process needed to achieve this. The more difficult and demanding it is for Rico to orient himself in his surroundings, the better the young reader can follow the process as from the perspective of an experienced expert – allowing the reader to focus on how Rico will solve this puzzle.

Place, space, and children's literature

The act of operating or making a map, called mapping, firstly presupposes a spatial understanding of one's concrete environment. After having gained this knowledge, the next step is building on it by understanding how intentional characters and symbols work on an abstract level. These are requirements for using maps to navigate unknown areas.

Urban spaces, which will be discussed below, are formed by human interactions. In contrast to places, which Michel de Certeau limits to being materially tangible and locatable, spaces are created: "Space occurs as the effect produced by the operations that orient it, situate it, temporalize it, and make it function in a polyvalent unity of conflictual programs or contractual proximities" (1988: 117). An active engagement in the creation of spaces is conducted for instance through walking, according to de Certeau a requirement for creating "a mobile organicity in the environment" (99). By actively participating in the environment, relations between different places are established and a virtual map emerges. In de Certeau's understanding, "*space is a practiced place*" (117, italics in original). In this way today's awareness of a street differs from yesterday's, even if the buildings and environments themselves do not change. By actually walking on the streets marked on a map, the walker absorbs impressions, interacts with other people, and, by doing so, turns the place into a space.

Yi-Fu Tuan also examines the interdependency between place and space. While places stand for security and stability, spaces symbolize freedom and

1. Rico's adventures are published as a trilogy, further consisting of *Rico, Oskar und das Herzgebreche* (Rico, Oscar, and the Broken Heart, 2009) and *Rico, Oskar und der Diebstahlstein* (Rico, Oscar, and the Theftstone, 2011a).

openness (2001: 6). According to Tuan, there is also a temporal aspect of place and space. Place is the condition of pause while space is connected to movement and change (6).

The highlighting of social processes in the formation of spaces is essential, according to Martina Löw. She claims that it is not enough to describe movement within just one given space, because that would limit space to something inflexible (2001: 67). She points out that there cannot be just one definable given space; the constitution of space always has to include a social process, and build on interrelations between places, time, and people (272). With regard to the child's perception of place and space, Tuan also highlights that children's spatial frame expands as they grow, normally from the known, safe place to the unknown and exciting – starting with the exploration tours as a toddler from their mother's lap, via the homey surroundings and garden, and extending into the neighborhood and more sophisticated places like a city (2001: 21–33).

Orientation problems are not unusual for children dealing with spatial mobility in an urban space, because of the complexity of sensory impressions. The ability to participate in city life is important for children growing up in an urban environment; however, this is easier said than done. Factors like the growth of the population and, consequently, an increase in traffic as well as the geographic expansion of the city call for a cautious introduction to the complexity of the city. In the western context, parents seek to bring up their children in an environment as protected and safe as possible. When examining the living conditions of children, Claire Freeman and Paul Tranter point out that children today have fewer opportunities for outdoor play than children a generation ago (Freeman & Tranter 2011: 23). It is not until children reach Rico's age of around eight to ten years of age that their range of exploration increases, while the parental supervision simultaneously starts to decrease (O'Brien et al. 2000: 259). This is the age at which children are starting to develop a keen interest in gaining map knowledge (Kümmerling-Meibauer & Meibauer 2015).

The novel by Steinhöfel addresses exactly this audience – children from 10 years of age. In the trilogy about Rico and Oskar's adventures, the range of travel of the two boys widens, starting with the local neighborhood, extending to other parts of Berlin, and finally including a journey to the Baltic Sea that the two boys undertake in the third part.

Achieving 'map literacy' in the sense of understanding how to use a map is a learning process. Bettina Kümmerling-Meibauer and Jörg Meibauer (2015) have shown in terms of picturebooks how mapping can be built up with the aid of children's literature. Maps, included as physical artefacts in picturebooks, draw the attention of the reader to different perspectives, that is, direction and distance. Kümmerling-Meibauer and Meibauer conclude that young readers can take in relevant information and develop mental or cognitive maps through the study of maps, illustrations, and texts. Just as map skills can be built up step by step with maps depicted in picturebooks helping this building process, written texts can help the reader reflect about spatial relations and can form the young reader's skills in developing mental maps. The construction of 'mental maps' is a "precondition for an understanding of real maps" (ibid). Marie-Laure Ryan, who uses the term 'cognitive maps,' defines these as "a mental model of *spatial* relations" (2003: 215, emphasis in text) that can represent the experiences with both actual places and imaginary ones. The term cognitive mapping has been used in different ways. For me the term implies the process of thinking about spatial relations and "how people learn, remember and process spatial information about an environment" (Kitchin & Freundschuh 2000: 2).

To move from a map as a two-dimensional object to a spatial understanding can be difficult for children (Liben 2009: 310). In addition, users must have learned to interpret map symbols correctly: "Interpreting spatial meaning requires users' spatial cognition just as interpreting the symbolic meaning requires users' representational insights and concepts" (311). The step of understanding the symbol of a road and a residential area on a map requires that the map users have developed the ability to interpret symbols, which is primarily based on an understanding of the spatial dimensions.

Regarding the ways children's literature and pictures of maps in books facilitate this process, I maintain that drawn maps are supporting tools but are not absolutely necessary for a young reader to build up a spatial understanding. Spatial and directional descriptions in the texts are adequate and can equally support the learning process. In children's literature, places are composed according to aesthetic and literary conventions. Places, streets, and surroundings are depicted in a certain way. Holly Taylor mentions that language is a useful device to describe how spatial relations can be used in different ways. For instance, different perspectives arise when speaking about the view from a roof, or about a route, where the reader can follow the protagonist along his way. It also makes a difference whether the focus is speaker-centered or addressee-centered. Language deals with a range of different levels of information, from simple object-to-object relations to complex environments (2000: 180).

Summing up the brief survey of findings about place, space, and children's literature, I conclude that mapping is a step-by-step learning process, in which children's literature can have a supporting function. Because place and space are intertwined and determined by social relations, it is not useful to analyze them separately. Imagine a scale which places safety and strict rules at one end and excitement and exploration at the other. I would define place as the environment at the safe end of the scale, where the child protagonist feels safe and secure, because s/he is familiar with it. Space is at the opposite end, and is more exciting and demanding; it is the place for new impressions and social contacts. A location can be placed anywhere on this scale, and has a mixture of qualities of the two extremes, all depending on the perception of the protagonist. Active exploration seems to be the key element that connects spatial experiences, surveys, and routes into a mental map.

In order to follow the process of mapping, I have chosen a detective novel, because the plot in detective novels is driven forward by the protagonists' desire to commit or solve crimes, and therefore they have to actively move around in spaces (Wigbers 2006; Löwe 2011: 52f.; Goga 2014, 2015). Melanie Wigbers emphasizes: "The crime novel asks of its protagonists that they take the space where the plot takes place seriously, examine it closely and intensively grapple with its peculiarities" (2006: 12).[2] Cities as a subject have a long history in detective novels. Stephen Knight (2012) describes it as the "Mystery of the City" genre. One need only think of Sherlock Holmes, who investigated in London, or the hard-boiled crime novels, in which portrayals of urban milieus are so important that these can be interpreted as the actual main characters, as Sara Kärrholm mentions (2011: 97). The descriptions of the urban environment are an essential part of creating suspense; detective novels often build upon the fact that the criminal case strongly affects the familiar world. The detailed description of places in detective novels, which often exceeds the actual sequence of events, reflects the intensity of the relationship between the protagonist and the venue. Quite often, role models outside literature are used as templates, which make them particularly "ambiguous and interesting" (Wigbers 2006: 13).

Although this chapter deals with a crime novel, I am not primarily interested in exploring spaces as crime scenes. Instead I intend to focus on the protagonist's intensive scrutiny of the city in order to gain a better understanding of how mental mapping processes can be portrayed in children's literature. What happens when the protagonist needs to step outside his comfort zone and explore the city? What places are important and how does the protagonist learn about the complexity of the city?

Overcoming obstacles

> Oh God, oh God!
> I'd never been out of my street by myself. I'd been with other people, though. Irina has a fast car, and on nice summer days Mom and I go for drives with her. We

2. All translations from German are by the author.

> cruise from Alexander Square to the radio tower and back, past the Brandenburg Gate and then into the center of the city listening to cool music. [...] But getting around Berlin by myself is another matter. The very idea of setting off to find Sophia without really knowing which way to go froze me to the sidewalk. I wasn't brave enough to open Mom's large A to Z of the city. All those lines and bright colors and the tiny letters and all those strange symbols. Not for Rico!
> (Steinhöfel 2011b: 104)

Steinhöfel's novel is an example of the many children's and youth novels that use cities as a setting where young protagonists are confronted with the complexity of urban life. The text describes the advantages of finding one's own way through a big city from a child's point of view. This story is special as its protagonist Rico, who in this case is the narrator, is a child with severe learning disabilities. The quotation indicates that orienting himself in the big city is difficult for him.

Several problems are mentioned: Rico, who is around nine years old, has never experienced Berlin on his own; at least he has not been outside of his home neighborhood *Kreuzberg* alone. Usually, when Rico meets the public urban space, he has adults accompanying him. They are driving him around in cars, which makes it difficult for him to learn the patterns of the city. His knowledge of the city seems to be limited to the names of sightseeing places like Alexander Square or the Brandenburg Gate. When Rico refers to Alexander Square, he describes a geographic location that he is not familiar with. In that sense the place for him is still not more than just a name on a map. Furthermore, he is described as insecure about reading maps. Throughout the story Rico has to get acquainted with the city of Berlin in order to face a number of challenges, and by doing so he improves his mapping skills.

Rico lives with his single mother, who is a bartender in a nightclub. His learning disabilities result in an overly long thinking process that hampers his completing his thoughts. His mom calls him a "proddity," the opposite of a child prodigy (Steinhöfel 2011b: 3). Despite his learning problems, he is a happy and curious child. Due to his mother's working hours, the boy is often on his own. He likes research of all kinds. On one tour through the streets he meets Oskar, another outsider. Being a child prodigy with a high IQ, Oskar is always aware of his surroundings and their risks, which makes him an isolated and unhappy child. The boys become friends, but one day, when Oskar is supposed to visit Rico, he does not show up. Rico is alarmed because in Berlin a child kidnapper (Mr. 2000) is striking terror into the hearts of the citizens. Now the story about friendship, loneliness, and being different transforms into a detective story. When Rico finds out that Oskar is the victim of Mr. 2000, he decides to rescue his friend, which takes him on a journey through Berlin. In the end, Rico manages to free Oskar and together they catch the kidnapper.

Rico follows in Emil's footsteps

Critics have drawn parallels between Steinhöfel's novel and Erich Kästner's *Emil and the Detectives* (1929), not only because of Berlin as the setting of a crime (Magel 2008; Menzel 2009). Although other novels had used this device before, Kästner truly managed to establish and popularize the city setting as a literary device in children's literature (see Kümmerling-Meibauer 2007; Löwe 2011: 102ff). Steinhöfel's text was published 90 years later and indeed there are analogies that show that the difficulties of orientation and getting to know the city have not changed. A parallel between Kästner's Emil and Steinhöfel's Rico is demonstrated in the ambivalent feeling about the city of both protagonists. Emil, coming from a small town called Neustadt, visits Berlin and is both impressed and overwhelmed. Emil's uncertainty in dealing with Berlin has its reasons in the sheer size of the city and also in the unfamiliar traffic, which stuns him:

> Motor cars rushed past with horns honking and screeching brakes. They signaled right-hand turns and left-hand turns, and swung off down side streets while other cars came swooping up behind them. The noise was indescribable, and on the pavements crowds of people kept hurrying by. Out of every turning vans and lorries, trams and double-decker buses swarmed into the main thoroughfare. [...] And all the buildings stretched up and up into the sky. So this was Berlin!
> (Kästner 2001: 69–70)

Gabriele Holzmann sees the reasons for Emil's problems in his lack of preliminary training in the perception of the city (2006: 105), which could be equated with a lack of mapping knowledge. But above all it is the anonymity in the big chaotic environment that worries the protagonists. In *Emil and the Detectives* it is expressed as follows: "The city was huge. And Emil was so small. Nobody cared about his having no money, or that he didn't know where to get off. [...] What would happen? Emil swallowed hard. And he felt so alone" (Kästner 1932: 88; my translation). The opposition between the child and the city is explained in short sentences. The passage ends with the recognition of Emil's feelings. He is completely clueless, without social contacts, and lost in the unknown environment. The English translation from 2001 is a bit more explanatory and it describes this scene from an adult's point of view: "Emil felt very small among them, in that big, busy city. Nobody cared about his having no money, or that he didn't know where he was going. [...] It was awful to feel so alone, and Emil wondered what would happen to him" (Kästner 2001: 77). Here, the question at the end can be interpreted as a cry for help. Both Rico's and Emil's inability to cope with the unknown surroundings could indicate that a certain level of emotional readiness and cognitive maturity is required in order to orient oneself in an unknown environment.

During the hunt for the thief who has stolen Emil's money, the boy, who is unfamiliar with the lifestyle of the city, gratefully accepts the help of a group of Berlin children who can navigate the city with ease. These children replace a 'real' map and function as ambassadors in Krämer's understanding. Supported by the children, Emil's daily range grows rapidly along with his familiarity with the urban space. With the assistance of social contacts, walking, and exploring the city by public transportation, Emil is able to build a spatial knowledge of the city. At the end, nothing is left of his uncertainty; he confidently shows the taxi driver the way (Kästner 1932: 175).

As in Emil's case, Rico's area of expertise is likewise limited to the city district of *Kreuzberg*, which could be characterized as a small town inside Berlin. He has to find his way on his own in the first part, which, similar to Emil, becomes easier in the following parts of the trilogy when his companion Oscar supports him.[3] The residential neighborhood, the streets, and finally the city become a place for social learning for Emil and Rico (cf. Kümmerling-Meibauer 2007).

Whereas Emil goes through the mapping process quickly and with great ease, Rico needs more training and repetition. His mother makes a joke of her son's sense of direction and compares it with that of "a drunken pigeon in a windy snowstorm" (Steinhöfel 2011b: 19). Rico works out the mapping step by step and the reader can follow him doing so.

Rico's home is his castle

The popularity of Berlin as a setting in children's books remains high. Berlin is an agile city of contrasts – from the metropolis, a city of constant changes, to the possibility of living a calm family life in the various neighborhoods, the so-called 'Kiez,' where people can feel at home and know each other.

The connection between urban space and private sphere is already established in the opening scene of Steinhöfel's novel. Rico finds a string of spaghetti on the street in front of his house, and searches for the owner, who is probably one of his neighbors. Rico uses the spaghetti – like Ariadne uses her thread in the ancient Greek legend – to explore the house and to enlarge his spatial net, going from flat to flat and meeting the neighbors. "I like visiting other people's apartments," he explains (6).

The safe harbor from which he starts his search and adventure tours is the apartment in which he and his mother live. "Human groups nearly everywhere tend to regard their own homeland as the center of the world," declares Tuan

3. In the second book, the two boys chase a scammer gang through Berlin. In the third book, it is the theft of a stone that they want to prevent which leads them all the way up to the Baltic Sea.

(2001: 149) and in Rico's case home means his apartment building and flat, where his favorite place is a cosy chair. The chair is a symbol for pause, where Rico can rest and philosophize. Symbolically, the illustrator Peter Schössow connects the chair to Rico's upbringing in *Kreuzberg* by shaping the chair like a typical *Kreuzberg* house (Steinhöfel 2008: 93). Rico feels a strong attachment to his apartment building and its residents. The flat and the house are his places of safety, but through the many contacts with his neighbors also a space in which he can already navigate.

That the house is more than just a living place is further highlighted with another illustration in the frontispiece of the book, a simple, childlike pencil drawing of a house, which shows the names of the people living in the house (Figure 1). The illustration not only emphasizes the importance of the house community for Rico, where Rico and his mother are placed in the center, but its placement at the very beginning of the book can be interpreted as an offer to the readers to familiarize themselves with the house as well through this simple 'map.' The homey surroundings give Rico a feeling of safety, because they act according to certain "rules of probability" (Wischmann 2003: 24), while the open space provides new and unknown challenges. Rico's focus on the spaghetti on the street hints at a passion for knowledge. It also shows that children experience places in a different way than adults, because they focus on other details (see O'Brien et al. 2000: 259).

Mastering the next step

Rico's comfort zone is of limited scope. *Dieffenbachstraße*, called Dieffe by the locals, the street on which the house stands and on which Rico found the pasta, is still in the comfort zone. The street is characterized as being crowded with people "sitting outside in front of coffee shops and restaurants, and music [coming] from the open windows of the apartments" (Steinhöfel 2011b: 18). It is striking that neither the house nor the street are described in detail besides these remarks. When asked in an interview why Berlin and *Kreuzberg* are more or less sparsely outlined in the novel, Steinhöfel answered that he did not want to be more specific because that would be unnatural for a child, who has always known his environment (Geissler 2009). This also adds to the process of mapping: the vague descriptions make the story more universal because readers from other cities or places can claim the street, and therefore also the story, as their own.

When comparing the English translation with the German version, one notices that there are slight shifts in meaning. For example the English translation "I felt good about myself" (Steinhöfel 2011b: 19) emphasizes that Rico left the house and managed to go shopping all alone, which shows that he appreciated the fact that he had left his comfort zone and faced the unknown. The German text instead

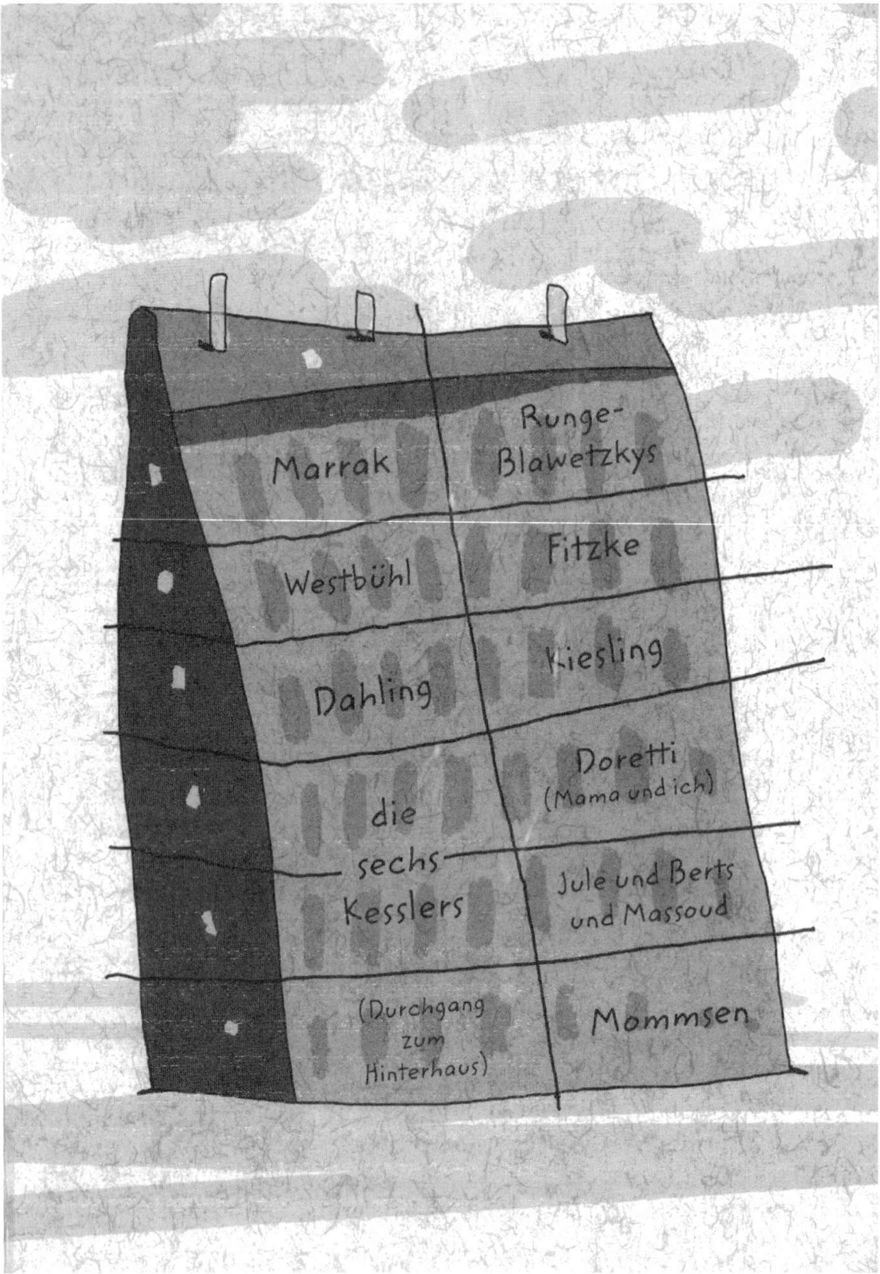

Figure 1. Frontispiece of Andreas Steinhöfel: *Rico, Oscar und die Tieferschatten*. Hamburg: Carlsen, 2008. © Carlsen Verlag GmbH, Hamburg 2008

underlines his feelings of safety when he stands on the street, his familiar place: "I felt safe" (Steinhöfel 2008: 29, my translation). We can see that the two different versions convey different messages to the reader. The German text would be more closely connected to place, while the English translation seems to be more closely connected to space. Another aspect is highlighted: the importance of feelings. To some extent, the child's own feelings and evaluation the situation can affect whether the location becomes a place or a space. The interconnection becomes even clearer in the description of how Rico navigates in his environment.

Rico's familiar environment extends further than just down the road. On well-defined routes, he is able to go shopping or to school:

> But from Dieffe Street I can actually go to school by myself. All I have to do is go out of the house, walk a little way to the drugstore on the corner and then turn off upward, in the direction of the canal. From then on I keep going straight, across the bridge to school. The street keeps going past the school, through Little Istanbul toward the subway station, but I've never been brave enough to go any farther than the kebab restaurant, just *before* the station.
>
> (Steinhöfel, 2011b: 19; italics in original)

Starting from his house he explains his path to school, which reveals how he orients himself in the city. The description primarily takes the form of a route through his environment and can be interpreted as an oral reproduction of a city map. Because of his learning disabilities, Rico explains and reflects more clearly upon what he is doing. This also helps the young reader to follow along the way. Children have to learn the concept of how to move from A to B, which explains why these very detailed descriptions are more prevalent in children's literature than in adult literature. The route description represents a general model for finding one's way in a modern city; therefore the streets and landmarks do not have names. It seems to be more important to acquire an understanding of how directions and distances can be linked together and characterized in words. Two steps in gaining spatial understanding become clear: first the orientation landmarks are put together into routes, contributing to a mental image of the city. The imaginary line from landmark to landmark creates a safety net for Rico's navigation in *Kreuzberg*. Then memorizing these routes consolidates the overall picture and forms a mental map.

It is noteworthy that landmarks are concretely specified in the German original. It is not just any arbitrary bridge, any arbitrary kebab restaurant, or any arbitrary station that Rico memorizes. Instead it is the *Admiral's* bridge, the *Doyum* grill house, and the *Kottie* station, places that Rico can directly relate to. Interestingly, the English translation omits the exact names of the places. Just the name of *Dieffe* Street is mentioned. As a result, the translation does not give the same atmosphere of familiarity as the original.

Especially the use of nicknames like *Kottie*, known in Germany for being typical *Kreuzberg* descriptions, indicates the spatiality and Rico's belonging to the place. The concrete designation of streets and landmarks gives the text authenticity. Furthermore the reader can, if interested, follow Rico's path to the school by using a Berlin city map.

Although some characterizations like "walk a little way" and "keep going straight" seem a bit vague (Steinhöfel 2011b: 19), they are expressions of Rico's individual exploration of space. Mapping is a way of structuring information and, in Rico's case, the symbiosis of certain landmarks and his own measurement of distance form a spatial web in his mind. Apparently the central aspect of his way of orienting is that he is walking. He first needs to build up a virtual map of the nearby surroundings in his mind before daring to expand his field of interaction. Furthermore, Rico seems to have a passion for structuring information, a strategy to overcome his learning disabilities. He writes his own dictionary entries, in which he defines difficult words like 'built-in teacher function' (37), 'partition' (59), and 'self-centeredness' (72).

Talking about orientation in the neighborhood means sequencing information, and thus being able to structure and to memorize it:

> Whether gleaned from maps, navigations, or descriptions, spatial information about entire environments cannot be processed all at once. To achieve a full, coherent representation, spatial information must be integrated over time. Through maps, information is acquired over successive eye fixations. In navigation and through texts, information is received sequentially. (Taylor 2000: 192)

Holly Taylor's observations on the different ways of processing information via text and maps can also be shown by another episode, which illustrates how Rico's map-reading skills develop. At one point, he shows the area to Oskar from the roof terrace of the apartment house. Almost like a tourist Rico begins to name the skyscrapers on Potsdam Square and the TV tower on Alexander Square (Steinhöfel 2011b: 56). Even though Rico has not yet understood the distances and routes leading to the sights, his mapping ability has increased because he recognizes landmarks from the roof terrace. The presented survey perspective can be interpreted as a first sign of understanding the three-dimensional map of Berlin.

The contrast between theoretical knowledge and intimacy with a place, however, is striking when the scope is reduced to his familiar little sphere of comfort. All of a sudden he eloquently explains how comfortable it would be to sit on the terrace with a comic strip, looking over the treetops and listening to the noises of the city (56). Another example indicating his improving skills in understanding maps is his response when his mother explains that she has to visit her brother. Rico mentions, as if he has a map in front of his inner eye, that "he lives somewhere in Germany down at the bottom at left" (71). Rico's skills clearly show his ability to navigate in his familiar environment. He has taken the first steps in mapping.

David Uttal and Lisa Tan describe the same steps in their research on the development of cognitive mapping in children. Children begin with orientation by landmarks. The next step links landmarks and leads to an understanding of routes and route-based representations of spatial knowledge. Finally, the recognition of locations from a bird's-eye view becomes possible and survey knowledge develops, which requires the ability to think abstractly (2000: 149–150).

In these three steps, gradually larger areas are opened up bit by bit, starting from the known and discovering the yet unknown – from the child's own apartment building to the city neighborhood (Löw 2001: 81; Tuan 2001: 30). As the story unfolds it will be revealed whether Rico has learned enough to move into unfamiliar terrain.

Leaving the comfort zone

Rico is confronted with a dilemma: on the one hand, he is afraid to leave his environment; on the other hand, he still wants to do so in order to be able to speak to the girl Sophia, to get clues about the kidnapper and the possible whereabouts of Oskar. His learning disabilities complicate his orientation because he constantly forgets relevant facts and he still considers a map to be an aesthetic artefact instead of a source of information (Steinhöfel 2011b: 106).

He knows that Sophia lives in another area of the city, which is an unknown territory for him. His strategy for mastering the problems involved consists in asking the neighbor for a ride. During the trip he is not able to remember the way. Instead, he concentrates on how it feels to drive in a Porsche and worriedly thinks to himself: "*You'll never find the way home*" (109; italics in original).

What this quote demonstrates in short is called urban-island knowledge of a city. According to Löw, the modern lifestyle affects the child's orientation in the city in this way, since children are nowadays usually driven by car to and from school and leisure activities and they are therefore not able to experience city life on their own. This lack of a general understanding of their surroundings restricts their knowledge to so-called urban islands (2001: 83).

In terms of orientation in the city, driving does not replace actual walking. Upon reaching his destination, Rico asks some children in front of a school where Sophia lives. Together they make their way to her, and he even manages to find his way back to where he met the children. Again the combination of social contacts and walking is helping him. However, new social contacts alone are not enough, since he fails to memorize the directions given by a shop assistant.

Similarly, the strategy to simply start walking and searching for the subway station fails as well, and he is relieved to finally find a taxi to take him home (Steinhöfel 2011b: 157–159).

It is illuminating how Rico acts in his neighborhood and how he tries to deal with foreign terrain. Life in the neighborhood is shown as a microcosm with a range of social relationships, in which Rico, despite his handicap, is well integrated. Gradually Rico expands his spatial range during the tours through the other neighborhoods. It is also important that Rico establishes social contacts in order to facilitate orientation. A central location, both spatially and socially, is and remains the apartment house. The travel through Berlin points out the limits of his spatial range. Outside his environment he has severe orientation problems, but his failure also means experience. However, the skills he has thus acquired cannot be easily transferred to other spatial experiences. It is evident that the skill of orientation must be practiced repeatedly. Meeting the challenge strengthens his self-confidence. Even though he fails to orient himself competently during his trip, he manages to fulfill his mission, because the trip gives him important clues about Oskar's disappearance. When he is home again in *Kreuzberg*, his increased confidence in his abilities is mirrored by the fact that he is able to concentrate better, combine the facts, and also manages to use his brain, or as the title of the English version indicates: "to use his noodle." His trip through the city is therefore an important piece of the puzzle in solving the crime.

The fact that the kidnapper is finally revealed as being a neighbor and the scene of the crime as a house close by facilitates Rico's liberation efforts, since he is well accustomed to this familiar environment. Furthermore, Steinhöfel plays here with the literary motif that danger might always be waiting around the corner.

Mapping a city – Concluding remarks

Topographical maps do not represent reality; instead they always represent knowledge about reality. A precondition for orienting oneself in a city is to obtain spatial perception and learn to navigate in the environment. The next step in mapping would be to match and transfer this knowledge to the symbols and the scale of a map.

As Steinhöfel's novel has shown, the mapping of the city is an important theme in children's literature. While Rico tries to experience the city and slowly and methodically approaches the urban space, by this means expanding his comfort zone, his familiar range is widened step by step, from the house to the street, from the street to the school, and then all the way to a full tour through the city. The reader is taken on a journey in which Rico gradually familiarizes himself with

Berlin. The text includes orientation by landmarks and route descriptions, which clarify the process of navigating in a city, as well as survey descriptions, which correspond to maps according to Taylor (2000: 193). Pausing, going back in the text, and re-reading it enables the young reader to understand the learning processes of orientation in a complex urban environment. Although Rico explores and finds his way around in Berlin, his approach is applicable to any exploration of other spaces as well.

Consequently, four aspects concerning the gradual discovery of a city play an important role. First, a desire for discovery and a feeling of curiosity are necessary. Second, walking seems to be an important piece of the puzzle, since it supports the process of spatial orientation, thus enabling the development of a mental map. Third, social contacts are a necessary precondition in order to discover unknown places and to adapt them into personal spaces. The fourth defining characteristic is that moving around in spaces generates knowledge and fosters identity development. Hence, reading about Rico's strategies allows young readers to imagine the urban space and by doing so to familiarize themselves with the concept of a city.

References

Primary sources

Kästner, Erich. 1932. *Emil und die Detektive*. Berlin: Williams & Co (first published 1929).
Kästner, Erich. 2001. *Emil and the Detectives*, transl. Eileen Hall. London: Red Fox.
Steinhöfel, Andreas. 2008. *Rico, Oskar und die Tieferschatten*. Hamburg: Carlsen.
Steinhöfel, Andreas. 2009. *Rico, Oskar und das Herzgebreche*. Hamburg: Carlsen.
Steinhöfel, Andreas. 2011a. *Rico, Oskar und der Diebstahlstein*. Hamburg: Carlsen.
Steinhöfel, Andreas. 2011b. *The Spaghetti Detectives. They've Got to Use Their Noodles!*, transl. Chantal Wright. New York NY: Chicken House.

Secondary sources

De Certeau, Michel. 1988. *The Practice of Everyday Life*. Berkeley CA: University of California Press (first published 1984).
Freeman, Claire & Tranter, Paul. 2011. *Children and Their Urban Environment: Changing Worlds*. London: Earthscan.
Geissler, Cornelia. 2009. Ein Kind, das langsam denkt, ist nicht doof, *Berliner Zeitung*. Retrieved from <http://www.berliner-zeitung.de/archiv/andreas-steinhoefel-gilt-als-der-neue-kaestner--mit-dem-schreiben-holt-er-sich-schoene-momente-seiner-kindheit-zurueck--seine-helden-findet-er-in-der-berliner-unterschicht--ein-gespraech-ein-kind--das-langsam-denkt--ist-nicht-doof,10810590,10631222.html> (19 December 2015).
Goga, Nina. 2014. Kart og krim. Litterære kart og steders betydning i krimserier for barn. *Tidskrift för Litteraturvetenskap* 2: 69–82.

Goga, Nina. 2015. *Kart i barnelitteraturen*. Kristiansand: Portal.

Holzmann, Gabriela. 2006. Berlinlektionen für Kinder. Erich Kästners Emil und die Detektive zwischen Provinz und Metropole. In *"Weltfabrik Berlin". Eine Metropole als Sujet der Literatur. Studien zu Literatur und Landeskunde*, Matthias Harder & Almut Hille (eds), 99–114. Würzburg: Königshausen & Neumann.

Kärrholm, Sara. 2011. Den hårdkokta deckaren. In *Kriminallitteratur. Utveckling, genrer, perspektiv*, by Kerstin Bergman & Sara Kärrholm, 88–104. Lund: Studentlitteratur.

Kitchin, Rob & Freundschuh, Scott. 2000. Cognitive mapping. In *Cognitive Mapping. Past, Present and Future*, Rob Kitchin & Scott Freundschuh (eds), 1–8. New York NY: Routledge.

Knight, Stephen. 2012. *The Mysteries of the Cities. Urban Crime Fiction in the Nineteenth Century*. Jefferson NC: McFarland.

Krämer, Sybille. 2015. *Medium, Messenger, Transmission. An Approach to Media Philosophy*. Amsterdam: Amsterdam University Press.

Kümmerling-Meibauer, Bettina. 2007. "…kommt nach Berlin und dreht gleich 'nen Film!": Berlin in der Kinderliteratur der Weimarer Republik. In *Berlin. Medien- und Kulturgeschichte einer Hauptstadt im 20. Jahrhundert*, Matthias Bauer (ed.), 189–206. Tübingen: Francke.

Kümmerling-Meibauer, Bettina & Meibauer, Jörg. 2015. Maps in picturebooks: Cognitive status and narrative functions. *Nordic Journal of ChildLit Aesthetics* 6. Retrieved from <doi: 10.3402/blft.v6.26970> (1 December 2015).

Liben, Lynn. 2009. The road to understanding maps. *Current Directions in Psychological Science* 18(6): 310–315. doi: 10.1111/j.1467-8721.2009.01658.x

Löw, Martina. 2001. *Raumsoziologie*. Frankfurt: Suhrkamp.

Löwe, Corina. 2011. *Von Jungen Pionieren und Gangstern. Der Kinder- und Jugendkriminalroman in der DDR* (Young Pioneers and Gangsters: Detective Novels for Children and Young Adults in the GDR). PhD dissertation, Stockholm University. Stockholm: Acta Universitatis Stockholmiensis.

Magel, Eva-Maria. 2008. Eine Fundnudel für ganz Berlin. *Frankfurter Allgemeine Zeitung*. Retrieved from <http://www.faz.net/aktuell/feuilleton/buecher/rezensionen/belletristik/eine-fundnudel-fuer-ganz-berlin-1549720.html> (19 December 2015).

Menzel, Hilde. 2009. *Empathie und Sprachwitz. Andreas Steinhöfel und die Nähe zu seinen Figuren. Rede aus Anlass der Verleihung des Erich Kästner Preises für Literatur an Andreas Steinhöfel*. Retrieved from <http://www.carlsen.de/uploads/Presse/Pressemappe_Andreas_Steinhoefel_neu.pdf> (19 December 2015).

O'Brien, Margaret, Jones, Deborah, Sloan, David & Rustin, Michael. 2000. Children's independent spatial mobility in the urban public realm. *Childhood: A Global Journal of Child Research* 7(3): 257–277. Retrieved from <http://chd.sagepub.com/content/7/3/257.full.pdf+html> (19 December 2015).

Ryan, Marie-Laure. 2003. Cognitive maps and the construction of narrative space. In *Narrative Theory and the Cognitive Sciences*, David Herman (ed.), 214–241. Stanford CA: CSLI Publications.

Taylor, Holly. 2000. A view of space through language. In *Cognitive Mapping. Past, Present and Future*, Rob Kitchin & Scott Freundschuh (eds), 179–196. New York NY: Routledge.

Tuan, Yi-Fu. 2001. *Space and Place. The Perspective of Experience*. Minneapolis MN: University of Minnesota Press.

Uttal, David & Tan, Lisa. 2000. Cognitive mapping in childhood. In *Cognitive Mapping. Past, Present and Future*, Rob Kitchin & Scott Freundschuh (eds), 147–165. New York NY: Routledge.

Wigbers, Melanie. 2006. *Krimi-Orte im Wandel.* Würzburg: Königshausen & Neumann.
Wischmann, Antje. 2003. *Verdichtete Stadtwahrnehmung. Untersuchungen zum literarischen und urbanistischen Diskurs in Skandinavien 1955–1995.* Berlin: BWV.

CHAPTER 6

"New York just like I pictured it – skyscrapers and everything"[1]

Anna Katrina Gutierrez

Maps of New York City, whether visual or verbal, evoke an abundance of scripts and schemas related to adolescent romance, adventure, and coming-of-age. Some of these are associated with iconic sights, for example, the Empire State Building and the 'romantic rendezvous' script. In these texts New York is a storyworld grounded on a map that exists outside of the narrative but is built from the blend of disparate New York schemas: those called upon by the focalizing characters and those held in the mind of the reader. In *Nick and Norah's Infinite Playlist* (2006) and *Dash and Lily's Book of Dares* (2010), the coming-of-age romance begins with a map, and the mapping of script onto storyworld is enriched by intertextual links with music, poetry, and literature. The intertextual meaning-making combined with the active blending of New York City schemas that occur in the background emphasize the complexity of intersubjective development.

New York City. The very words evoke images imprinted in our collective memory, so often have they been repeated in media: the neon lights of Times Square illuminating the awestruck faces of tourists; the grim, grey, and noisy subways; spontaneous song and dance numbers in Central Park; the steadfast Statue of Liberty standing guard over the city and its dreamers, and on and on. Adolescent fiction draws from such iconic images when recreating a real city into a storyworld. Storyworlds refer not only to landscape and physical matter but also to conceptual patterns attached to these, creating a mental map of events and circumstances that set up narrative expectations (Herman 2009: x). New York City, located at the intersection of reality and narration, is able to hold a variety of story scripts from all kinds of genres and cultures. Stevie Wonder's description – "skyscrapers and everything" – summarizes the city's grand narrative: a place where anyone can reach for the stars, where anything can happen. A specific example would be the variety of story

1. *Living in the City*, Stevie Wonder. Quoted in *Nick and Norah's Infinite Playlist.*

DOI 10.1075/clcc.7.07kat

scripts associated with the Statue of Liberty: new beginnings in immigration stories, independence in young adult stories, while its destruction in dystopian science fiction – half-buried in sand in Pierre Boulle's *The Planet of the Apes* (1963); floodwater up to her nose in John Bowen's *After the Rain* (1958) – symbolizes a cynical view of democracy or of the future. Characterized by tenacious possibility, New York is an appropriate setting for YA novels across genres, from brooding realism as in J. D. Salinger's *Catcher in the Rye* (1951), to Rick Riordan's fantastical New York in the *Percy Jackson* series (2005–2009), and to romantic adventures, as in my focused texts, Rachel Cohn and David Levithan's *Nick and Norah's Infinite Playlist* (2006) and *Dash and Lily's Book of Dares* (2010).

This chapter examines cognitive mapping in coming-of-age narratives that are grafted onto a location rich with meaning in fiction and in reality. In Cohn and Levithan's novels, the symbols and stories attached to the New York cityscape guide the reader's understanding of each character's maturation. The authors collaborate on alternating chapters, with Cohn writing Norah's and Lily's pages and Levithan responding in the voices of Nick and Dash. To direct an understanding of cognitive mapping, I will begin with a discussion of related terms, in particular schemas, image-schemas, and scripts. These definitions are put into the context of the novels in the sections that follow. I examine the way Cohn and Levithan graft adolescence onto the idea of Manhattan as a place of excitement and opportunity. Through specific examples from each novel, I present the authors' use of symbolic New York spaces to facilitate dialogic growth in the third section. *Nick and Norah's Infinite Playlist* and *Dash and Lily's Book of Dares* (referred to as *Infinite Playlist* and *Book of Dares* from this point forward), furthermore, draw on musical and literary storyworlds linked to the cityscape to enrich the protagonists' maturation. In the final section, I explore the depth of meaning that arises from the interaction of intertextual storyworlds with each character's experience of the cityscape.

A cognitive map of young love in New York City

Adolescent fiction is primarily concerned with mapping a young person's development into a mature and socially aware subject (Stephens 1992: 3) in dialogue with others, with the past, with language, and with the world (McCallum 1999: 3). Young adult novels that open with maps of New York City, whether these maps are visual or verbal, elicit a number of patterns, technically referred to as schemas and scripts, associated with aspirational themes, for example, adolescent romance, family sagas, and "American Dream" stories. Schemas and scripts are generalized knowledge structures, what David Herman calls "experiential repertoires," through which we filter our expectations and make sense of stories (2002: 89).

They provide a framework for the relations between physical things and abstract concepts. A script is composed of a network of schemas, whereby a schema is “a static element” within our list of experiences and “a script is a dynamic element, which expresses how a sequence of events or actions are expected to unfold” (Stephens 2011: 14). Underpinning *Infinite Playlist* and *Book of Dares* are schemas and scripts of young love, many of which are attached to the sights and streets of New York, developing in readers a kind of map wherein topography and existence are understood in connection to one another.

Schemas at their most basic refer to memory patterns for objects, people, generic procedures, sequences of events, and precepts, which are then filled out with the particularities of the represented item or event (Herman 2002: 89; Johnson 1987). They are frame-like, referencing reality from a specific perspective. The basic schema for an apartment, for example, is a set of private rooms, including a bedroom, a kitchen, a living and dining room, and a bathroom, inside a residential building. When thinking of a New York City brownstone, however, the basic apartment schema is typified with a beautiful brick façade, larger rooms, a fireplace, hardwood floors, and high ceilings. George Lakoff and Mark Johnson insist that this generalized schema theory be complemented and enriched by image-schemas. These are gestalt representations – unified wholes that are perceived as more than the sum of their parts – that organize information “at the level of *bodily* experience and movement” (Johnson 1987; italics mine). An example is up-down, wherein our understanding of upward and downward movements is integrated. Tied to our mental and motor perceptions, image-schemas allow us to modify knowledge patterns according to experience and how they might apply to different situations. Lakoff and Johnson include embodied concepts of spatial orientation (up-down, in-out, near-far, and so on), ontological concepts emerging from experience (for instance, entity, container), and structured experiences and activities (for example, moving) among the image-schematic source domains, that is, the conceptual basis for metaphor (1980: 195; 2003: 10–11, 15, 30). These and other recurrent image-schemas provide rich imagery that “dynamically structure[s] our perception, action, and cognition” (Kimmel 2009: 159). For example, in *Book of Dares*, when Dash states “my name is a connector of words” (61), he ostensibly provides a literal definition of his name, but by drawing on container (name) and conduit (connector) image-schemas he first reveals his adolescence, a state of liminality, and second a desire for connection and communication, wherein the target is a sympathetic other.

Scripts are structured as interconnected “slots” or “terminals” (Herman 2002: 98), each of which is filled with appropriate schemas that form event sequences with standardized conditions and expected outcomes. The schemas that fill one slot affect what can fill another (Johnson 1987). We comprehend a specific situation or procedure when we make connections between each frame. In other words, human cognition completes the story-meaning of the semantic network (Trites 2014: 40). The coming-of-age romance script that runs through *Infinite Playlist* and *Book of Dares*, for example, relies on a structured schema with typical characters (a male and female teenager), and a setting reflective of their liminal states (the culturally diverse New York City), arranged in a stereotyped sequence of events (the "meet cute" – the comical yet charming introduction of the lead characters to one another; a date that leads to a misunderstanding between them; the second date and 'second chance'; and so on) leading to the predetermined goal: first/true love.

The networks created and the meanings activated form a cognitive map, which Marie-Laure Ryan argues is "a mental model for *spatial* relations" that is representative of bodily experiences and preconceptions of environments real and imagined, and wherein the graphic map or verbal recreation of space becomes "a stage for narrative events" (2003: 215). Cognitive mapping helps readers situate themselves in relation to the New York storyworld temporally and *spatio*-temporally, generating a deeper understanding of the narrative (Herman 2001: 535). Such representations are linked to temporal information through two discourse strategies. These are the 'survey' (also called the map), which provides a bird's eye viewpoint of space, and the 'route' (also called tour), which presents the perspective of a moving object (such as a traveler) (Ryan 2003: 218). What is perceived through survey and route becomes meaningful when it triggers associations that effectively shape or alter the perceiver's understanding of a given event in the framing narrative. While it may seem evident, the effects of links made between the geographical map of New York City and its iconic features and the scripts and schemas elicited by those features upon meaning-making need further exploration. To illustrate, when featured in a romantic comedy, the Empire State Building triggers the romantic rendezvous script from *An Affair to Remember* (dir. Leo McCarey, 1957), but in migration and self-actualization narratives evokes American Dream scripts. Even everyday, ordinary spaces can activate experiential blueprints. A youth narrative that centers on a basketball court in Brooklyn, for example, invokes a basketball script representative of the youth culture unique to that specific area of New York. The schemas and scripts associated with the eclectic streets of the Lower East Side, known as much for its immigrant and Jewish roots as for its alternative music and art scenes, would be different from those associated with the sleek avenues of the Upper East Side, lined with beautiful brownstone apartments and designer stores. The expected outcomes of a coming-of-age romance would be affected by the set of schematic patterns embedded in the area (posh Upper or diverse Lower East Side) on which it is charted.

When a young adult novel is set in New York City, then, place-related scripts and schemas activate a cognitive map that is fundamentally linked to the growth and maturation of the adolescent characters. Roberta Seelinger Trites maintains that adolescence is linguistically represented as embodied metaphors, for example, journeying, confining, adventuring, and awakening. Such movements draw on conceptual metaphors structured from spatial, ontological, and experiential image-schemas as source domains, for example, UP IS GOOD, MENTAL PROGRESS IS A JOURNEY, and LIFE IS A JOURNEY, that underscore a cultural bias towards images of upward and forward momentum (2014: 20–22). Coming-of-age scripts and schemas, then, necessarily denote transition and growth, and easily plot onto the image of New York, with its climbing skyscrapers and "everything," as a place of convergence and opportunity.

In *Infinite Playlist* and *Book of Dares*, the coming-of-age romance script specifically contextualizes the New York storyworld. In both storyworlds, New York City is grounded on a map that exists in reality, outside of the narrative, but is built from the blend of disparate New York City schemas and scripts: those called upon by the focalizing characters and those held in the mind of the reader. The spatio-temporal movements of the adolescent protagonists in both novels trigger place-associated schemas held by the reader, which the characters corroborate or challenge as their journeys through the city shape their intersubjectivity. For both novels, a map of assumptions and expectations related to New York is more important than a topographical map. Only the movie tie-in edition of *Infinite Playlist* (2008) provides a sketched map pointing out some of the key locations of the story, focusing on Midtown, the Lower East Side, the East Village, and the Times Square and Theatre Districts. This map is not available in other editions of the book, which indicates that it is of secondary importance to verbal and cognitive mapping. The same conclusion can be made of *Book of Dares*, which does not provide a city map in any of its editions. The book covers, however, specify the location. The original hardcover edition (2010a) portrays a typical New York street corner with skyscrapers in the background; the Australian edition (2010b) and the Kindle edition published by Ember (2014) include sketches of the New York City skyline on their covers, while the MiraInk Kindle edition (2012) has the Statue of Liberty in silhouette. These iconic images are enough to trigger for some readers scripts and schemas related to place and genre.

The cross-mapping of coming-of-age romance and New York storyworld is further enriched by intermedial links with music in *Infinite Playlist* and intertextual allusions to poetry and literature in *Book of Dares*, whereby the interweaving of place with specific imagery from stories, poems, and songs reflects and/or affects the mental and emotional progress of the young protagonists. Intertexts and intermedia also prompt cognitive mapping, activate scripts and schemas, which are either strengthened or undermined, and infuse new meaning into the real world and the narrative landscape. These references also function as links to other storyworlds and the experiences contained within. This form of cognitive mapping draws on "conceptual blending," coined by Gilles Fauconnier and Mark Turner to describe our minds' ability to automatically fuse selective elements from discrete domains, or "input spaces," and from this blending create a new meaning that adds to the significance of its parent components (2002: 17–38, 47–49). The difference between conceptual metaphor theory and conceptual blending theory is that metaphor is "typically concerned with entrenched conceptual relationships and the ways in which they may be elaborated whereas the latter often focuses on novel conceptualizations, which may be short-lived" (Yu 2009: 122).

In the following discussion, I examine how both novels prompt dialogic reading practices, engaging readers in (a) the negotiation of each intertext's conceptual world with elements associated with the New York storyworld constructed from the blend of reader and character-held New York schemas; and (b) an interpretative play of musical and literary intertexts and how these are used to create relationships between characters and place. The intertextual meaning-making that occurs in relation to the blending of genre- and place-related schemas and scripts emphasizes the complexity of intersubjective development.

"The real wild" and "the center of the world": Manhattan as spectacle

Cohn and Levithan focus on the Manhattan landscape, which they cross-map with area-specific scripts and schemas to set the narrative stage. In both novels, the coming-of-age romance pivots on the repeated invocation of Manhattan as a place of discovery and infinite possibility because of the narrative and symbolic patterns grafted onto its iconic spaces. This anticipatory feeling is magnified by each teenager's search for a romantic love that is dialogic. Their struggle to understand themselves in relation to the world is expressed in vocabulary associated with maps. In effect, the desire for a map to guide them through the murky pathways of maturation becomes linked to an already mapped out place, whereby the anxiety of self-searching finds some relief in being anchored to an existent space. The back-cover text of my copy of *Infinite Playlist* (2010b) charts the complications of adolescent romance onto a spatio-temporal scenario. The eventful journey towards mature intersubjective dialogue spans Manhattan:

> Nick and Norah **set off on an uncharted adventure called the "first date"** that will turn into an **infinite night** of **falling in and out (and in and out, and maybe in and maybe out)** of love […] As Nick and Norah **wander** through the

> **middle-of-the-night mystic maze** of Manhattan, they share **the kind of night you never want to end**, where **every minute counts** and every moment **flickers between** love and disaster. [ellipsis and bold in this and all other quotes are mine]

Falling, wandering, finding one's way out of darkness, and the equal possibility for love or disaster develop from path, in-out, and moving source domains that characterize the complexity of the characters' experience. The known parameters of the "first date" script are overturned by the qualifier "uncharted adventure," which is grafted onto Manhattan. The path, in-out, and moving schemas are elaborated in spatio-temporal succession, with several sudden changes in direction ("falling in and out"), with the threat of abruptly ending ("flickers," "every minute counts"), and with the attempt to extend, and the hope of making permanent ("infinite"), the thrill that comes with authentic dialogue. Describing Manhattan as a "middle-of-the-night mystic maze" diagrams the sensory and spatial perception of their emotional development. That Manhattan remains a mystery underscores that topographical maps are not exhaustive, which, when related to the "first date" and coming-of-age scripts, highlights the unexpected delight that comes with realizing that a person, like a mapped out place, is both known and ultimately unknowable. Related imagery across *Infinite Playlist* corroborates the spatial orientation of intimacy. Following their first unsuccessful venture at a date, Nick's decision to find Norah after she unceremoniously leaves him is physically located: "I look back to the sidewalk" and "map the possibilities" (2006: 101). Sidewalk and map serve as terms that link the coming-of-age romance to the path image-schema and hint at growth and forward momentum.

Related imagery mapping the convolutions of adolescence can also be found throughout the text, as when Norah describes Manhattan as "the real wild" (2006: 37). "Wild" activates the urban jungle metaphor and points to her feelings of vulnerability and insecurity, and "real" suggests that she is representative of typical adolescence in the storyworld and in actuality. It is Norah who quotes Stevie Wonder upon meeting Nick: "Here I am in Manhattan, like Dad's favorite Stevie Wonder song goes: *New York, just like I* ***pictured*** *it –* ***skyscrapers and everything.*** Shit is supposed to be ***happening*** here" (italics in this and all other quotes from the primary texts are in the original) (2006: 31). "Skyscrapers and everything" invokes a tourist gaze that triggers "spectacle/spectacular" New York schemas, which when later qualified by "wild" and "happening," is injected with a frenetic but purposeful energy. In the quotation, container, structure, and path logic form a complex image of Norah's in-betweenness and her longing to become part of the action.

Lily and Dash also invoke the tourist gaze in *Book of Dares*. Lily declares that Manhattan is the "center of the world" (Cohn and Levithan 2010b: 201). Like Norah, she draws on the container schema (through "center") to situate her growth within the heart of modernity, thus implying her progressive personality. Dash, on the other hand, focalizes the chaotic wonder of Times Square as a study of performance vis-à-vis authenticity:

> *Having* ***grown up*** *here, I always wonder what it would be like to see the city as a tourist. Is it ever a disappointment? I have to believe that New York* ***lives up to its reputation****. The buildings really are that tall. The lights really are that bright. There's truly* ***a story on every corner****. But it still might be a* ***shock****. To realize* ***you are just one story walking*** *among* ***millions****. To not feel the bright lights even as they* ***fill*** *the air. To see the tall buildings and* ***only feel a deep longing for the stars****.* (174)

Dash alerts readers to their (assumed) usage of the tourist gaze and questions expectations attached to the Manhattan as center (of stories, in which stories are people) schema. "Grown up" relates with "tall buildings," thus blending Dash's subject-formation with the progressive and upward development of the city. Looking through the eyes of a tourist, however, indicates a certain detachment from the space. He draws from container ("a story on every corner"), person ("lives up to its reputation"), structure ("buildings," "lights"), multiplex-mass ("one story walking among millions"), and path ("walking," "longing for the stars") source domains to elucidate his existential angst and loneliness in spite of the dense activity that characterizes Manhattan. What is missing is a connection image-schema, whereby the exchange of stories might possibly bring the stars that much closer, as intersubjectivity revitalizes the experience of the self, of others, and of places that have become ordinary to him.

Mapping possibilities for growth onto real world locations

In both novels, intersubjective intimacy is contextualized in locations that reveal something about the characters. Most of the action in these books takes place on the Lower East Side, in the East Village, Midtown, and in the Times Square and Theater Districts, but Nick and Norah often reference New Jersey, where they both live, and parts of Dash and Lily's story take place on the Upper East Side and in Brooklyn. In most of *Book of Dares*, Dash and Lily are not in the same scene; rather, they take turns sending one another to places representative of facets of their personalities or current emotional and mental states. In *Infinite Playlist*, Nick and Norah make assumptions about one another based on place – where each one lives, goes to school, and so on – which are then overturned when set against the places they escape to or find themselves in while on their date. Revelatory moments become fused with landmarks and topographic distinctions, enriching both real world and storyworld. Ryan states that the annexation of parts of real world places with fictional storyworlds is appealing because these novels "invest in a sense of place that already exists in [readers'] minds" (2012: 112), and the use of an iconic space as the location for the dramatic turns of each character triggers special meanings for each reader, some personal and some communal, which makes the characters more relatable as well as renders both storyworld and real world more tangible and authentic (2003: 236; 2012: 110). This affective quotient is part of cognitive mapping (Miall 1989: 61–63) and deepens connections to both actual and narrative topographies, whereby readers comprehend characters through the schemas activated by their emotional attachment to landscapes real and imagined.

Emotional growth and other-awareness is mapped on the following types of interrelation between character and place:

1. *Stereotypical associations* based on place are undermined when combined with other place-based tropes, or when character-place interplay results in the character going against type;
2. *The (re)discovery of place*, when a character interacts with a place through the other's perspective and/or when one character shares with another the special meanings s/he associates with a specific place;
3. The instantiation of place through *intertextual and intermedial connections* made by the character.

Each character's maturation generally adheres to the coming-of-age romance script wherein the search for the beloved other equates with the discovery of self. The twisting and turning, backwards and forwards movement inherent to the coming-of-age romance script (that mainly draws from path and connection image-schemas) is charted onto existent places that are colored by the judgments and experiences of the characters.

In *Infinite Playlist*, Nick and Norah's first meeting is influenced by assumptions made about the other based on where they met – at a punk rock club on Ludlow Street on the Lower East Side – and where they think the other is from. Nick can tell from Norah's haircut that she goes to a private school, which he later guesses is in the wealthy part of New Jersey, and that she is trying to hide this by wearing dated clothing (2006: 7). Norah confirms his observation in her own narration, describing herself as a Jewish princess from Englewood Cliffs, one of the most affluent boroughs of New Jersey. Norah first notices Nick while he is playing bass guitar for his queercore Jewish band, and infers from his unfashionable outfit that, in addition to being non-queer and non-Jewish (9), "he has to be from Jersey" (10). Her derision masks a growing interest that is partly rooted in the commonality of the places from which they come and the place they choose to be. For both Nick and Norah, the Lower East Side counterculture gives them the freedom to express their adolescent anxieties better than the tranquility of Jersey suburbia. Their presence at a chaotic club located at the edges of Manhattan, where they listen to and perform anti-establishment music, playfully pushes the boundaries of the stereotypes they rely on to measure relationship potential. They meet when Nick, in an effort to make his ex-girlfriend jealous, propositions Norah, whom he has never met, if she will be his girlfriend for five minutes. Norah initially hesitates, but guesses that if Nick is from Jersey then he must have a van (10), and her more immediate and urgent need for a ride home moves her to respond to his request with a deep kiss. What follows is an awkward attempt at a first date that ends in disaster, which Nick manages to salvage when he follows Norah to Veselka, an iconic 24-hour Ukrainian eatery in the East Village. Veselka, with its "great borscht and clean bathroom" (109), is where Norah and her friends recharge and recover before they begin the long journey home. It suggests a halfway point between the brightness of suburbia and the shadows of Ludlow Street, reflecting Norah's own unguarded liminality. That Nick makes his way to her in a place representative of comfort and friendship implies that he is plotting their relationship on more substantial ground; and indeed, he asks to start over and re-introduces himself to her formally (121). From this point, they walk the same path towards intersubjective maturity.

Book of Dares similarly operates on stereotypical associations based on place, which are then upended when experienced through the other's perspective. If in *Infinite Playlist*, the protagonists experience Manhattan as a mystic maze, in *Book of Dares*, Manhattan is the site of a scavenger hunt. The prize is intersubjective intimacy, qualifying the scavenger hunt as a rich image for path and connection logic that undergirds the coming-of-age romance script. The novel is bookended by a specific location: the Strand bookstore. Dash finds Lily's red notebook on a shelf of old Salinger editions. He is intrigued by the challenge on the cover – "Do you dare?", an intertext to T. S. Eliot's *The Love Song of J. Alfred Prufrock* (1915) and Robert Cormier's *The Chocolate War* (1974) – and enticed by the game she offers to, in the words of Eliot's poem, disturb his known universe: "I've left some clues for you if you want them … turn the page" (2010b: 4). Lily's game involves cobbling together a message by finding the correct words within the pages of obscure books. Her idea of a perfect match also rests on a schema of the bookish teenage boy typically found at the Strand. The message tells Dash to leave the notebook with the store's personnel, and wait for word at her own convenience. But Dash subverts Lily's expectations and decides to continue the game. He leaves a set of his own literary-inspired clues for Lily that leads her to a new location representative of himself, in which he has hidden the notebook. Thus begins a game of discovery, wherein the experiences and feelings shared within the notebook become irrevocably intertwined with the places each sends the other to. They give one another a fresh set of eyes with which to experience the city, but the tourist view is undermined by the place-related story each one shares. The personal meanings they attach to such landmarks peels back scripts of "grandeur and glitz" (73). In uncovering the city, they lay their innermost selves bare. Dash sums up the cross-mapping of person and place in a notebook entry while in front of one of Lily's favorite places – the most excessively decorated house on Dyker Street, Brooklyn, a destination street for lovers of Christmas lights and representative of commercialized cheer: "But whether or not you are here, you are here – because these words are for you, and they wouldn't exist if you weren't here in some way" (95). Though schematic of manufactured Christmas, Dyker Street is changed for Dash through its association with Lily. The schema is infused with her personality, thereby undermining the tourist view through intersubjective dialogue.

Cross-linking storyworlds: Intertexts and intermedia

The dialectic between place-related schemas and each character's experience of place sometimes references other texts, the allusion to which further enhances intersubjectivity. The collaboration between the New York storyworld of the title characters, the intertextual and intermedial storyworlds, and the real world context highlights contrasting relationships between characters and foregrounds the ideologies that underlie the primary storyworld. Such interchanges in each novel, furthermore, transform the city into a third character that impacts upon the intersubjective formation of the adolescent protagonists. When Nick asks Norah for a second chance, he includes the city in his proposition: "You, me, and the city" (2006: 139). Lily's fierce claim of ownership – "*my* city, Manhattan" (2010b: 73) – when threatened with her family's possible move to more tropical climes underscores her identity's dependence on the landscape.

Nick and Norah initially use what Norah calls their "Manhattan music scene" to set the coordinates that mark their understanding of one another. Just as *Book of Dares* is bookended by the Strand, Nick and Norah's first date adventure begins and ends at Ludlow Street, where edgy bands like The Velvet Underground once lived and performed. The anti-establishment musical soundtrack (Nick's band plays songs with lyrics like "Fuck the Man" (9); the Foo Fighters and Green Day are among the bands Norah references) points to their non-conformist ideals. As they get to know each other better they find that each one's musical tastes are rich and varied, thus adding depth and dimension to their characters.

Norah finds out that Nick is the musician ex-boyfriend of her 'frenemy' Tris, and that he was the one who made the music mixes and wrote the songs that Tris used to make fun of but that Norah secretly loved. Upon learning this, Norah imagines herself in a relationship with him. It is clearly fantasy, based on a mishmash of music-and-romance scripts grafted onto places that are meaningful to her. She:

> fantasized about [...] going all the way punk with him to a fucking *jazz* club in the Village or something. Maybe I would have [...] walked along Battery Park with him at sunrise, holding his hand, knowing I would become the one who would believe in him. (18)

Norah combines punk and jazz to convey the boundary-breaking relationship she imagines they would have, but at the same time draws it back into the margins of familiar romantic schemas (walking along Battery Park at sunrise, holding hands). Later, when they give their first date a second try, Norah describes the tourist view of Times Square in vocabulary related to music so as to convey her growing intimacy with the city through her rediscovery of the space with Nick:

> Here I am at the crossroads of the world with shining red-and-white neon lights and yellow taxis, **humming** with action and **pulsing** with music and people, danger and excitement [...] (153)

Nick similarly fuses his tumultuous yet maturing relationship with Norah with Ludlow Street and the punk rock schema associated with it:

> *ON LUDLOW*
> *THERE'S A SHADOW*
> *THAT LETS THE TRUTH SHOW*
> *AND WE WERE WRONG WRONG WRONG*
>
> [...] *on Ludlow*
> *it's just a stone's throw*
> *from where we could go*
> *to where we are.* (114)

Even readers unfamiliar with the destination street's music scene will realize that Nick is drawing from New York counterculture. The punk rock schema he invokes informs their relationship and intersects with as well as pushes the boundaries of the scripts from which Norah draws her initial fantasy. The raw emotion and the clarity of the message he expresses further underscores the value of the genre as Norah sees it (14). The playlist or imagined soundtrack Cohn and Levithan interweave into the narrative characterizes Nick, Norah, and the city as boundary-bending. For example, they have drinks at a club featuring transsexuals performing songs from *The Sound of Music* while dressed as nuns. When Norah inspects Nick's notebook of CDs, she "flip[s] through his musical life, getting to know him through his tastes" (180). She finds "the usual suspects in there, Green Day and The Clash and The Smiths, yeah, but there's also Ella and Frank" (180). It is an extraliterary mode of storytelling that adds to the overall narrative in the same way a movie soundtrack does, which, for musical readers in particular, evokes emotions that enhance the dramatic turns and the personalities of the focalizing protagonists.

The imagery of hand holding (first mentioned in Norah's fantasy) is repeated throughout as Nick and Norah lose and find one another, long to know what the other thinks, feels, and believes, and culminates in the actualization of Norah's fantasy: a sunrise walk from Midtown back to Ludlow Street, and in Nick's invocation of the Beatles' "I Wanna Hold Your Hand" as a script for "what we all really want" (176): connection. Norah, however, once again defies popular opinion and declares that the Beatles are overrated. Nick drops her hand, but rather than falling into another round of will-they-or-won't-they, Norah's disagreement adds texture to their relationship, and furthermore, emphasizes that intersubjectivity develops the self even as it creates a 'we'. Towards the end of the book, they choose to take the subway home. Nick's subway card has enough fare for only one person. He holds out his hand and urges her to jump over the turnstile but Norah, recognizing the symbolism, hesitates.

> If I make this jump, then this is real, he is real [...] I should just [...] let Nick go [...]
> If I do this, it will be like jumping into the middle of the mosh pit. Dangerous. Exhilarating. Terrifying. It's only a [...] turnstile, but what if I don't make it to the other side? Some people never make it out of the mosh pit alive [...]
> Nick says, "Are we in this or not?"
> To throw myself into the breach of our great divide will be a leap of faith.
> I grab hold of his warm hand. (183)

The New York City subway triggers scripts of connection, transience, and isolation, bringing together distant places but through links that are "distinctly embodied and partial" (Stalter-Pace 2013: 49). Norah describes her indecision through a series of intertexts that, especially when grafted onto the liminality of the subway, magnify the blind trust associated with holding hands, jumping, and the belief that the subway will take you to your destination. Her 'yes' indicates intersubjective growth.

In *Book of Dares*, the subway station is also symbolic of Lily's liminal position. While waiting for the train that will take her to the latest destination on Dash's list, Lily shares with him her longing for authentic connectivity by referencing her "personal anthem book" (2010b: 22), Salinger's *Franny and Zooey*, even though at this point Dash's name and face are still unknown to her:

> [...] *there's a line where he* [Zooey] *talks about Franny going to the phone and becoming "younger with each step" as she walked, because she's making it to the other side. She's going to be okay. At least that's what I took it to mean.*
> *I want that. The getting younger with each step, because of anticipation, in hope and belief.*

> [...] *I want to believe that, despite all evidence to the contrary, it is possible for anyone to find that one special person. That person to spend Christmas with or grow old with or just take a nice silly walk in Central Park with.* (75)

In cross-linking *Franny and Zooey* with her own life experience, Lily becomes important to Dash, who astutely recognizes that he "was starting to confuse Lily with Franny" (86). With only locations of significance, the red notebook letters, and the referencing of favorite books and poems (set in or about New York) to go by (for instance, *What the Living Do*, 1998, by Marie Howe, *The Tender Bar*, 2005, by J. R. Moehringer), Dash and Lily inevitably attempt to comprehend the information gathered about the other within the lines of available schemas and are repeatedly warned by friends and family to let go of preconceived notions. Based only on his letters, Lily imagines Dash as an artist living in "swank [...] Chelsea [...] playing the trumpet and wearing a beret" and surrounded by family (103), which is far from reality. When Dash meets Lily's Great-aunt Ida, whom she fondly calls Mrs. Basil E. (like the character in E. L. Konigsburg's *From the Mixed-Up Files of Mrs. Basil E. Frankweiler*, 1967, for she is artistic, eccentric, and perceptive, and aids Lily and Dash in keeping their mystery game in play), he realizes that to truly know Lily he must approach her as "Completely uncharted territory [...] *Terra enigma*" (153). Even though he relies on schemas and scripts, he must be ready to break free from these to achieve true intersubjective intimacy. Similar to the way Norah draws from punk and pop music imagery to make a leap of faith, Dash elaborates on his anticipation of authentic connection on the level of semantics:

> It's like when you're starting to read [...] You know that c-a-t leads to cat [...] But then you have to make an extra leap, to understand that the word, the sound, the "cat" is connected to an actual cat [...] It's that leap, that understanding, that leads to meaning. (86)

Through Dash, Cohn and Levithan eloquently explain the way we imagine, understand, and believe. Dash expresses the value of communication: the way words map schematic patterns, are spatially (even geographically) oriented, and trigger meaningful relationships. He shares the hope we all have that these verbal maps create genuine links between the self, space, and society.

A specific experience of space and time

The theoretical model discussed, when applied to other children's and YA fiction set in real locations, underscores the cognitive network created between texts, society, landscape, scripts, and schemas, and the importance of dialogic meaning-making. The blending of New York storyworld and real world, the scripts and schemas associated with them, and the cross-linking of intertextual and intermedial worlds create a tangible map that illuminates the twists and turns of the coming-of-age romance script. The Manhattan in-jokes in *Infinite Playlist* and *Book of Dares* might leave some readers cold, but more likely Cohn and Levithan's smart and energetic take on YA romance ensures that such witticisms are always in service to the recognizable romance and maturation scripts. Their choices of musical and literary references are especially significant in that they map for young readers not only space, but the cultural significance of a specific place at a particular time, and remind readers of the value of going off-map and experiencing places and people as wonderful enigmas.

References

Primary sources

Cohn, Rachel & Levithan, David. 2006. *Nick and Norah's Infinite Playlist*. New York NY: Knopf.

Cohn, Rachel & Levithan, David. 2008. *Nick and Norah's Infinite Playlist* (Movie tie in edition). New York NY: Ember.

Cohn, Rachel & Levithan, David. 2010a. *Dash and Lily's Book of Dares*. New York NY: Knopf.

Cohn, Rachel & Levithan, David. 2010b. *Dash and Lily's Book of Dares* (Australian edition). Crows Nest NSW: Allen and Unwin.

Cohn, Rachel & Levithan, David. 2012. *Dash and Lily's Book of Dares* (Kindle edition). MiraInk.

Cohn, Rachel & Levithan, David. 2014. *Dash and Lily's Book of Dares* (Kindle edition). New York NY: Ember.

Secondary sources

Fauconnier, Gilles & Turner, Mark. 2002. *The Way We Think: Conceptual Blending and The Mind's Hidden Complexities*. New York NY: Basic Books.

Herman, David. 2001. Spatial reference in narrative domains. *Text* 21(4): 515–541.

Herman, David. 2002. *Story Logic: Problems and Possibilities of Narrative*. Lincoln NE: University of Nebraska Press.

Herman, David. 2009. *Basic Elements of Narrative*. Chichester: Wiley-Blackwell. doi: 10.1002/9781444305920

Johnson, Mark. 1987. *The Body in The Mind: The Bodily Basis of Meaning, Imagination, and Reason*. Chicago: The University of Chicago Press. doi: 10.1017/S0047404500014317

Kimmel, Michael 2009. Analyzing image schemas in literature. *Cognitive Semiotics* 5: 159–188. doi: 10.3726/81609_159

Lakoff, George & Johnson, Mark. 1980. The metaphorical structure of the human conceptual system. *Cognitive Science* 4: 195–208. doi: 10.1207/s15516709cog0402_4

Lakoff, George & Johnson, Mark. 2003. *Metaphors We Live By*. London: The University of Chicago Press. doi: 10.7208/chicago/9780226470993.001.0001

McCallum, Robyn. 1999. *Ideologies of Identity in Adolescent Fiction: the Dialogic Construction of Subjectivity*. London: Garland.

Miall, David S. 1989. Beyond the schema given: Affective comprehension of literary narratives. *Cognition and Emotion* 3(1): 55–78. doi: 10.1080/02699938908415236

Ryan, Marie-Laure. 2003. Cognitive maps and the construction of narrative space. In *Narrative Theory and the Cognitive Sciences*, David Herman (ed.), 214–242. Stanford CA: CSLI.

Ryan, Marie-Laure. 2012. Space, place and story. In *Medienkonvergenz-transdisziplinär*, Vol. 1, Stephan Füssel (ed.), 109–127. Berlin: de Gruyter. doi: 10.1515/9783110262094.109

Stalter-Pace, Sunny. 2013. *Underground Movements: Modern Culture on the New York City Subway*. Amherst MA: University of Massachusetts Press.

Stephens, John. 1992. *Language and Ideology in Children's Fiction*. London: Longman.

Stephens, John. 2011. Schemas and scripts: Cognitive instruments and the representation of cultural diversity in children's literature. In *Contemporary Children's Literature and Film*, Kerry Mallan & Clare Bradford (eds), 12–56. Basingstoke: Palgrave Macmillan.

Trites, Roberta Seelinger. 2014. *Literary Conceptualizations of Growth* [Children's Literature, Culture, and Cognition 2]. Amsterdam: John Benjamins. doi: 10.1075/clcc.2

Yu, Ning. 2009. Nonverbal and multimodal manifestations of metaphors and metonymies: A case study. In *Multimodal Metaphor*, Charles J. Forceville & Eduardo Urios-Apatisi (eds), 119–146. Berlin: De Gruyter.

CHAPTER 7

Itineraries and maps

Walking as a means of building mobile cartographies in Peter Sís' *Madlenka* and *The Three Golden Keys*

Anna Juan Cantavella

This chapter is based on two works by Czech author-illustrator Peter Sís, *Madlenka* (2000) and *The Three Golden Keys* (1994), in which the act of walking the streets of two cities becomes the main theme. Both works can be seen as a fragment of Sís' personal cartography. The chapter pays particular attention to scholars from the fields of social anthropology and cultural studies. In doing so, the aim is to underline the marked subjectivity of space, a suggestion that is present in all of Peter Sís' works, but which is especially relevant to these two picturebooks, dedicated to the two cities that have featured most strongly in the author's own life.

Introduction

This chapter is based on two works by Czech-born American author-illustrator Peter Sís, *Madlenka* (2000) and *The Three Golden Keys* (1994), in which the act of walking the streets of two cities becomes the main theme. Both works can be seen as fragments of the author's personal cartography, a map-making that is born of the act of walking and which conceives the itinerary – as Jacques Mullender (1980) claims – as the degree zero of cartography. In presenting these observations, the chapter draws on different disciplines and pays particular attention to researchers from the fields of social anthropology and cultural studies. In doing so, the aim is to underline the marked subjectivity of space, a suggestion that is present in all of Peter Sís' works, but which is especially relevant to these two, dedicated to the two cities that have featured most strongly in the author's own life.

DOI 10.1075/clcc.7.08jua

The importance of the journey in the poetics of Peter Sís

The importance of travel is a key element in all of Peter Sís' work. His books contain geographical journeys, spatial journeys, and journeys through time. These journeys guide the reader through wide exterior spaces and, at the same time, through the inner recesses of Sís' characters or of Sís himself. The author's taste for travel comes – as he admitted himself in an interview (Host 1996) – from his childhood, when his father, a great explorer, told him stories of his adventures in such places as Borneo, Tibet, and France. These stories helped to develop Sís' curiosity and opened doors to fragments of other cultures and other lives that seemed fascinating and new (Meunier 2011). In all of these journeys, exploration is a theme made explicit in various ways, and travel becomes inextricably bound up with the idea of freedom that the Czech-born author has forged since his own adolescence. The importance of travel to Sís also seems to be a direct consequence of his own life. His childhood and youth, marked by the secrecy, control, and censure of communist Czechoslovakia (Scharioth 2009), turned him into an emigrant, a forced exile, obliged to find a new homeland in that image of America that he had idealized from the other side of the iron curtain. The pleasure found in the discovery of other cultures is therefore combined with the need to understand himself so as to be able to explain to his own children, born in a very different context, who he is (Sís 2009).

In this way, all of his journeys in picturebooks explore identity and the limits of the genres of biography and autobiography, themes that Sís has developed in a complex manner in his various books. Genres – biography and autobiography – link his works through recurring themes such as the forced differentiation between a secret and a public life, the transcendence of censorship in different historical moments, the importance of following your dreams, the desire for discovery, or the necessity of doubt to banish prejudice and achieve freedom. His autobiographical stories also show the need to find new perspectives from which to observe and inhabit the world. The young Sís abandoned his native Czechoslovakia in 1982 in search of a place where thinking differently did not mean automatic condemnation.

This poetics of displacement results in books that are full of what Christophe Meunier (2011) has called "geo-graphisms": diverse expressions of *species of spaces*. The journeys that Sís proposes often start long before what is conventionally understood as the beginning of the story. Maps and plans are used not only to trigger or synthesize the story; they are also essential to telling it, and are placed throughout his works for this very reason. This is fundamentally due to another of the aspects analyzed by Christian Jacob in his book *L'empire des cartes* (1992): "The first question we ask of a map," the French writer suggests, "is 'Where am I?

I am here' and the deictic element designates a point, but also a time of repose during the walk"[1] (428). The hypothesis of this chapter is that in Peter Sís' biographical picturebooks, and particularly in his autobiographical works, the response to this "Where am I?" and its accompanying "I am here," leads, in part to the question "Who am I?," which is omnipresent in his work. Memory and the imaginary, essential components of his identity are for Sís – as Maurice Halbwachs (1925) already showed in the twentieth century – examples of topophilia. They need to be anchored to lands, to itineraries, and to public space in order to develop. This logic inextricably joins time and space, memory and place, history and location; and it converts spatial displacement into the degree zero of cartography and the most basic instrument to support and configure his stories. Trajectories offer anchorage points to tell a character's story or to recall fragments of the author's life. This is where the peripatetic nature of the stories comes in. Sís conceives his works as the luck of the path chosen, as an itinerary – spatial, but also mental – throughout which the story takes shape.

Maps and itineraries have distinct functions in Sís' works. While geographical maps and plans are used to situate the reader in the story and the historical moment in which the action develops, as well as to evoke the sense of adventure that each journey possesses, the mental maps, and in particular the use of itineraries, serve to focus the reader on the character's interior life, and likewise serve to underline the nomadic nature of every identity. In the same way, the importance – as outlined by Bettina Kümmerling-Meibauer (2010) – of fragmentation and overlapping play with the reflection of this identity. Michel De Certeau (1990) affirms that itineraries allow the point of view to be located at ground level, at the same level as everyday developments, the stomping ground of the most typical forms of cartography, which are revealed to us through the experience of the walker, that "daily commuter who speaks space and by doing so creates landscapes and mobile cartographies" (Delgado 1999: 46).

Walking as map-making in two stories by Peter Sís

Madlenka and *The Three Golden Keys* were chosen for the common elements they share that make them interesting for my analysis. While most of Sís' works feature stories that develop across multiple cities, countries, and even continents, these two stories each take place in a single city and the action is restricted to a few streets. The cities in question are the two that have been most pivotal in the author's life: Prague and New York.

1. All translations of quotes that appear in this text are my own.

The urban spaces that Sís and Madlenka move through are not only the stages on which the action unfolds or decorative or atmospheric elements that situate the reader in a chronotope; they are active participants in the story. More than simply forming the exterior world, the wanderings of both protagonists constantly lead to interior spaces and reveal the sensations that are created by the act of wandering. Sís has said of *The Three Golden Keys* that, "after various books that told stories of journeys to faraway places, I decided to focus on a man who goes further still, to a world that is entirely unknown, and entirely the product of his own mind" (Host 1996: 52).

With these two books, Sís demonstrates how cities, beyond their streets and buildings, are also formed of images, created due to the daily habits and interactions of places with their people. His New York and Prague become dense and overflowing when they take on the heterogeneous fantasies and individual and collective fictions of their inhabitants and their visitors. The very walls and stones that form his buildings and monuments play a highly relevant role. This means that for Sís, territory is understood in a similar way to the definition put forward by Allan Corboz: "territory, weighed down as it is by the traces of past readings, seems more than anything to be a palimpsest" (2001: 24). The cities in *Madlenka* and *The Three Golden Keys* are somaticized; they acquire weight and significance while their respective protagonists move through them, and these protagonists in turn discover pieces of other worlds and other times. In these urban wanderings, route and itinerary are not only resources used to tell the story; they become the axes, the main elements of the story, which is the experience of a journey. The act of walking itself gives the story shape. To read *Madlenka* is to accompany the protagonist on her journey, so much so that in order to read the book and follow in the young protagonist's footsteps, the book must entirely turn its back on its urban island setting. The narrative experience, which consists in a circular journey around Madlenka's world, becomes a physical experience, highlighting the importance of walking and of exploration.

Walking is important in both books due to their marked liminal character. Anthropologist Victor Turner (1969) best analyzes the middle and indeterminate period of every rite of passage, known as the liminal period. During this period, Turner claims, the identity of the person undergoing the rite is ambiguous and lacks most social attributes: they are no longer what they were, but neither are they what they will become. They are caught between two points and this position carries a certain provisional lack of definition as well as the potential to become, after having crossed the border, a different person. In this sense, the characters in *Madlenka* and *The Three Golden Keys* are individuals in transit, characters who have embarked upon a path and find themselves deviating from it, people in search of old or new elements that will allow them to redefine their identities. Madlenka's journey begins with her losing her first tooth (a strong symbolic rite of passage in our society), while Sís' imaginary return to his dreamlike Prague is sparked by the author's need to explain the city of his childhood to his daughter, so as to be able to define himself as a father and an immigrant. In *L'imagier du monde* Sís explains:

> *The Three Golden Keys* is a letter to Madeleine written in secret, for in some moment I realized that she, beautiful and American as she is, might one day wonder 'who is this man who is my father?' (Host 1996: 50)

In this way, urban space is transformed, in both books, into liminal, fringe space, while walking becomes a rite of passage. After her walk, Madlenka will have reconfigured her imagination, and this will have allowed her to grow. Passing through the streets of Prague allows Sís to situate himself between various points: between the past and the present, but also between that which belongs to him and that which belongs to other people, what is known and what from a distance seems strange. These divisions let him try to understand and to recover some fragments of the Prague that affected him as a child and which have followed him into adulthood. The liminal nature of the walk turns the subjective gaze into an essential element of the telling of both stories. Beyond their graphic composition and choice of narrator, what connects the two books is the fact that Sís offers a very particular and personal vision of the two cities. More than a historical perspective, he tries to express what Prague and New York mean to him, or meant to him at a particular moment of his life.

In this regard, the documentary aspect of the works is not as relevant here as in *Tibet: Through the Red Box* (1998) – as shown by Kümmerling-Meibauer (2010), in *The Wall. Growing up behind the Iron Curtain* (2007), or in Sís' biographical pieces. The construction of these two stories therefore distances them from Sís' more documentary works. Both *Madlenka* and *The Three Golden Keys* give precedence to the imaginary. Even so, this gaze, subjective and not overly attentive to factual reliability, offers tools for understanding the workings of the processes of semanticizing and resemanticizing locations, and, more concretely, the social construction of urban space. Sís' characters could very well be the ordinary practitioners in De Certeau's city, whose footsteps participate in the multiple urban texts that they write without ever becoming entirely conscious that they do so. De Certeau insists that such practices are necessary to analyzing and understanding space beyond the abstract geometry of modern maps. It is walkers who create this degree zero of cartography known as an itinerary. Both of the works discussed here can be seen as fragments of the author's personal cartography, and both serve to reveal elements of his personality.

The Three Golden Keys, or the city as a mental map

The Three Golden Keys, as explained above, tells the story of Peter Sís' wanderings through a dreamlike and phantasmal Prague. It is a Prague empty of people, but plagued by memories that materialize in the walls and within certain buildings that the protagonist passes through, accompanied by his old black cat. As the story develops, we learn that the apparent emptiness of the streets is due to the fact that this is not the real Prague; it is instead an internal Prague. This is the Prague that has been conserved in the author's memories, the Prague of his childhood, a Prague marked by silence, a dark city that the epilogue of *The Wall* defines as "full of fear, suspicion and lies." It is a Prague that he yearns to offer to his daughter so that she may alter, if she can and wishes to, parts of the stories that forged her father's identity; the old Prague that it is difficult to return to and which makes walking neither quick nor safe, but slow and shaky. This is a walk that reconstructs, and as he walks, Sís rewrites his home town along the lines that he creates, recovers fragments of his childhood scattered between the buildings, and rediscovers the old stories and legends that his father told him when he was a child. He is a vagabond who carries the present to the past, in order to place it in a new present during this liminal journey. In this sense, it is worth highlighting how the author knits together the sensations that come from his memories through the use of verbs that evoke the movement of walking. Travel, make a detour, wander, roam, run, cross, come, slip, find, follow, wait, continue, and stroll are only some of the verbs that appear in the text next to the word "memories." In this way, the author constantly and energetically relates space, movements, and memory.

The structure is similar to that of *Tibet: Through the Red Box*: a framing story contains three stories within it, using three small tests that recall the structure of traditional folk tales. The protagonist must find the three golden keys of the city. The three keys are offered as three stories, and the three stories are the keys to understanding the Prague of Peter Sís. It is a journey that mixes characters and spaces together into a kind of daydream, where connections do not stem from any particular cause, but respond to the diffuse logic that governs dreams and old memories. The author narrates the walk in the first person, and as he advances, he recalls piano lessons, birthday cakes, the smell of lemon tea, expeditions with his friends to places that then seemed far away, frost-bitten ears, and the colors of spring. All of these memories stem from encounters with characters who seem to spring from Arcimboldo paintings. These acquire the function of donors: the librarian, the emperor, and the chief of the robots. They open doors to the legends and histories of the Charles Bridge, of Prague during the reign of Emperor Rudolph II, of the Golem, of Prague's Jewish neighborhood, of Hanouch and his marvelous astronomical clock. The text is short and evocative. The sentences seem to emerge and throng without leaving room to breathe or reflect; in this sense they are like memories. The narration is openly fragmented and disorganized. Just as the story follows the rhythm of Sís' steps through the city, the stories that emerge do not come in chronological order. The only thing the reader knows (through language but also through the colors of the images) is that the seasons are changing as the story moves forward. And then the walk seems to stop in the very moment that Sís' need to forget is unleashed: in that tragic spring in Prague in which blue gave way to a violent red and everything seemed to melt into black.

What kinds of cartographies are featured in the text and what functions do they fulfill in the story? In *The Three Golden Keys*, the reader finds various maps of Prague, many mental maps and multiple urban landscapes, drawn from different perspectives, all towering around a small protagonist.

Upon opening the book and passing the wall that is represented by the dust jacket (a wall that appears fissured and that seems to be mental as well as physical), the reader comes across a detailed plan of the center of Old Prague. This is not a planimetric map, but one in which buildings and monuments can be observed in relief. It is a "pictorial map" – in Jacob's words – that shows the main stops along the way in Sís' stroll through Prague from an external point of view, (and is not located anywhere, as Louis Marin (1973) would say). According to Jacob "landscape-maps" always depend on the story in question and make no sense beyond the boundaries of that story. They help the reader to visualize the scene and accompany him during the reading, anchoring the interior images in a kind of summary-diagram that constructs a vision of the whole. At the same time, the map that opens *The Three Golden Keys* is introduced as a kind of warning. That the map is drawn in relief (which distances it from an objective view), and the directions that appear on it, with the cat winding its way down the alleyways and the important elements marked in red, warn the readers that what they will find within the book is the story of a ramble, the story of a route. This route will take shape in parallel with the map of the city of Prague that lives in Sís' memory.

As with the rest of the book's illustrations, this first map is superimposed onto a kind of parchment scroll, which surrounds it, making reference to the general theme of overlapping and superimposition. Territory is a result of condensation, and reading the folds of this palimpsest, and unfolding them, can help us to understand it. This idea also appears in the execution of the map itself: although it resembles the true image of a map of Prague, Sís uses an ashy blue color and adds drawings that shape it as a phantasmagorical space. An angel, a cat, and a circle formed by multiple faces overlie the map, as though they were transparent beings. They underline the importance of overlapping and hint that this is a story of ghosts, and a story of memories.

There are also numerous mental maps in the book. Jacob describes them as "representations [...] entirely social, sentimental and symbolic readings of the world" (1992: 435). In some senses they represent Sís' personal view of the world and allow the reader to come closer to the jumble of elements forming the author's viewpoint. If these mental maps meddle with the urban landscapes that the protagonist moves through, Sís also uses them elsewhere: they appear in the introduction and epilogue of the story, and are also a resource to introduce the city legend that is told each time the protagonist finds a golden key. Seen this way, the title page and the epilogue are made up of two doublespreads in which, on a background of parchment, a series of symbols (Hebrew but also Tibetan) are inscribed. These form part of the story that will be revealed in Prague, hinting at the cultural apathy that the story Sís wants to tell is built upon. It is part of his identity, which is a central theme.

The essential elements of the story are urban landscapes, from which Sís composes his itinerary. He makes use of what in cinematography would be considered a *tracking shot* to develop the tone of the story and unfold its central theme. It is the walk itself that is important, and the author announces as much on the front cover, which shows an urban landscape in black and white seen on a map from a slightly elevated perspective. There is a stone door bearing hieroglyphics that are more or less legible. In the middle of a plaza is a small human figure, looking up (into the reader's eyes) with a disoriented expression. This is the only person on the cover. The city appears to be asleep and only an enormous cat, which forms part of the walls of the buildings and of the asphalt on the streets, seems to be alive, along with this small individual that transmits fragility and a certain expression of loss. With this first illustration, Sís situates the readers at the beginning of the route and does so via an oblique perspective so as to explain two key elements of the story: that they can expect to lose themselves in the urban streets of Old Prague and that the book will tell of an unsettling journey, in which the protagonist does not set off from a known location, but rather moves forward accompanied by doubt and hesitation.

Prague appears throughout the book as a labyrinth. The protagonist's sense of hesitation and indecision is revealed in a number of ways. These include: (a) plans seen from above or below (only occasionally does the reader observe the city at eye level) that emphasize the protagonist's vulnerability in a world that is often phantasmagorical; (b) the illustration of wide swathes of the city that show a jumble of roofs blocking a clear view of the streets, or of the streets themselves that seem to turn into alleyways or snaking paths; (c) the mixture of standard with specific maps, to focus the reader's attention on a concrete space, or to decentralize the gaze, opening it wider and showing us things we were not aware of before; and (d) the protagonist's location, which is always in the lower part of the image, making the urban landscape appear even larger and leaving the character in a state of constant insecurity. A good example of this is the double-page illustration on pages 5–6, in which the city appears as a labyrinth and Sís is located – following William Moebius (1990) – in one of the most unstable places possible within the graphic codes of picturebooks: on the lower left side of the doublespread, dwarfed by a landscape that seems more like an imaginary vision than a city map. These maps and perspectives mark the tone of the piece and position it as a story of discovery and exploration. It is important to remember that Sís conceived of the book with his daughter in mind and that in the prologue he encourages her to discover the mysteries hidden in this Prague that he has drawn and written for her. As readers move progressively deeper into the maze of Prague's streets, their understanding of the weight and density of the walls of the buildings and monuments grows. The importance of physical structures is emphasized by the lack of people: in Sís' internal Prague, other people do not wander as he does; rather they appear like spirits among the stones, as invisible footprints (Figure 1). There, semi-transparent, are dragons, people, animals, symbols, shadows, and bodies that accompany Sís or wait for him to rescue them from being forgotten. These illustrations show that cities are composed of the images recorded in our memories: the people, the words, and the symbols give them shape through a condensation of meanings.

What the reader glimpses in the journey is a complex, magical, and mysterious city, a city that is more than what its exterior features show. It is a space that is

Figure 1. Prague as a labyrinth. Illustration by Peter Sís from *The Three Golden Keys*. New York NY: Farrar, Straus and Giroux, 1994. © 1994, Peter Sís. All Rights Reserved

difficult to decipher, contradictory, and not entirely understandable, given that it is only a map created by Sís' memory, and composed of many other memories. Even so, the text gives information about objects, monuments, buildings, and characters that are important in the history of the city and the author. It introduces a Prague of alchemy, sciences, and arts in the court of Rudolph II (the Arcimboldian characters are found there, but also buildings or legends related with that time); the Prague of Rainer Maria Rilke and Franz Kafka (found in monuments and phrases about the city); the Prague of secrets, wars, revolts, and resistances. This last may be the most important side of Prague with regard to Sís' biography, and the author marks key moments, presenting stories of resistance with text and images. The references to the 27 crosses close to the main square with the astronomical clock underline the importance that monuments recalling the resistance and the Czech identity have for Sís. The 27 crosses are a monument erected to the Czech noblemen executed in the seventeenth century for their resistance to the Habsburg monarchy, which was trying to unify all the Germanic people under the Catholic faith. This is also why the journey ends with Prague's bloody spring, and the images go from being a sky blue, evoking hope and struggle for liberty, to a dark red, in which tanks, symbols of power and inflamed passions, open a path through a shadowy city, and in which even the graves in the Jewish cemetery come alive to remember the miseries of its history.

The act of walking, the central motif of this book, pauses three times to encompass three smaller stories within the larger one. As in his other works, Sís uses different narrative focuses to tell the story, and different typography to distinguish each voice and underline the fragmentary and polyphonic nature of his work – as Kümmerling-Meibauer (2010) shows in reference to Sís' book *Tibet: Through the Red Box*. So the walk is narrated in the first person (showing an internal focalization), while the three stories about Prague are written in the third person (marking an external focus). As though they were storyboards, each smaller story occupies two pages, in which the composition is always the same: an old scroll bearing the form of a large golden key and a fragment of text written in different types of letters is superimposed on a background colored in shades of ochre and black. The scroll explains parts of the stories of buildings and people in Prague. The author uses texts by Rilke, André Gide, or Albert Camus, or historical facts to briefly introduce the legend, and these later give way to hand-drawn letters – surely a sign that these are the words of the author's father – and narrative snippets, without time connectors and almost always ending in ellipses points that the reader must put together with the help of graphic vignettes that surround the text. The doublespread is therefore conceived as a kind of mental map, providing essential elements of Sís' memories, which request the reader to relate the words and images to form a continuous story.

Madlenka, or walking as map-building

Unlike Peter Sís' journey in *The Three Golden Keys*, Madlenka's walk around the block she lives in is not situated between the past and the present but between the present and the future. And it is not a reconstructive or internal journey so much as a journey of creation. Madlenka makes sense of her world, the streets of her neighborhood, and by extension the city itself with every step forward as she comes across the people who live, or walk through, the places near where she lives. Enthusiasm and emotion guide her journey of discovery, which is much less hesitant than that of her father in Prague: it is an optimistic, rather than nostalgic, walk. To some extent, Madlenka's walking recalls the Dadaist practice of trying to stimulate, through entertaining and artistic walking practices in urban spaces, the marvelous in the day-to-day reality that every city hides.

Madlenka has lost her first tooth. She is excited and wants to declare to the world that she is growing up. As she goes through the streets of her Manhattan neighborhood of NoLiTa she meets various neighbors, each of a different nationality, who tell the little girl stories about the countries they are from. When Madlenka returns home, she can truthfully tell her parents that she has been around the world. The structure is similar to that of *The Three Golden Keys*. The walk forms the story, and smaller stories, narrated by Mr. Gaston, Mr. Singh, Mrs. Grimm, Eduardo, Mrs. Kham, and Cleopatra appear within it. The journey ends where it began, in Madlenka's home, but Madlenka herself is not the same. As suggested by her losing her tooth, she has grown, and the walk around her neighborhood has also caused her to grow. To tell this story, Sís uses different kinds of maps, plans, and urban landscapes. Examining these shows to what extent the little girl's walk can be read as a foundational journey, a journey in cartography.

Sís' extensive use of cinematic language to build his stories is well known. There are some elements of this in the maps of *The Three Golden Keys* and the use of tracking shots to follow the footsteps of the protagonist through a dreamlike Prague. The beginning of *Madlenka* is one of the best-known examples of this technique in recent children's literature. Sís makes use of the zoom technique to focus the reader's attention on a particular object, in this case a pink dot that, when zoomed in upon, shows itself to be the book's small protagonist. Once again, the author uses peripheral text spaces to introduce his first maps and plans, elements that he employs to locate the story in a concrete space and to build the reader's expectations. Zooming in on the planet Earth allows his reader to catch a glimpse of the map of a city that will quickly, on turning the page, acquire an identity. A few street names included on the map on the title page show the reader that this is New York, and the text begins by explaining what is already known: "In the universe, on a planet, in a country, in a city [...] a little girl named Madlenka". The zoom ends with an American shot that shows a glimpse of a window with a little girl leaning out of it, pointing a finger towards her mouth. To underline the circularity of the journey, Sís ends the story by zooming out, whooshing the reader away from the little girl to show once more a planet floating in the universe.

From this moment on, the urban landscapes, shown with long shots and close ups, are mixed in with planimetric maps of the block where Madlenka lives, and a type of mental map known as an "ethnoscape." This term has been coined by Arjun Appadurai when he was researching the images that immigrants create of their culture when they are far from home: "the landscape of persons who constitute the shifting world in which people live" (1996: 68). With the "ethnoscape" concept, Appadurai refers to both the exteriority of the landscape that the immigrants come from and the interpretation that these groups or people project onto it. Immigrants frequently mix stereotypes with cultural and symbolic elements, often in contradictory and ambiguous ways. These reinforce and shape their itinerant identities.

Sís uses maps to introduce readers into the action and resituate them each time a narrative sequence begins. These show the city block from a slightly elevated perspective, so that the reader glimpses the global nature of the urban area that Madlenka walks through and can also keep track of what is happening where, and locate Madlenka in a drawing that resembles reality more than it does a planimetric map. Zooming in again, Sís converts the long shot into a close-up to center in on one of the shops in the neighborhood and so introduce the various characters. Rather than being an important element of the storytelling, the urban landscapes serve as elements to orient young readers and introduce them to the story. The meat of the story is narrated using planimetric maps of the block and its buildings and the mind maps of neighbors.

In the case of the planimetric maps of the block, Sís' pages are always composed in the same way (Figure 2). The facades of the different buildings are drawn in pencil on a white background. Madlenka, in full color, is in the middle, in varying positions, accompanied by her magical object, the yellow umbrella that she always carries with her. On the edges of the page, surrounding the map, there are smaller drawings – in black and white or color – that fill the page, along with texts written in different lettering styles. These texts consist of phrases spoken by the characters, or simply of single words. To read everything and take in all that is happening on the page, the reader must turn the book around completely, and so accompany Madlenka on her circular journey. To some extent, these maps blend with the first draft of a mental map, built with some elements that belong to Madlenka and other elements that belong to her neighbors. Accordingly, each neighbor's personal world comes preceded by an introduction, albeit a fragmented one, to the space that Madlenka is about to enter.

Figure 2. Planimetric map of the block. Illustration by Peter Sís from *Madlenka*. New York NY: Farrar, Straus and Giroux, 2000. © 2000, Peter Sís. All Rights Reserved

In this way, the protagonist arrives at the mental maps or the "ethnoscapes" of the inhabitants of the neighborhood. Sís has made cut-out windows, and the little girl peers through these from her place in the street, seeing the interior reality of each of the secondary characters. To accompany Madlenka through these windows is to enter worlds where spatial references are distorted and where objects, fantastical characters, buildings, and animals mix exuberantly to show the social, sentimental, and symbolic sides of each of the cultures that Madlenka experiences thanks to the tales, stories, and legends told by her neighbors.

Madlenka learns about the Little Prince, Hansel and Gretel, the Bremen town musicians, and Struwwelpeter through these ethnoscapes. In this same way she visits the Eiffel Tower, the Taj Mahal, the Mayan pyramids, and the Tower of Pisa, discovers the Andes and the African savannah, encounters Tibet and the Great

Wall of China. The doublespreads dedicated to the ethnoscapes show, through their use of deterritorialization, the degree to which these are remembered and reinvented images, to what degree the information Madlenka is discovering is just a small part of a much more complex whole, and to what degree these stories that she is told become an imagined reality, in which it is nonetheless difficult to establish limits and classify elements in an orderly way. These full-color doublespreads – distinct from those that represent the real world, drawn in black and white – are where Sís unfolds his knowledge of different cultures and presents them through a number of more or less recognizable references.

Throughout the process, the reader notes that the pages dedicated to the planimetric maps change, not only because the drawings framing them change, but also because the walls of the buildings become denser and heavier as Madlenka's adventure moves forward. In this way, on the first of these pages, most of the building facades are drawn but not painted. By the end of the story, when Madlenka has listened to all of her neighbors, all of the walls of the street have been shaded in, appear heavier, and are full of meaning. In the wake of studies on urban anthropology (Augoyard 1979; Corboz 2001; Rautenberg 2003), *Madlenka* demonstrates the degree to which the city acquires meaning when we practice it, when we feel it, and when we experience it through our bodies. The urban imaginary landscape develops with every footstep, glance, and interaction. In moving through the streets, city-dwellers interact with them and with other passers-by (something that is demonstrated in the second book in the series, *Madlenka's Dog*, 2002), and the city becomes firmly lodged within the reader's mind in the form of images. From that moment on, urban space ceases to be an objective fact and transforms into a part of life, into a place where memory and imagined worlds live.

It is in this way that Jean-François Augoyard's observation acquires its relevance: "The city cannot be perceived in its entirety, it becomes unimaginable. Only lived spaces have a concrete existence" (1979: 132). This idea gains force in an illustration in *Madlenka* that in the American edition of the book is the cover image, but in the Spanish edition appears on one of the courtesy pages just inside the cover (Figure 3). The illustration, which can be read as a kind of epilogue, is different in certain ways from others in the book. The author's usual style of framing, used to contain spaces or conceptions of the world, is absent here, and the image spills over the page. By suppressing his usual framing techniques, Sís allows the reader to enter the illustrated world with no barriers, and reinforces the idea that this is the fruit of a little girl's overflowing imagination. Readers find themselves within a kind of landscape-map, drawn in relief and showing the contours and geographic accidents of what appears to be an island. Here and there can be found some of the monuments and animals that appear in the stories that the neighbors tell Madlenka. And so, as with the pictorial map in *The Three Golden Keys*, Madlenka's

Figure 3. Madlenka's walk. Illustration by Peter Sís from *Madlenka*. New York NY: Farrar, Straus and Giroux, 2000.

journey is synthesized. But, unlike in Prague, this is not the map of a city but rather that of a continent that does not seem to follow the laws of any known continent. Looking again at the first picture of Madlenka's street, when Sís is still zooming in, the reader notes that the shape of this imaginary continent greatly resembles the forms of the buildings and the trees. And this continent-world that Madlenka has drawn in her imagination is strongly connected to the experience of walking. It is a world in which everything that she has just learned mixes together and in which imagination and fantasy are greater than reason and representation. This illusion shows the world as Madlenka learns it: the square city block grows round, becoming a continent that is home to many different cultures. On this continent is Madlenka, alert and happy, at times seeming to float with the help of her umbrella.

This demonstrates the territorial connections that a six-year-old girl is capable of establishing, where distances and shapes reorganize themselves with the force of her internal world. The urban walk has become the starting point of cartography. Such maps exist as a result of walking, and spaces acquire meaning only when they are experienced. With her walk around the block, Madlenka lays the cornerstones of what in the future will form part of her memories.

Madlenka and *The Three Golden Keys*: Mapping the memories of Peter Sís

And so, these two walks by Sís build and materialize two different, and personal, ideas of the world. As Sís explains in a note to the reader, *The Three Golden Keys* is a secret letter to his daughter, meant to provide her with clues to her father's identity. In a sense, *Madlenka* functions the same way, though Sís has not made it explicit to his readers in this case. And while the first story takes the reader to the Prague of the author's childhood memories, in *Madlenka*, in the guise of a stroll through the streets of NoLiTa, Sís offers his daughter another element of his internal world, different fragments of the memories that have made him who he is. The result is two stories with a marked autobiographical bent, arising from the Czech author's memories and imagination. Prague and New York can be seen in these works as two sides of the same coin, as fragments of his life, as maps to a memory that Sís is telling his daughter, and, with her, his readers.

References

Primary sources

Sís, Peter. 1994. *The Three Golden Keys*. New York NY: Farrar, Straus and Giroux.
Sís, Peter. 1998. *Tibet: Through the Red Box*. New York NY: Farrar, Straus and Giroux.
Sís, Peter. 2000. *Madlenka*. New York NY: Farrar, Straus and Giroux.
Sís, Peter. 2002. *Madlenka's Dog*. New York NY: Farrar, Straus and Giroux.
Sís, Peter. 2007. *The Wall. Growing up behind the Iron Curtain*. New York NY: Farrar, Straus and Giroux.

Secondary sources

Appadurai, Arjun. 1996. *Modernity at Large: Cultural Dimensions of Globalization*. Minneapolis MN: University of Minnesota Press
Augoyard, Jean-François. 1979. *Pas à pas, essai sur le cheminent quotidien en milieu urbane*. Paris: Éditions du Seuil.
Corboz, Allan. 2001. *Le territoire comme palimpsest*. Besançon: Les éditions de l'imprimeur.

De Certeau, Michel. 1990. *L'invention du quotidien*, Vol. 1: *Arts de faire*. Paris: Gallimard.

Delgado, Manuel. 1999. *El animal público*. Barcelona: Anagrama.

Halbwachs, Maurice, 1925. *Les cadres sociaux de la mémoire*. Paris: Presses Universitaires de France.

Host, Michel. 1996. *Peter Sis ou l'imagier du monde*. Paris: Grasset.

Jacob, Christian. 1992. *L'empire des cartes. Approche théorique de la carthographie à travers l'histoire*. Paris: Albin Michel.

Kümmerling-Meibauer, Bettina. 2010. Remembering the past in words and pictures: How autobiographical stories become picturebooks. In *New Directions in Picturebook Research*, Teresa Colomer, Bettina Kümmerling-Meibauer & Cecilia Silva-Díaz (eds). 205–215. New York NY: Routledge.

Marin, Louis. 1973. *Utopiques, jeux d'espaces*. Paris: Editions de Minuit.

Meunier, Christophe. 2011. Géo-graphisme(s): Représentations et perception du monde dans Madlenka de Peter Sís. *La Revue du Livre pour Enfants* 259: 87–93.

Moebius, William. 1990. Introduction to picturebook codes. In *Children's Literature. The Development of Criticism*, Peter Hunt (ed.). 131–147. London: Routledge.

Mullender, Jacques. 1980. Connaissance et surveillance de la terre. In *Cartes et figures de la terre*, by Jacques Mullender, VII–IX. Paris: Centre George Pompidou.

Rautenberg, Michel. 2003. *La rupture patrimoniale*. Grenoble: Editions à la Croisée.

Scharioth, Barbara. 2009. Peter Sís. A quest for a life in truth. *Bookbird* 47(3): 29–39. doi: 10.1353/bkb.0.0169

Sís, Peter. 2009. My life with censorship. *Bookbird* 47(3): 42–45. doi: 10.1353/bkb.0.0171

Turner, Victor. 1969. *The Ritual Process*. Chicago IL: Aldine.

CHAPTER 8

Bruno Munari's visual mapping of the city of Milan

A historical analysis of the picturebook *Nella nebbia di Milano*

Marnie Campagnaro

Bruno Munari was one of the most pioneering and ingenious thinkers of the twentieth century. Pablo Picasso called him "the new Leonardo" and Pierre Restany "the Leonardo and the Peter Pan of Italian design." During his long career as an artist and a designer, Bruno Munari achieved a special bond with the infant universe. He explored the area of visual narration in children's literature with sublime results. Munari's witty picturebooks pay special attention to young readers' capacity to organize and orientate their reading experience by means of visible and invisible details. This chapter examines the picturebook *Nella nebbia di Milano* (The Circus in the Mist, 1968). The aim of the chapter is to provide an overview of Munari's original approach and of his capacity to visualize and map places in children's everyday lives.

Maps enable us to assemble, organize, store, remember, and handle information about spatial environments. They are useful tools in children's books because they help readers to deal with the text and orient themselves when the story is developed in a large geographical area. However, some authors like Bruno Munari, who deeply explores the area of visual narration in children's literature, make different use of maps: they reproduce real landscapes and transform them through imagination into "geographies of the mind" (Watkins 2006: 59) in order to emphasize the relationship that links a landscape to the quality of people's life. This chapter aims to provide an analysis of Munari's original approach to visualizing and mapping places in picturebooks, with a particular reference to his work *Nella nebbia di Milano*.[1] In this picturebook Munari adopts this kind of narrative mechanism.

1. The Italian title literally means *In the Fog of Milan*, but the official English translation of the title is *The Circus in the Mist*.

DOI 10.1075/clcc.7.09cam

The Circus in the Mist describes a journey through the milky opacity of Milan's fog. The young reader is stimulated to actively enter into the story through a series of pictures and prompts, created by different types of pierced and perforated paper, and is invited to undertake an original and challenging discovery of the city. The lively urban landscape created by Munari becomes a character in itself, which attracts the child's attention and tests his or her sensory receptiveness. A series of different elements are scattered through the pages of this picturebook – that is, visual spatial information (the geographic name of the city, distinctive atmospheric conditions, urban and natural architectures), verbal spatial information (prepositions of place and prepositions of movement), visual travel instructions (traffic lights, road signs, arrows, etc.), and original details about the final destination. These elements are not only designed to amuse young readers, but also to educate them about how to find their way in the world of narration and in real life.

Bruno Munari and the futuristic heritage

Bruno Munari's research and creativity have a wide scope, which ranges from literature to didactics, from drawing to photography, and from design to sculpture. Munari may be defined, at the same time, as a designer, artist, author, teacher, experimenter in techniques and materials in the visual communication field, and inventor of plastic fantasies and artistic paradoxes: for instance, Munari's suspended artworks, which belong to the same period as Calder's famous mobiles (Fiz 2000a: 20); his *Macchine aritmiche* (Arithmetic Machines), which gave significant input to the artistic experimentation of Swiss sculptor Jean Tinguely; his *Sculture da viaggio* (Sculptures of Travel), which were created in the 1950s and may be directly compared to Marcel Duchamp's *Boîte en valise* (Box in a Suitcase; see Fiz 2000a: 20), to Balla's games, or to Albers Bauhaus' exercises (Tanchis 1986: 78). He is also generally considered "a child prodigy of Italian painting, graphics, and design […], who has always remained a child – thanks to his liveliness, helpfulness, promptness in inventing new forms, new didactic methods" (Dorfles 1998: 33).[2]

Munari was in charge of the graphic design management for the publishing house Einaudi. He created illustrations for the famous children's author Gianni Rodari and invented didactic games for the toy manufacturing company Danese. Numerous workshops in different countries, not only for children, have been inspired by his pedagogical artistic laboratories and visual education methods. Munari first tested these at the Pinacoteca di Brera in Milan in 1977. His method has been tested not only with several thousand primary school children, but also

2. All translations from original Italian sources are mine.

at meetings and courses with several hundred teachers. The purpose of his workshops, held all over the world, was to promote a new way of teaching visual arts and to broaden children's sensitivity, imagination, and dynamism. During these laboratories, teachers are asked not to give examples which are destined to be copied by children, but to conduct experiments and invent new examples, so that everyone can try out new ways of making visual communication. Each individual personality may thus be stimulated and fully developed (Maffei 2008: 232).

For Munari, artistic work was closely tied to life experience. He started his career at the early age of nineteen. He wanted to become a painter, and, for this reason, he left his Venetian hometown of Badia Polesine in 1926, where his parents owned a hotel, and settled in Milan. In this culturally animated city, Munari very

Figure 1. Cover of Bruno Munari: *Nella nebbia di Milano*. Milan: Emme Edizioni, 1968.

soon joined futurism, one of the most important and driving artistic movements in Italy at that time.

During this preliminary stage of his career, he developed his typical experimental attitude: some examples of his inexhaustible experimentation capacity include his rigorous study of matter and materials, the search for simple and essential solutions, the graceful and light-hearted playfulness of his surprising and demystifying creations, the active involvement of children, and his witty irony (Maffei 2008: 26–34). The futurists inspired his eagerness and desire to learn and to experiment: "The heterogeneity of their methods, their ability to mix different art forms and techniques, their exploration of new media and new avenues of expression [...] were quite congenial to his own conception of art" (Antonello 2012: 95). Futurism and other avant-garde movements also played a role as far as Munari's irony and playfulness in an urban, machine-oriented milieu were concerned.

Munari became one of the front-runners of the second futurist movement led by Filippo Tommaso Marinetti, but, at a certain point, he gradually started distancing himself from it. His relationship with futurism and its heritage may therefore be considered as rather complicated (Antonello 2012: 95). As Marco Meneguzzo (1995: 5) remarked, Munari simply did not accept the fact that his long prolific artistic career, which lasted for over sixty years, might be superficially categorized as a derivate of futurism. Nevertheless, it is undoubted that Munari was able to achieve results that many other futurists failed to reach: "Whilst other ex-futurists continued to recycle the movement's vocabulary of mechanical and geometric forms in their curiously nostalgic paintings, Munari's work encapsulated the truly revolutionary message of futurism: that art should be a joyful and integral element of daily life – not something detached, austere and elitist, arbitrarily cut off from the real world by the artificial borders of the picture frame" (Cremoncini 2012: 7). Munari succeeded in expressing this revolutionary message even in his children's picturebooks, and *The Circus in the Mist* (Fig. 1) is an iconic representation thereof.

Munari's innovative children's books

Munari had a special relationship with books: he illustrated or planned over sixty volumes, forty of which he wrote himself. His prolific editorial production was due to the fact that books played a fundamental role for Munari. According to Giorgio Maffei (2008), they represented his "personal diary," where he used to take notes, record events, and write down his experiences. The ethic imperative underlying his whole production was the need to explain himself properly, to clarify his thoughts, to make his work intelligible, readable, and usable (12). This is the reason why he dedicated so many books to children, even toddlers, many of which draw their inspirational potential from the fact that they challenge "not only the boundaries between adult books and children's books, but the boundaries of the book itself" (Beckett 2012: 20).

Childhood is part of Munari's work right from the beginning. He illustrated his first book, *L'Aquilotto implume* (The Unfledged Eaglet; see Maffei 2008: 26), in 1929, at the age of 22. During the tragic years of World War II, Munari frequently turned his attention to children's books, and published the educational volumes *Mondo Aria Acqua Terra*. (World Air Water Earth, 1940) and the two children's books *Le macchine di Munari* (Munari's Machines, 1942a)[3] and *Abecedario di Munari* (Munari's ABC Book, 1942b).

In 1945 Munari designed and partly published with Mondadori a collection of books which called into question the very idea of a children's book (Maffei 2008: 27). Illustrations and short sentences metaphorically chase each another across large colored pages and small hidden inserts of these picturebooks, thus they represent a direct legacy of the surrealist *boîtes* (27). By opening some unexpected windows or flaps that can be lifted, children are involved in an ironical discovery game: they find special animals that reveal their desire to be other animals, and special suitcases that hide cats, lions, and giraffes.

Munari's action is revolutionary in these creations. He "disempowers" words and gives the leadership to pictures, which have their own communicative autonomy and are able to establish a direct dialogue with children and encourage their curiosity. Besides narrating stories, books thus become toys and surprise boxes. The idea of inventing these innovative books, which are still in print in Italy and abroad, came from the desire to create some thought-provoking books for his son Alberto, who was five years old at the time. Thanks to the help of the very first theories on childhood (particularly those developed by Piaget) and of his empirical investigation skills, Munari used irony and playfulness in these picturebooks to increase children's curiosity. These books were destined to renew the concept of children's picturebooks in Italy and abroad (Maffei 2008: 27). Munari's clean lines, his playful irony, and skilled use of simplification in creating picturebooks still continue to be elements of inspiration for children's book authors now: the works of Katsumi Komagata, Suzy Lee, and Alessandro Sanna may be mentioned here.

Munari's editorial production continued incessantly until his death, but his most intense and poetic books appeared between the late 1950s and early 1980s. The picturebook *The Circus in the Mist* was published by Emme Edizioni, an

3. This book contains a series of tables showing obscure devices, which carry out surreal actions. The futurist myth of machinery thus turns into a series of merry objects, which serve no other purpose than creating a playful surprise (Maffei 2008: 26).

intrepid publishing house destined to revolutionize children's literature in Italy (Farina 2013), which was guided by the young and tenacious editor Rosellina Archinto. This square-shaped picturebook[4] consists of 56 large format, 21.5 x 21.5 cm, pages. It includes paper of different densities and colors, with special perforated and cut-out pages. The somehow inappropriate use of materials and printing techniques creates a work that contains a whole repertoire of inventions.

The Circus in the Mist is at the same time Munari's homage to his city, Milan – the biggest industrial center in Italy, the center of his entire artistic activity, and the city that offered him the opportunity to make his wishes come true (Tanchis 1986: 11) – and to the little country village where he spent his childhood, Badia Polesine, a rural municipality not far from Padua, situated along the river Adige, in the southwest of the Venice region. Both of these geographical settings – the city and the country – may well look familiar to any child.

The picturebook does not aim at evoking a symbolic opposition between city and country, between mechanical and natural (Watkins 2006: 67). Quite the contrary, besides offering a good story for children, Munari considers some fundamental changes of his time. These social, cultural, and economic changes were caused by the so-called 'Italian economic miracle' and referred in particular to the years 1950–1963. This phase of Italian history represented not only a cornerstone in the economic and social development of the country, which was transformed from a poor, mainly rural country into a major industrial power, but also a period of exceptional flowering in arts and culture. In his view, the urban and industrial development may involve great dangers, but it does not necessarily mean the destruction of the vital force of nature. Progress may well coexist and be reconciled with nature.

Munari's imaginative background is an open-air landscape characterized by long roads lined with trees, sounds of running river water, and simple shapes of old wooden mills (Tanchis 1986: 6–8). Munari's attention to physical perceptions is not only limited to the five senses, but also includes other stimuli like the sense of rhythm, the sense of temperatures, the sense of weight, and the sense of balance.[5] Thus the simultaneous presence of rural and urban sceneries encourages a vast repertoire of feelings towards landscapes and the possibility of engendering "ways of seeing and being in the city [...] reminiscent of the *flâneur*" (Mallan 2012: 58).

4. The square shape was Munari's "favorite" geometric form (Maffei 2008: 23).

5. Munari was aware that mental elasticity is first developed when children are at a preschool age. Only at that stage do humans have an awareness of the surrounding environment through all their sensorial receptors and not just sight and hearing; they can also perceive sensations of touch, heat, material, sound, and smell (1981: 228–229).

The structure of the picturebook *The Circus in the Mist*

The Circus in the Mist describes an original exploration of the Milan landscapes by using different printing materials and typographic solutions. The picturebook consists of three sections, each one representing a different landscape and a different way of exploring the city: the first section is a journey through the foggy urban landscape of Milan, the second section is a journey through the bright life of the circus, and the third and last section is a journey through the park. Munari created an object-book that involves the reader in an active and physical experience at the same time:[6] these three lively landscapes become characters that attract children's attention, test their sensory receptiveness, stimulate their imaginative background, and help them to connect visual narration to spatial orientation.

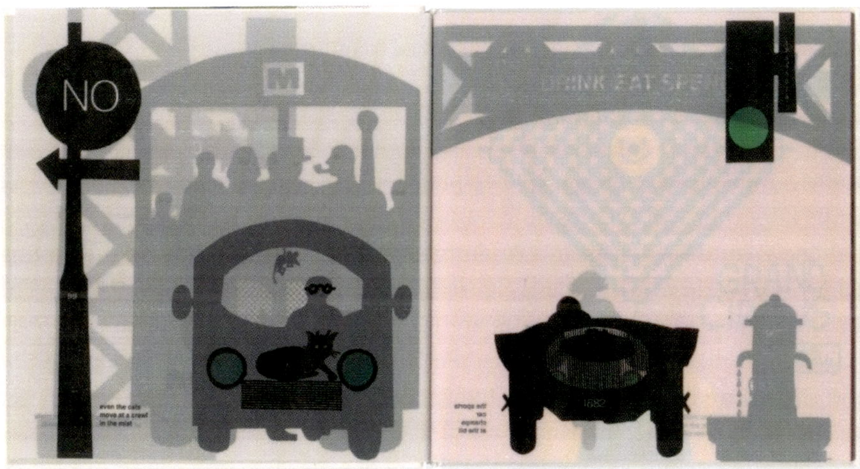

Figure 2. The fog in Milan. Doublespread from Bruno Munari: *Nella nebbia di Milano*. Milan: Emme Edizioni, 1968. © 2016 Bruno Munari. All rights reserved to Maurizio Corraini srl. Mantova

The first section depicts the story of an *ordinary* journey in a foggy Milan: the fog is a personifying element of the city of Milan. Munari uses tracing paper to represent Milan's fog (Figure 2). A rigorous repetition of black colored geometric and mechanical forms represents the urban landscape: squares and rectangles are elements that "dominate the shape of our cities, our buildings, our roads" (Kress & van Leeuwen 2006: 54). The cityscape is reconstructed through the visual representation of its transportation network, of the different means of transport and

6. Munari himself once declared that all different kinds of colors, materials, and forms may be developed into a language that all people understand. This language reveals a powerful and promising creative potential (Maffei 2008: 22).

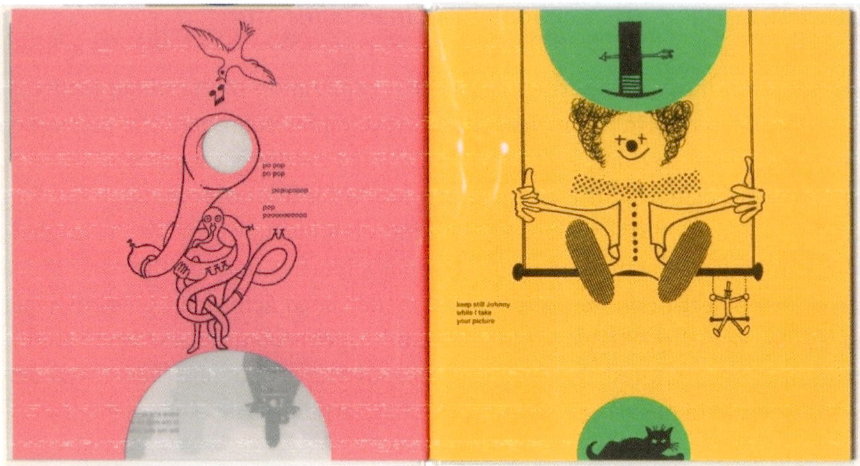

Figure 3. The world of the circus. Doublespread from Bruno Munari: *Nella nebbia di Milano*. Milan: Emme Edizioni, 1968. © 2016 Bruno Munari. All rights reserved to Maurizio Corraini srl. Mantova

of their traffic flows, which are a metaphor for physical and mental "mobility" and for its importance in everyday life.

The second section is an *extraordinary* colorful journey inside the whimsical artistic world of the circus (Figure 3). Bright multi-colored cardboards containing sequences of die-cut holes are used to emphasize the amazing acrobatic skills of the characters in the circus tent. The sinuous, irregular, and joyful lines and shapes are light-heartedly counterpointed to the rigorous repetition of geometrics and mechanical forms of the first section. The choice of these audacious and daring drawings emphasizes the distinctive freedom and the immeasurable value of art, which is – in Munari's view – not a purely meditative or consolatory activity but a necessary, participatory activity, which is deeply rooted in humans (Tanchis 1981: 15).

The third section is an inspiring journey through the park (Figure 4). Munari uses tracing paper and black forms to portray the natural open-air landscape. The style and layout of the pages are completely different from the previous sections. Munari uses light fanciful and lopsided lines to give shape to nature. This choice highlights the proximity between the natural world and the world of art. Trunks, branches, and leaves, which spontaneously stretch out from one side to the other of the doublespread pages, have dynamic and curved forms. These curved silhouettes are associated with an organic and natural order as well as with organic and natural growth (Kress & van Leeuwen 2006: 55). While geometrical forms build a sort of mechanical frame around human life in the urban space, natural forms are

Figure 4. Journey through the park. Doublespread from Bruno Munari: *Nella nebbia di Milano*. Milan: Emme Edizioni, 1968.

part of the human life situated in the country: trees, birds, and a small child and his dog belong to the same unique landscape.

The divergent landscapes embody the multifaceted world we live in and emphasize the importance of encouraging the child's natural propensity for flexible thinking, and its readiness to adapt to experience and knowledge (Munari 1981: 231). The reader is taken for a stroll through different places and situations, which are recognizable not only thanks to the illustrations and the (few) written indications at the beginning of the story, but also due to the changes in the material quality of the book. This reading experience can lead to a new physical, visual, and mental awareness.

Since our world is often shrouded in opacity, a stroll through different cityscapes and more generally through different urban spaces is an activity that can offer children the opportunity to become critical observers of the city and of its people. The child *flâneur* observes, records, and reports, he "does not just live in the city and walk through its streets, but also subjects it to his or her critical gaze [...] or engages in some way with writing, art, or the imagination as a means of contending with and mastering the city and modernity" (Tribunella 2010: 70). This type of character has already been investigated in children's literature and, as Kerry Mallan points out, "unlike the worldly urban stroller that Baudelaire and Benjamin wrote about, a different kind of *flâneur*, a neo-*flâneur*, appears in recent picture books, which can be argued is part of a (post)modern figuration of the urban condition" (2012: 58). A detailed analysis of the child *flâneur* is outside the scope of this chapter. However, the studies on this character draw our attention to the fact that, in 1968, Munari was fully aware of how a children's book could convey the dialogic relation between children, urban spaces, and the different modes of seeing and being in the city, because in Munari's view, mobility and visualization are inextricably connected.

Munari's visual mapping of the city of Milan

In *The Circus in the Mist*, Munari creates a map of the city of Milan by visually depicting three different landscapes. The protagonist finds the most suitable way home, wandering through these different cityscapes, and the fact that an image of the child protagonist never appears in the visual narration is motivated by Munari's intention of identifying the protagonist with the "real" child who is reading the story.

In his essay "Homelands: Landscape and Identity in Children's Literature," Tony Watkins (2006) observes that

> the stories we tell our children, the narratives we give them to make sense of cultural experience constitute a kind of mapping, maps of meaning that enable our children to make sense of the world. These maps contribute to children's sense of identity [...]. Some narratives [...] shape the way children find a 'home' in the world. (59)

The Circus in the Mist is an example of this kind of narrative and reveals some typical features of Munari's approach as far as visual mapping is concerned.

The sense of direction is built thanks to some key aspects which include developing and protecting flexible thinking (Munari 1981: 231); helping children to undertake "research" itineraries, especially but not exclusively in their everyday experience, by means of such experiences as "crosswalks," "extra-territoriality," and "globality" (Meneguzzo 2000: 26); and teaching them to learn through ludic experimentation (Meneguzzo 1993; Restelli & Sperati 2008).

Munari adopts his "special" object-books in order to enable children to make sense of the world through their visual skills. Thanks to these multimodal creations, young readers have the possibility to explore ordinary places and circumstances in extraordinary ways. As the critic and art historian Filiberto Menna points out, as early as 1966, Munari did not wish to "produce any kind of collective amazement [...] on the contrary, he wished to create little fantastic worlds for a domestic and everyday use, places which should be contemplated, psychically inhabited, enchanted" (1966: 15). This is the reason why the adventures of Munari's characters cannot be considered as everyday experiences, even though they take place in everyday places and settings, either green spaces, which represent the pleasure as well as the wilderness of the overgrown wild spaces, or roadways, such as city centers and urban streets. These settings are not extraordinary in the sense of fantastic spaces, but they owe their unusual dimension to Munari's choices as far as time (nighttime, for example) or weather conditions (for instance, foggy or snowy places) are concerned (Campagnaro & Goga 2014: 80). Munari makes careful choices about the everyday situations portrayed in his stories, to the extent that his landscapes somehow become characters in themselves, by attracting children's attention and testing their sensory receptiveness.

The visual mapping of Milan in *The Circus in the Mist* is not comparable to any ordinary map. It does not follow the rules of cartography. Rather than presenting a bird's eye view, Munari's map offers a close view, full of urban and natural details: a schematic, but still realistic representation of the city. This special map of a foggy Milan landscape could prove to be difficult to read, because fog makes things hazy, vague, and obscure. Yet on the contrary, the book content, shape, and materials have an immediate, clear, and precise effect, in perfect compliance with the fundamental technical map-making requirements: that is, clarity, completeness, and precision. Everything – from humans to animals, from architectural elements to vehicles – is represented through minimalist and highly readable, linear, and geometric pictograms. Much like road signs, pictures become easily readable orientation tools.

The presence of visual and textual information about both the geographic and atmospheric setting plays a similar role. The city of Milan is described not only through its geographic name, but also through its distinctive atmospheric conditions (for instance, the fog). The same completeness is present both in the colorful central part, dedicated to the circus, where lines become less clear and, at the same time, more sinuous and curving, and in the final part of the journey through the park.

In this picturebook, Munari's visual mapping emphasizes two fundamental aspects. The first aspect is the importance of mobility and nomadism in everyday life. The whole narration is a poetic statement of the importance of wandering. Upon closer inspection, movement and constant transformation, accompanied by a touch of ironic light-heartedness, represent the most typical topics of Munari's entire artistic production. Like the protagonists of his books, Munari is a wanderer (Meneguzzo 2000: 26), and, through his artistic creations, he proves that being able to find one's way in life is an essential survival skill, even in the most unpredictable and undetermined situation.

The second aspect refers to the fact that, in order to find their way in an urban area, children need to have direct experience with the world around them and develop their personal autonomy. Munari manages to visually emphasize this aspect, insisting on the role of direct experimentation with materials. As far as *The Circus in the Mist* is concerned, he declares that all sorts of paper convey different messages: from printing paper to wrapping paper, from tracing paper to textured paper, rough or smooth, recycled paper, tissue paper, paraffin paper, tar paper, plasticized paper, pure cellulose, rag paper, straw paper, natural paper, man-made paper, soft, hard, or flexible paper, and so on ad infinitum. Different discoveries can be made thanks to these different qualities. If paper is transparent, it communicates its transparency; if it is rough, it communicates its roughness, and so on. If many sheets of transparent paper, that is, the sort used by architects and engineers for their drawings, are positioned one above the other, they create a filter and can give an idea of fogginess: turning those pages is like walking through the fog (Munari 1981: 219). Thanks to the use of these different papers (and it should be remembered that this happened back in the 1960s) children can literally undertake a sensory journey. By turning every single page, readers have the possibility to undertake a physical experience of discovery. They can admire a sequence of changing shapes: the overlapping pages reveal different urban architectures, formed by street and traffic lights, bridges, and all sorts of vehicles including busses, cars, and motorbikes (which once again refer back to the concept of locomotion and mobility). When colors and geometric shapes (circle, square, equilateral triangle) interact in rigorous and scientific combinations (emphasized by the use of black surfaces and the creation of visual geometric schemes), this interaction gives shape to typical urban settings. When colors and geometric shapes interact in free and playful schemes (emphasized by the use of bright colors and the ironic and bizarre elements), this interaction contributes to depict the joyful atmosphere of the circus. The readers' ears can capture the unexpected sounds produced by the compact cardboard or the flying flimsy paper. Their fingers can touch different materials: the foggy translucent softness of the flimsy paper, the sturdiness of the colored cardboard, the emptiness of the holes, and the bizarre shapes of the circus.

Another significant element of Munari's work consists in the possibility of experiencing limits (Meneguzzo 2000: 28). Munari's characters are traveling children (Cf. Campagnaro & Goga 2014: 80), who move towards the borders of the available space, and possibly try to cross those borders. The event of experiencing a limit plays a fundamental role in the discovery of new itineraries, in the extraordinary exploration of territories which are which are off the beaten path.

The event of experiencing a limit in children's search for autonomy and exploration of urban areas is underlined both visually and verbally in *The Circus in the Mist*. Visually, this concept is represented by means of the picturebook's graphic layout: no frames or margins delimit the pages. Through these pictures, which reach beyond the margins of the pages, Munari metaphorically invites children to go beyond their limits and to reach towards mobility, freedom, and discovery.

Autonomy is also highlighted by Munari's skillful use of visual travel instructions (for example, traffic lights, road signs, arrows, signs). These indications, which are very much present at the beginning of the story, contain mandatory or prohibitory instructions (such as the "no entry" sign), which indicate and influence the itinerary. However, as the exploration goes on (from the foggy city of Milan to the circus and then back home), the mandatory signs first become sparse and then disappear, indicating that children have developed their autonomy and broadened their horizons, thanks to this journey. The search for autonomy and direct experience is finally emphasized by Munari's choice to adopt a special representation style, which aims at the readers' involvement, with no free margin for perspective. As Gunther Kress and Theo van Leeuwen rightfully point out, "perspective puts a barrier between the viewer and the represented participants […] the viewer looks at the represented participants and has an attitude towards them, but does not imaginarily engage with them" ((2006)140). Munari chooses a direct frontal angle, because the frontal angle is the angle of maximum involvement (145). By using this graphic layout, it seems that objects and shapes move either backwards or forward in the viewer's comfort zone, thus creating a sense of optical instability, depending on the different points of view (see Casciani 1988).

Verbally, the concept is represented through the skillful and careful use of verbal and linguistic register, enabling Munari to invite the protagonist/reader, for example, to learn how to move in all directions: upwards, downwards, towards the center, around, and so on. On the front cover flyleaf, the narration starts as follows:

> When the summer sunshine makes everything bright and makes the sand scorching hot under the feet, nature is awake and very active: new leaves grow on the trees, birds make long flights, animals and insects run and jump, and children discover a world of new things around them. In winter nature sleeps, and fog appears when it is dreaming. Walking in the fog is like peeping into nature's dream: birds make short flights, so that they won't lose their sense of direction, the road signs disappear along the streets, the vehicles travel slowly and as soon as you can recognize them, they disappear. Red, green, yellow lights make the fog colorful, everything becomes unreal. Only in the houses, do people and animals go on with their activities. (Munari 2008)[7]

In fifteen lines, divided into two columns, Munari introduces a sequence of verbs of movement, such as push, fly, run, jump, come out, walk, go, and continue; verbs of transformation, such as disappear, color, and become; verbs of exploration, such as light up, discover, dream, lose one's direction, recognize, and browse around;

7. This is the only text in the picturebook and supports the understanding of the picturebook's meaning.

and prepositions of place, which offer information on the area where the action takes place: in, under, outside, around, and inside.

In Munari's view, children do not need many verbal explanations to understand things: for them it is much more useful to look and observe. Nevertheless, words are not modest signs used to convey meaning; they are also powerful transmitters of feelings, beliefs, values, and dispositions to act in certain ways. Another aspect, which is also strictly connected with the importance of ludic experimentation, refers to the role of simultaneous contrast (see Munari 1989). This element can be investigated thanks to the book structure, which presents three different environmental settings. As Munari himself reminds us, "an ancient rule of visual communication is simultaneous contrast. Thanks to this rule, two components of a dichotomic couple enhance and intensify each other's communicative potential. The contrast is not limited to formal or material elements, but it also includes semantic oppositions" (Munari 1968: 355). Munari defines the technique of "simultaneous contrasts" as the first law of communication, applicable to all creative disciplines. The simultaneous contrast generates a kind of responsive energy, which produces some kind of memory once the contrast itself has been experienced – that is, seen, touched, or perceived.

The Circus in the Mist is a good example of the power of this mechanism of visual communication. By exploring the story, it is possible to see how Munari makes use of the entire repertoire of simultaneous contrast mentioned in his famous book *Design and Visual Communication* (1968), published in the same year as *The Circus in the Mist*. The three sections of the picturebook are based on this rule of visual communication. The regular, geometrical, and mechanical forms of the first section, for instance, form a contrast with the irregular, sinuous, and natural lines of the second section; the stable, heavy, and static architecture of the urban landscape forms a contrast with the light, unstable, and moving profiles of the natural landscape. The narrative role of these contrasting couples consists in the fact that they can somehow be considered as a litmus test. Finding out one's direction and being able to move in space implies the necessity of coming to terms with different environments: from flat country to mountain areas, and from urban streets to narrow paths through the woods. No single landscape is totally devoid of asperities and dangers. It is utterly important to bring harmony into the great variety of situations where a contrasting pair is involved. The capacity to create a balance between opposing issues is a much sought-after talent, even in everyday life. From this point of view, the functionality of different means of transport in urban areas, for example, may be reconciled with the freedom of a contemplative stroll in the park.

In *The Circus in the Mist*, Munari creates a poetic analogy between urban and natural landscapes, between mechanical and organic elements, between technology and nature, between city and countryside. The general sense of the work is thus conciliated, that is, reunited, in an ever-changing balance: the functionality of technology (expressed by the vehicles in the first section of the book) is accompanied by the gratuitous nature of games (expressed by the circus performance in the second section) and the freedom of contemplation (expressed by the walk through the park). The book appears as a visual map, which offers children an explanation of the fact that black and white are inextricably connected with colors, pictures with their background, concave with convex surfaces, positive with negative sides, and the knowledge of rules with the possibility of breaking them.

Engendering new aesthetic dimensions

It is a known fact that one does not really learn how to experiment by simply looking at a master's experiment or by repeating a prearranged exercise. On the contrary, it is important that children enjoy freedom of action, "a playful process of negotiation, imagination, orchestration, interpretation and experimentation, using visual strategies of noticing, searching, exploring, hypothesizing, comparing, labelling and strategizing" (Salisbury & Styles 2012: 79). A foggy landscape is typically disorienting and confusing. It is the ideal metaphor for crawling, for children's feeling around. Any reference point is inevitably lost in foggy landscapes, and it is difficult to identify the appropriate physical and geographical coordinates. Fog determines and transforms the perception of one's surroundings.

Even in such a disorienting situation, which is so similar to some situations of human experience, Munari believes that it is possible to learn how to find one's direction. Nowadays urban areas are constantly expanding and overlapping, and it is difficult to find a map which can ideally guide us in our approach to the reality around us. Wandering and experiencing one's limits are important. Thanks to these experiences, in fact, we can avoid the repetitive schemes created by our habits: infinite possibilities are automatically sacrificed by going to the same places, by doing things in the same old way. Moreover, new experiences may engender the aesthetic dimension.

The Circus in the Mist portrays the movements of nature, experienced during Munari's happy childhood in the Venetian countryside. Since pictures do not represent a predetermined itinerary, it is essential to have a map. Munari's readers are thus expected to manipulate the map, to change points of view together with the different addressees, who thus gain first-hand experience, both through the mechanisms of narration and through the mechanisms of their own perceptions (Tanchis 1986: 88). In the description of this urban world, art and nature are not excluded from human life. On the contrary, they form part of the phenomenological reality and of the flow of everyday things (25). *The Circus in the Mist* invites the reader to reconsider the relationship between man and nature. Nature should not be dominated, but man should learn how to live "inside" nature. The preposition "nella" ("in the"), contained in the Italian title of Munari's picturebook, conveys this noble value.

In the absolutely modern framework of *The Circus in the Mist*, Bruno Munari reveals a fundamental teaching. According to Umberto Eco, Munari's man (and child), need to have a "thousand eyes: on their noses, on the nape of their necks, on their shoulders, on their fingers and under their bottoms. They are restless inhabitants of an expanding universe" (1962: 187). A visual map may prove to be a useful tool in this expanding universe.

References

Primary sources

Munari, Bruno. 1940. *Mondo Aria Acqua Terra*. Milan: Italgeo.

Munari, Bruno. 1942a. *Le macchine di Munari*. Torino: Einaudi.

Munari, Bruno. 1942b. *Abecedario di Munari*. Torino: Einaudi.

Munari, Bruno. 1968. *Nella nebbia di Milano*. Milan: Emme Edizioni.

Munari, Bruno. 2008. *Nella nebbia di Milano*. Mantova: Corraini.

Romeo-Toscano, Giuseppe & Munari, Bruno. 1929. *L'Aquilotto implume*. Milan: Ambrosiana Editoriale.

Secondary sources

Antonello, Pierpaolo. 2012. My futurist past, present and future. In *Bruno Munari. My Futurist Past*, Mirolava Hájek & Luca Zaffarano (eds), 95–103. Cinisello Balsamo MI: Silvana Editoriale.

Beckett, Sandra. 2012. *Crossover Picturebooks: A Genre for All Ages*. New York NY: Routledge.

Campagnaro, Marnie & Goga, Nina. 2014. Bambini "in cammino" nella letteratura per l'infanzia. Forme e figure nei libri illustrati. In *Le terre della fantasia. Leggere la letteratura per l'infanzia e l'adolescenza*, Marnie Campagnaro (ed.), 73–98. Rome: Donzelli.

Casciani, Stefano. 1988. *Arte industriale: Gioco, oggetto, pensiero. Danese e la sua produzione*. Milan: Arcadia.

Cremoncini, Roberta. 2012. Introduction. In *Bruno Munari. My Futurist Past*, Miroslava Hajek & Luca Zaffarano (eds), 7. Cinisello Balsamo MI: Silvana Editoriale.

Dorfles, Gillo. 1998. Quell' eterno ragazzo prodigio che custodiva il segreto del gioco. *Corriere della Sera*, October 1, 1998: 33.

Eco, Umberto. 1962. *La forma del disordine, Almanacco Letterario Bompiani*. Milan: Bompiani. Retrieved from <http://p-dpa.net/download/almanacco-letterario-bompiani_1962.pdf>

Farina, Loredana. 2013. *La casa delle meraviglie. La Emme Edizioni di Rosellina Archinto*. Milan: Topipittori.

Fiz, Alberto. 2000a. Bruno Munari tra spiazzamento e demistificazione. In *Omaggio a Bruno Munari*, Albert Fiz (ed.), 15–21. Milan: Mazzotta.

Kress, Gunter & van Leeuwen, Theo. 2006. *Reading Images: The Grammar of Visual Design*. London: Routledge.

Maffei, Giorgio. 2008. *Munari i libri*. Mantova: Corraini.

Mallan, Kerry. 2012. Strolling through the (post)modern city: Modes of being a flâneur in picture books. *The Lion and the Unicorn* 36: 56–74. doi: 10.1353/uni.2012.0002

Meneguzzo, Marco. 1993. *Bruno Munari*. Rome: Editori Laterza.

Meneguzzo, Marco. 1995. *Bruno Munari. Opere 1930–1995*. Bergamo: Fumagalli.

Meneguzzo, Marco. 2000. La libertà e il limite. Munari, l'arte, il metodo. In *Omaggio a Bruno Munari*, Alberto Fiz (ed.), 25–29. Milan: Mazzotta.

Menna, Filiberto. 1966. Bruno Munari o la coincidenza degli opposti. La botte e il violino. *Repertorio Illustrato di Design e di Disegno* 8: 11–18.

Munari, Bruno. 1968. *Design e comunicazione visiva*. Rome: Editori Laterza.

Munari, Bruno. 1981. *Da cosa nasce cosa*. Rome: Laterza.

Munari, Bruno. 1989. *Simultaneità degli opposti*. Mantova: Corraini.

Restelli, Beba & Sperati, Silvana. 2008. *A che gioco giochiamo?* Mantova: Corraini.

Salisbury, Martin & Styles, Morag. 2012. *Children's Picturebooks. The Art of Visual Storytelling*. London: Laurence King.

Tanchis, Aldo. 1981. *L'arte anomala di Bruno Munari*. Bari: Laterza.

Tanchis, Aldo. 1986. *Bruno Munari*. Milan: Idea Books Edizioni.

Tribunella, Eric L. 2010. Children's literature and the child *flâneur*. *Children's Literature* 38: 64–91.

Watkins, Tony. 2006. Homelands: Landscape and identity in children's literature. In *Children's Literature. Critical Concepts in Literary and Cultural Studies*, Vol. 4, Peter Hunt (ed.), 57–81. London: Routledge.

PART 3

Fictional seascapes and landscapes

CHAPTER 9

"An island made of water quite surrounded by earth"

Mapping out the seascape in nonsense literature

Olga Holownia

This chapter examines the ways in which geography functions in nonsense verse, prose and illustration, and more specifically, in the representations of seascapes. The key purpose of maps, toponyms and topothesia, which conventionally help the readers envision and navigate a fictitious world, tends not to be fulfilled in literary nonsense, even when maps or detailed descriptions are provided. Focusing on the genre-defining nineteenth-century works and their twentieth-century visual re-interpretations, this chapter outlines selected common features of nonsense geography and shows how the nonsense game has since been followed in our own time, using a popular example drawn from contemporary literature.

Let me propose the following conditional statement. If Jonathan Swift's *Gulliver's Travels* (1726) and Robert Louis Stevenson's *Treasure Island* (1883) set a benchmark for sea voyage stories featuring maps, Lewis Carroll's mock-epic *The Hunting of the Snark* (1876) plays the same role within the genre of literary nonsense (see the definition by Tigges 1987, 1988). The "perfect and absolute blank" (Carroll & Holiday 1876: 16), which is to guide the Snark hunters, underscores one of the key features of the genre, namely its penchant for challenging and, indeed, frustrating readers' expectations (Tigges 1988: 41). Appearing early in Carroll's poem, Henry Holiday's iconic ocean-chart (Figure 1) is also symptomatic of the succinct verbal mapping which follows. Edward Lear's five nonsense books (1846–1877), on the other hand, are replete with real and imaginary toponyms and even they seem to provide as little in terms of coherent, mappable secondary worlds as Carroll's blank map does. Geography, as so much else in nonsense, turns out to be about play with words and sounds.

Against this background, I aim to explore the role maps, topothesia (a description of an imaginary place), toponyms and illustrations play in literary nonsense,

DOI 10.1075/clcc.7.10hol

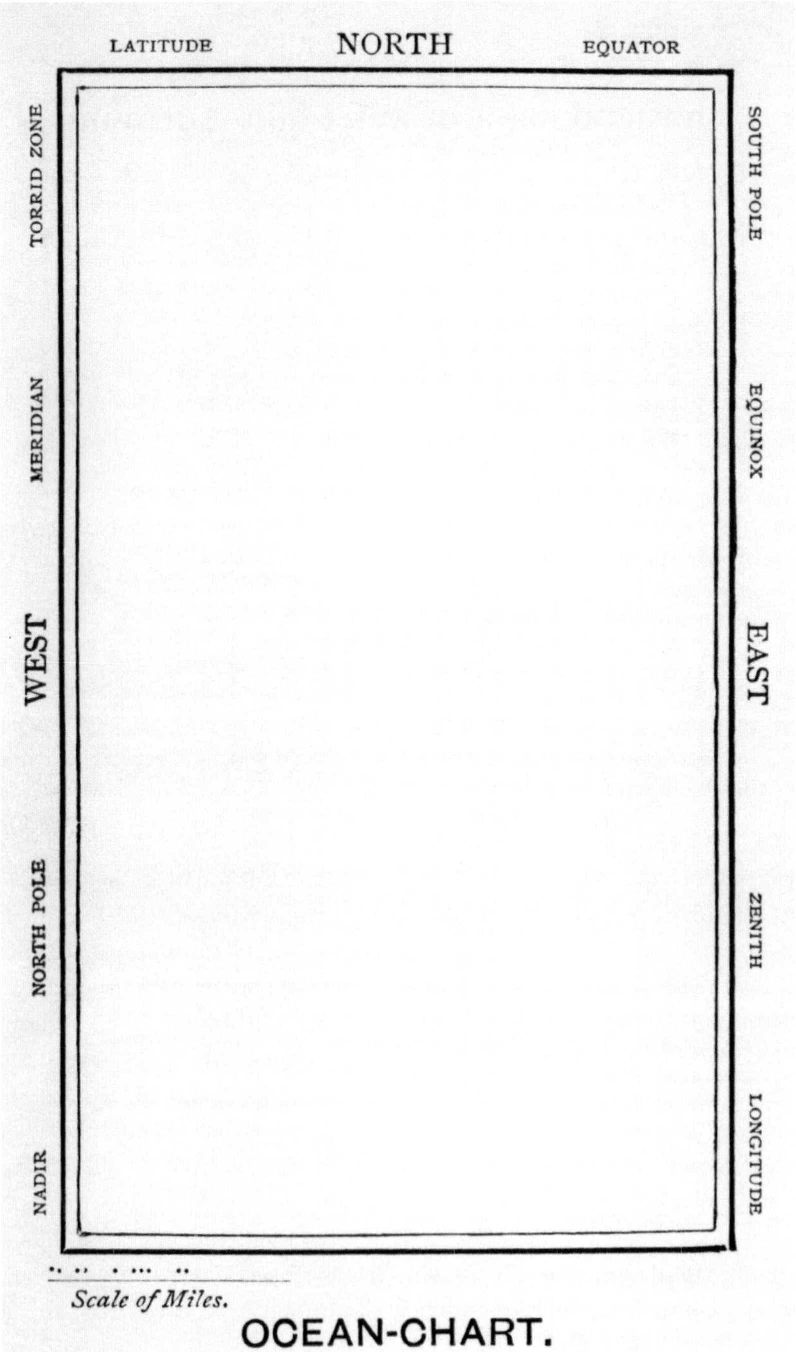

Figure 1. Illustration by Henry Holiday from Lewis Carroll: *The Hunting of the Snark*. London: Macmillan & Co, 1876

focusing primarily on sea voyages. To do so, after introducing the nautical theme, I first look at Lear's and Carroll's genre-defining examples before moving on to their visual re-interpretations offered by the twentieth-century practitioners and aficionados of literary nonsense including Mervyn Peake, Edward Gorey, and Quentin Blake. In the final part, I demonstrate how the classic nonsense strategies are deployed in a contemporary nautical setting, namely in Walter Moers' fantasy crossover. Although far from being exhaustive, a close examination of these examples offers an opportunity to delineate a number of common features which give insight into nonsense geography – a subject little studied so far in the critical literature.

Nonsense geography: Seascapes and soundscapes

If we think of the most popular nonsense poems, sea adventures are likely to strike us as one of the recurrent motifs – a subcategory of quests or voyages widely present in the genre (cf. Tigges 1988: 77–78, 256). Carroll's eclectic crew embarks on a sailing expedition in their pursuit of the Snark. The Owl and the Pussy Cat go to sea, as do the Jumblies, Quangle-Wangle and the Pobble. Notably, for their journeys Lear's and Peake's protagonists borrow objects from the domestic domain – a common practice in nonsense (Sewell 1952: 97–114) – and thus churns, teakettles, sieves, crockery jars, and "a table of a rare design" (Peake 2011: 78), along with the company of "twelve peaches, / A sofa and a swan" (167), belong to the nonsense seascape (Figure 2). The spirit of sea escapades, often interpreted as a manifestation of escape (Heyman 1999: 120, 210), certainly is strong in nonsense literature, but how much can we infer about the setting and the course of these journeys? It varies, but the short answer is "not much."

Figure 2. Illustration from Edward Lear: *Nonsense Songs, Stories, Botany, and Alphabets.* Boston: James R. Osgood and Company, 1871

A paucity of verbal mapping and descriptions is one of the features of the nonsense works discussed here. One may, at least in part, attribute it to the form. With the exception of *The Snark*, nonsense poems about sea voyages are relatively short. Even the longer prose pieces such as Lear's "The Story of the Four Little Children Who Went Round the World" (henceforth "The Story") tend to have an episodic structure with few logical links. Moreover, unlike most quests, these journeys need not have a purpose, lead to any specific destination or reach a dénouement. In terms of verbal mapping, where one may expect topothesia to create a coherent setting, the nonsense writers appear to be more interested in the toponyms' aural rather than semantic properties. Wordplay and soundplay prevail in these travel accounts as some of the main formal features of the genre come to the fore, including "lumped use of alliteration, a love of exotic names, and a delight in neologisms" (McGillis 2002: 159). In the best nonsense, argues Wim Tigges, sound dominates the meaning (1988: 20), and the genre's "emphasis, stronger than in any other type of literature, upon its verbal nature" constitutes one of its main characteristics (55). As will be demonstrated, in nonsense toponyms evoke an aural rather than visual setting. Moreover, accumulation of place names, often adding nothing to the story and not relating locations to each other (cf. Wolf 2013: 156), signals the presence of another nonsense device: stringing or seriality (Tigges 1988: 55), which Moers, for instance, uses abundantly to great effect.

Lear's limericks

Numerous place names appear in Lear's limericks, first published in 1846. Elizabeth Sewell contrasts Carroll's "map of a vacuum" with what she refers to as "Lear's precise Nonsense geography" (1952: 152). His topographic limericks were no coincidence – Lear was one of the great Victorian travelers and travel-writers, as well as a landscape painter (Lear 1828–1887, see e.g. Maxwell 2010). While his limericks can be mapped and geocoded, such a detailed image is of little consequence and exposes the way nonsense engages with geography. The main justification for the presence of a specific toponym is its aural quality – the feature of nonsense mentioned earlier and the validation of the claim that nonsense's "first allegiance is to rhyme rather than reason. Or rather, rhyme *is* its primary reason" (Sonstroem 1967: 198).

In terms of illustrations, as a rule, Lear's limericks, unlike his travel journals, display an intriguing paucity of land- and seascapes. If one appears, it is merely sketched in the background (Figure 3). One may also question the characters' interest in the actual voyage: as Lisa Ede points out, even the lady of Portugal "[w]hose ideas were excessively nautical" focuses on the tip of the branch, not the

Figure 3. Illustration from Edward Lear: *A Book of Nonsense*. London: Thomas McLean, 1846

sea beyond it (1987: 106). Indeed, one of the features of Lear's limericks is a certain disregard not only for the setting but also for the actual voyage: despite their professed intentions, his protagonists hardly ever leave the shore. Sea adventures abound, however, in Lear's later nonsense books. The aforementioned prose piece "The Story" tells of a round-the-world voyage, and happens to provide exemplary study material for all nonsense devices (Tigges 1988: 148–149), while a number of resonant place names, which recur in his songs, suggest the presence of a mappable nonsense universe.

Imprecise nonsense geography and soundscape

The beginning of Lear's story provides an apt example of the way nonsense voyages indulge in inconsequentiality and resist the purpose of mapping: "So they bought a large boat to sail quite round the world by sea, and then they were to come back on the other side by land" (Lear 2006: 218). This introduction is followed by a series of encounters which one could probably sequence in a random order. The children, who pursue their adventure "with the utmost delight and apathy" (222), visit various lands and islands, but it is impossible to locate them even on an imaginary route, and juxtapositions of geographic zones (Arctic Bears live next door to Tropical Turnspits) preclude a sense of orientation. Curiously, despite his fondness for exotic toponyms, Lear opts for imprecision. The children simply visit "a country," "some land" or "a narrow part of the sea." Unnamed but described in some detail is "an island made of water quite surrounded by earth … bordered by evanescent isthmuses with a great Gulf-stream running about all over it" (Lear 2006: 219) – one of the highlights of nonsense geography. What distinguishes these places is their inhabitants (Blue-Bottle Flies, Co-operative Cauliflower, Seeze Pyder). Otherwise the descriptions focus predominantly on food – one of nonsense's favorite subjects – and, fulfilling the rule of seriality, everything comes in countless multitudes.

Aural richness is another characteristic feature of Lear's seascape and he uses it with great virtuosity in "The Story." It is particularly evocative in the classic nonsense scene in which the Blue-Bottle-Flies begin to buzz

> in a sumptuous and sonorous manner, the melodious and mucilaginous sounds echoing all over the waters, and resounding across the tumultuous tops of the transitory Titmice upon the intervening and verdant mountains with a serene and sickly suavity only known to the truly virtuous. (Lear 2006: 227)

This is an excerpt from a long passage dominated overwhelmingly by strings of adjectives and adverbs the presence of which seems to be triggered by their sound rather than their meaning (Heyman 1999: 172; Ede 1975: 56–7; Anderson & Apseloff 1989: 59). The rhythm of the sentence becomes clearer when it is read out loud. Clusters of alliterative sibilants and plosives are elegantly interspersed with languid gerunds that actually refer to sound ("echoing", "resounding"), and two nouns related to landscape. But "the waters" and "verdant mountains" remain tertiary to the memorable soundscape that emerges while the "tops of the transitory Titmice" ensure the balance between the absence and presence of meaning.

The above and other descriptions from "The Story" are humorous in a purely nonsensical way, but here one should also note nonsense's complicated relationship with parody. According to Tigges "it is the prime characteristic of nonsense not to make a 'point' or draw a moral, not to satirize, to ridicule or to parody, and not even primarily to entertain" (1988: 50; cf. Hildebrandt 1970: 47–49; Heyman 1999: 13–65). And yet one cannot deny the presence of a strong parodic undercurrent in *The Snark*, "The Story" and other sea voyages discussed here. Nonsense scholars have, indeed, suggested such an interpretation of Lear's prose piece, not least its style, seeing it as "a parody of Robinson Crusoe exoticism, and of the rather pompously written travelers' tales of which the British reading public was inordinately fond in the nineteenth century" (Lecercle 1994: 58–59; cf. Anderson & Apseloff 1989: 59). Even Tigges admits that Lear "pokes fun" at this type of style, but, as he stresses, "the Story rises above the level of mere parody, because the description creates its own reality" (1988: 149). Commenting on the Blue-Bottle Flies' evening song, Ede makes an important point about Lear's intentions: "He seems most intrigued with the possibilities for word play that parody offers, rather than with making a comment about the original form" (1975: 56). This is certainly true of the realm located somewhere around the Torrible Zone.

There is no question that sound plays a significant role in Lear's geography. He successfully creates aural rather than visual sea- and landscapes through the use of alliterative and rhyming toponyms, some of which rank among the finest imaginary places (Manguel & Guadalupi 1999). Alongside generic names (the Lakes, the Western Sea) we also find neologisms such as the City of Tosh, the Zemmery Fidd, the Land of Gramblamble, and the Soffsky-Poffsky trees, some of which recur in Lear's songs about sea voyages. These include the Chankly Bore, the Bay of Gurtle, the Isles of Boshen, the Coast of Coromandel, the Torrible Zone and the Great Gromboolian Plains. Michael Heyman considers all these places to be various manifestations of "Lear's mythical land of romantic escape and adventure" (1999: 116). Indeed, the way these toponyms recur hints at the presence of some – let us risk saying it – coherent world but, as before, with the exception of a few epithets, it remains resolutely undescribed. This pared-down approach to the setting is best encapsulated in the famous refrain "Far and few, far and few / Are the lands where the Jumblies live" (Lear 2006: 252). Lear uses illustrations sparingly too, focusing on his characters rather than their surroundings. We can recognize its idiosyncratic soundscapes, but otherwise this world remains visually indeterminate and unmappable – a feature addressed by the twentieth-century illustrators of Lear's work. The tension between the original intent and the subsequent practice of re-illustration of classic nonsense is discussed in the second part of this chapter.

Carroll: Maps as concepts

The Carrollian type of nonsense is classed as rational (Tigges 1988: 85–87). It not only plays with words but also explores paradoxes and logical problems. Crucially, maps are part of this preoccupation. Two examples include the blank ocean-chart from *The Snark* and a 1:1 scale map as described by Mein Herr in *Sylvie and Bruno Concluded* (1893), both of which have become a staple of cartographic discussions on reality versus representation, as well as an inspiration for literature and visual arts.[1] When Mein Herr is asked about the fate of the 1:1 map, he admits that "[i]t has never been spread out, yet [...] the farmers objected: they said it would

1. Carroll's concepts still surface in cartographic debates, and Holiday's map graces book covers (see Stockhammer 2007; Dodge, Kitchin & Perkins 2009; Brotton 2012). In the 1960s the conceptual group Art & Language produced a series of works inspired by the blank map. We find echoes of Mein Herr's map in Luis Borges' "On Rigour in Science" (1964) and Umberto Eco's "On the Impossibility of Drawing a Map of the Empire on a Scale of 1 to 1" (1982).

cover the whole country, and shut out the sunlight! So we now use the country itself, as its own map, and I assure you it does nearly as well" (Carroll 1893: 169). Since turning the symbolic depiction into reality proved impractical, at least according to the sensible farmers, reality became its own symbolic representation. The implementation of this cartographic experiment brings to mind a common nonsense device – the inversion of metaphor whereby the comic effect is achieved when a figurative expression is taken literally and the meaning is made material and factual (Stewart 1979: 77–81).

It would seem that in *The Snark* Carroll plays with the opposite concept to that of mapping everything. But is that the case? Initially, the blank ocean-chart seems to be a prank played on the crew and the readers, but while nautical maps can be very detailed, arguably a fragment of a simplified 1:1 scale map of the ocean would indeed show exactly that: a blank space. The humor of Holiday's illustration (approved by Carroll) derives from the fact that he does retain some of "the conventional signs" , albeit arbitrarily arranged, lacked by the map as described in the poem. Crucially, *The Snark*, with its most recognizable map of the genre, offers the only cartographic specimen, at least within the original editions of the classic repertoire.[2] As such it can be taken to show that the main function of maps – "to provide structure to an imaginary world" (Wolf 2013: 156) – seems to go against the grain of nonsense, in which "no consistency is offered by way of foothold to the reader" (Tigges 1988: 85).

This may be of no consequence in *Sylvie and Bruno Concluded*, in which the map is not meant to play any role in the story, but the situation is different in *The Snark* because the captain supposedly uses the chart to navigate. Additionally, since there is an illustration, we may expect the map to help us envision the imagined world of the poem. It certainly evades doing so in a conventional sense, but the emptiness does reflect the amount of knowledge we acquire about Snark Island and its whereabouts. Carroll's sparing use of topothesia leads Elina Druker to write about "total loss of environmental depiction" (2006: 115). As a matter of fact, the poem's key topothesia is limited to what sounds like an alliterative formula. Upon landing the crew face a view described as consisting of "chasms and crags" (Carroll & Holiday 1876: 19). This hendiadys is split in the final scene, in which the Baker finds himself on top of a crag and eventually plunges into a chasm. Holiday's main focus is on the protagonists, but the dark and massive crags are there to form the background of three illustrations (41, 52, 82). Crucially, as a result of Carroll's verbal frugality, the world of the poem remains rather indeterminate and can

2. Among more recent works, there are examples of maps which integrate nonsense devices, for example, Niki Daly's *A Wanderer in Og: An Amphigory Devised for Your Amusement* (2005) and Jack Prelutsky's *Scranimals* (2002) illustrated by Peter Sís, the author of many surreal maps.

reconfigure itself with each new reading. It certainly does so with new sets of images – the illustrators are literally given carte blanche to create their visions of the Snark's world.

The ongoing practice of re-illustrating is an important aspect to consider with respect to nonsense geography, not least because of the aforementioned tension which arises between the authors' intent and the illustrators' approach to geographic indeterminacy. For over a century both Carroll's and Lear's works have received new visual interpretations, many of which attempt to fill the gaps left by the authors or even, as is the case with the Gromboolian poems, provide coherence to the poet's nonsense universe through the use of pictorial maps. As will be shown, these new takes on the classics may add an interesting perspective to the study of both seascape and maps in nonsense literature.

Emptiness (re)imagined and a new nonsense seascape

Numerous versions of *The Snark* provide a fascinating field of enquiry (see Goodacre 2006). Here, however, only two aspects are of direct relevance: the map and the seascape. Holiday's ocean-chart is probably as well-known as the line of the poem it refers to. Peter Newell, the first to illustrate *The Snark* after Holiday in 1903, even "quoted" the original image within his own work. The majority of subsequent illustrators followed the idea that the "absolute blank" should be framed as a map, thus confirming the lasting appeal of Holiday's concept. Some artists, however, including Danny Kerman, Helen Oxenbury and Ami Rubinger, remained faithful to the text of the poem, while, for instance, Tove Jansson chose to completely ignore the iconic cartographic artefact. She does, on the other hand, create a whole fantastic seascape out of the cryptic "chasm and crags" line. Her crags of monstrous features tower over the island while the hunters are portrayed as tiny dots. Quentin Blake gives us his take on emptiness in the very first spread, which is almost completely devoid of detail: a small ship sits on the line of the horizon, which is strung between the outlines of two crags framing the image. This minimalist approach is already present on the cover (which has no lettering) and continues throughout the book as the scenes gradually become darker. But in terms of nonsense's growth as a genre, it is Mervyn Peake's best-selling 1941 edition of the poem which creates a new iconic seascape – one he consistently developed throughout his works, many of which continue the sea voyage theme.

The sea was a subject of fascination for Peake. It informs not only his own works but also the choice of books he illustrated, among them *Treasure Island* (1949) and *The Rime of the Ancient Mariner* (1943). Importantly, his works, like Edward Gorey's, bring in a much darker tone to nonsense (Heyman 2003: 14) exemplified by poems such as "O'er Seas that have no Beaches," or "Sensitive, Seldom, and Sad," which echoes over "the sneezing sea." In a genre defined by "lack of emotional involvement," a sense of isolation seems to be the only permitted emotion (see esp. Sewell 1952: 145; Ede 1975: 14–15; Tigges 1988: 54). In Peake's illustrations it takes the very distinctive shape of a tall and convoluted rock formation, usually placed in the middle of the sea. This characteristic crag, possibly the most recognizable feature of Peake's land- and seascape, is already present in his early *Moccus Poems* (c. 1929), in which a melancholic creature called Maranesa is perched on top of "a kind of pointed stone" (Peake 1981: 101), and recurs throughout his work, including on the cover of *Peake's Progress*, "Ride a Cock-Horse" (Peake 2011: 27), "I Wish I Could Remember" (99), "The King of Ranga-Tanga-Roon" (114) and the final image in *Captain Slaughterboard Drops Anchor* (1939). A different variant of it is a brilliantly inverted seascape of islands floating on top of the waves (Peake 1981: 27). In *The Snark* the crag looms in the background (Fits the First and the Fifth) before it eventually becomes the central stage in the final scene, in which the Baker is shown on top of it right before his demise. In this take on the poem, Carroll's and Peake's nonsense universes coalesce and the seascape is more clearly tinged with new melancholy.

Lear's realm re-illustrated and mapped

Over the years Lear's poems and prose stories have been re-illustrated in many variants of his selected works. The 1960s, the key period for the post-war development of nonsense (Reynolds 2007: 56), revived "The Story," which was illustrated first by Stan Mack (1967) and later by Arnold Lobel (1968). Crucially, Edward Gorey, considered to be (together with Peake) one of the "great, direct inheritors of the nonsense method and style" (Heyman 2003: 14), produced an outstanding version of *The Jumblies* (1968), which was followed by *The Dong with a Luminous Nose* (1969) and first published as one book in 1982. Gorey always admitted his indebtedness to Lear (see Shortsleeve 2002: 32) and, like Carroll and Peake, this was another perfect union of two nonsense sensibilities, with Gorey imbuing the world of his predecessor with characteristic darkness.

A detailed pen-and-ink illustration accompanies every stanza of each poem. Gorey's take on Lear is recognizably idiosyncratic, aesthetically cohesive and faithful to the original in spirit, a quality appreciated in the book's reviews (see Fisher 1974: 200–201; Shortsleeve 2002: 34). There is great attention to detail, not least in the depiction of the sea with the waves in various stages of animation, ranging from stoic to stormy. Importantly, each poem comes with its own panoramic map. Each is composed of three parts: the Western Sea, a line of nondescript mountains and the sky above them which takes up two thirds of the image. The place names hover over mountains. The clouds are light and scattered in the Jumblies' map showing a slightly ruffled sea, dark and brooding in the one with the curiously calm sea. Apart from the expressive clouds, both maps look very similar. Interestingly, the Jumblies' map does not show their land but three places they supposedly visited (all mentioned only in passing), including the Hills of the Chankly Bore where the Dong lives. The places are precisely marked on the map but inconsistently with the Dong's map – the same Hills differ a little while the Lakes and the Torrible Zone are replaced by the Great Gromboolian Plain. Is it the same place? Does it matter? "[A]n unresolved tension between the presence and absence of meaning" (Tigges 1988: 55) seems to be preserved in the willfully (mis)matched referents. The maps at once suggest and avoid precision. As a result we do not really get a coherent topographic representation of the poems' land, and this is in line with the geographic indeterminacy suggested in Lear's songs. What we do get, however, is the atmosphere. Like Peake, Gorey's lucid yet predominantly dark illustrations make the seascapes feel detached, melancholic and brooding.

Without making any sweeping claims about further developments in nonsense geography, one could argue that in the subsequent decades the tendency has been towards making Lear's world more accessible, coherent and, above all, colorful. We find the most systematic attempt at organizing this world in *Edward Lear's Gromboolian Poems* (1983), in which Jenny Thorne brings together his poems linked by recurrent characters and place names. A map (Figure 4) printed on both endpapers includes the key landmarks of Lear's nonsense. It is a pictorial map, which may serve as a table of contents with the main protagonists of the poems placed in different parts of the Western sea. In terms of the map's "conventional signs," the illustrator plays with the units of scale, expressed in Gromboolian miles, as well as with the directional indicator – she pairs South with West and North with East, and where we would expect North, the compass rose points South. Richly colored illustrations within the book present more detailed topographic views of the nonsense places (predominantly seascapes) and are complemented by flora and fauna derived, mostly, from Lear's poems and his *Nonsense Botany* as well as additional inventions included in book's notes to the illustrations.

Thorne uses Lear's drawings as the basis for her own visual representations. The fact that they appear in vivid colors and often in new juxtapositions makes them distinctly different from the original editions. As I argued, Lear's sparing use of images seems deliberate. The relation between various toponyms remains ambiguous and the soundscape comes to the fore. Once we finally see Lear's places and characters captured on one arbitrarily organized map, the readers' expectations are fulfilled. This seems, however, contrary to what we expect of nonsense literature. Somehow, one would want this world to remain in Lear's head. And this

Figure 4. Endpapers from *Edward Lear's Gromboolian Poems*. First published in 1983 by Macmillan Children's Books, an imprint of Pan Macmillan, a division of Macmillan Publishers International Limited. Illustration copyright © Jenny Thorne 1983

is indeed Thorne's take on maps and nonsense. When we look at it upside down, the Gromboolian Plain turns out to be the profile of Lear's head while the two isles of Boshen are the outlines of the poet's glasses. This is a cunning concept, although Thorne does what nonsense geography resists doing: she creates coherence, giving the readers a foothold.

The infinite eclecticism of Zamonia

In the final section of this chapter we venture out of the field of classic nonsense into new territory. As I tried to suggest, navigating through nonsense geography to some extent reflects the trajectory of the genre. After Lear's and Carroll's "golden age", it was in decline in the first half of the twentieth century before taking off again with the works of Spike Milligan and Dr. Seuss, among others, and in the much more sinister and adult-oriented mode of Peake and Gorey (Heyman 2003). Today, as Heyman argues, nonsense as a genre occupies a niche position. It is, however, possible to find works which tap into the repertoire of nonsense devices, not least with respect to geography, and this certainly is the case with Walter Moers' Zamonia series.

Before the publication of his first novel, Moers had been known in Germany for his satirical characters, among them Adolf and Asshole. The latter featured in Moers' parodies of famous works of art (*Arschloch in Öl*, 1993). Six novels about a continent called Zamonia, five of which have been published in English, continue to highlight his predilection for parody, both verbal and pictorial, and are clearly aimed at a dual audience. Sandra Beckett discusses them under the rubric of "comic fantasy crossovers" together with Terry Pratchett's Discworld series (2009: 147–148). The following analysis focuses on *The 13 ½ Lives of Captain Bluebear* (1999; henceforth *Captain Bluebear*), Moers' popular first novel based on a TV series for children. In the spirit of nonsense, it is a quest with no suspense. We know from the start that Bluebear cannot perish since every bluebear has twenty-seven lives, and what we read is a 700-page account of half of them, retold in 13 ½ chapters, the first and the final of which take place at sea, where Bluebear encounters a number of creatures and one voracious island.

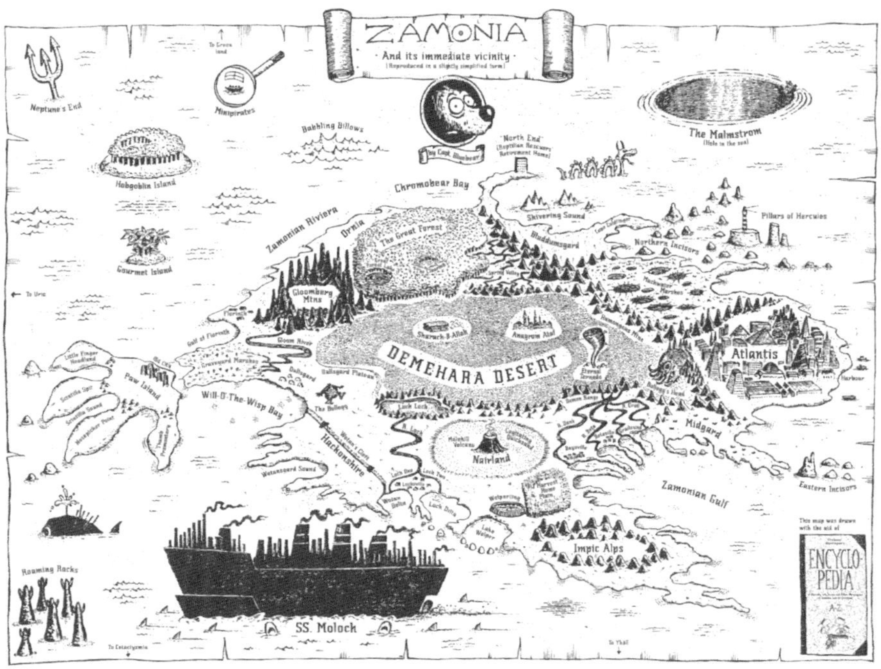

Figure 5. Double spread from Walter Moers: *The 13 ½ Lives of Captain Bluebear*, translated by John Brownjohn. Published by Secker & Warburg and reproduced by permission of The Random House Group Ltd.

Generously detailed maps play a significant role in the Zamonia series (Lembke 2011), as does nonsense (Oppermann 2011). *Captain Bluebear*, abundantly illustrated by the author himself, contains two maps on the first and the last endpapers, which appear to fulfil the usual role of laying the land. The first pictorial map quotes and parodies the cartographic tradition of fantasy literature, not least in its eclectic allusiveness. In terms of toponyms, it is a hotchpotch of nonsense wordplay, various traditional mythologies, and imaginary and real names. There we find Atlantis, the Pillars of Hercules, Cogitating Quicksand, Midgard, Bluddumsgard, Muchwater Marshes, and the cluster of Lochville, Loch One, Loch Two, River Loch, and Loch Loch, to name just a few examples. This pictorial representation of Zamonia is produced in the tradition of "maps of space and time" which, apart from providing an outline of the imaginary realm, also include "major characters and significant objects at important plot junctures" (Kelen & Sundmark 2013: 267). It is the books' non-linear table of contents. Significantly, while in fantasy maps the sea is usually left blank, Moers adds as much detail to the seascape as the early cartographers used to. Given the range of his allusions, this may be the tradition to which he is referring. Notably, just like Olaus Magnus on his Carta Marina (1539), Moers pins down the elements which are not static, including the Babbling Billows, the Minipirates, and Zamonia's "infurno" in the shape of the colossal SS. Moloch. The map does indicate that certain elements of the seascape have an active role to play. In fact, just like in Gorey's version of Lear, the sea itself becomes one of the book's protagonists. Each wave is described as possessing "not only a face of its own but an individual hairstyle in the shape of the foam on its crest" (Moers 2001: 22). The two most significant features of the seascape are the Malmstrom, a gigantic whirlpool, and SS. Moloch, which haunt Bluebear throughout his journey: a predominantly black illustration of the Malmstrom appears as the second double spread (after the map) and is soon followed by a similarly dark frame showing SS. Moloch or, rather, a small part of it. This is a mock-seascape in which tiny white portholes in the side of the black ship resemble stars in the night sky. Positioned in the north-east corner of the map, the Malmstrom is Zamonia's Snark and Boojum in one. Bluebear survives his eventual encounter with it because in the looping logic of Zamonia "the Gates into Hell" turn out to be an entrance to another dimension. Although very specific in its depiction, Moers' map expands the conceptual repertoire proposed by Carroll by playing with various aspects of infinity, other dimensions and maps within maps.

As emphasized before, this is not a nonsense novel, but it feeds on the repertoire of nonsense devices. Eva Oppermann focuses on Moers' indebtedness to Carroll, in particular the techniques and themes used in his *Alice* books (wordplay, intertextual parodies, palimpsests, illustrations). I would argue that the Learian elements are equally prominent, not least if we compare Moers' novel and "The Story." Like Lear's and Carroll's sea voyages, *Captain Bluebear* reveals a highly episodic structure, to the extent that most of the episodes can be shuffled almost at random. While the book's first map may give some information about Zamonia, its structure almost completely ignores the spatial relations presented there (Lembke 2011: 94), which is in line with nonsense's nonchalant disregard for readers' expectations. Characteristically, there is almost no emotional involvement and the hero's adventures seem to have no purpose. They are a string of haphazard events, many of which seem to exist for the sake of creating a multitude of background characters and phenomena which play little or no role in the story. Along with arbitrariness comes seriality. Echoing "The Story," countless creatures, plants, places and natural phenomena populate Bluebear's intensely detailed and digressive travel narrative. Moers draws not on one myth-kitty but on dozens of them, surfing on the edges of several genres simultaneously. As a result, *Captain Bluebear* is an overwhelming mixture of styles, intertextual references, nonsense, fantasy, and elements of sci-fi. In short, this is infinite eclecticism.

To further complicate the structure, Moers introduces two parallel narratives captured by the book's subtitle: "being the demibiography of a seagoing bear, with numerous illustrations and excerpts from the 'Encyclopaedia of the marvels, life forms and other phenomena of Zamonia and its environs,' by Professor Abdullah Nightingale." Bluebear's account is interspersed with entries from the said Encyclopaedia. Oppermann discusses these inserts, composed in an "exaggerated" style, as one of the nonsense devices (2011: 128). Most of the book's wordplay, often reminiscent of Carroll, can be found in this catalogue of marvels. Nonsense indulges in lists and useless details (Lecercle 1994: 63). This practice is taken to the extreme in Moers' excess of information and meticulously precise descriptions, many of which are irrelevant to the story. One such example is the Encyclopaedia's entry on Atlantis, the capital of Zamonia. It lists its many districts arguably just for the sake of wordplay, as all the names are anagrams of Atlantis. This systematic division is subsequently undermined by the following statement: "From the air Atlantis looked like the toy collection of a demented giant" (110).

Moers plays not only with words, images, and typography but also with perspective and time. Throughout the book, we see Zamonia from all possible points of view. On top of that he adds time travel and parallel dimensions, more maps, plans and labyrinths. Mein Herr's discussion of maps is taken to another level as we meet Planmaker, who changes shape and texture and can morph into a map. Not one map, of course: "Then the surfaces changed once more. They now displayed a chart, a timetable, and a view of some solar system or other" (419). In his article about Zamonia's cartography Gerrit Lembke demonstrates the different roles which maps play in each of Moers' novels. In *Captain Bluebear*, like in *The Snark*, they are meta-fictional or meta-artistic figures. Lembke's conclusion aptly sums up their function: "[t]hey serve less to direct – either the characters or the reader – but instead to provide pleasure in the act of reading. They are not intended as functional objects, but rather as a card*game*, free of purpose" (Lembke 2011: 116, my transl.). "Karten*spiel*" can be also understood as "map*game*," which is what the book ultimately offers and adds to nonsense geography. The metafictional argument becomes even more convincing once we look at the final map showing Zamonia in relation to the world. It is a slightly more crowded version of our world with some real (Africa, North America, Eurasia) and less real (Greater Trollia, Fridgia, Zombia) continents.

"Navigation was always a difficult art"

By taking a tour through a set of selected examples of sea voyages, this chapter has aimed to outline some common features of nonsense geography and the way it has developed over time, including new illustrated versions of the classics. Firstly, we find maps featuring as metafictive devices, with the authors, such as Carroll and Moers, playing with cartographic concepts. Secondly, in terms of the seascape, literary nonsense offers two extremes: on the one hand paucity of visual and verbal mapping or, if it exists, deliberately misleading topothesia, and on the other, excess of irrelevant detail, which achieves a similar effect. Furthermore, nonsense's propensity for wordplay and soundplay creates an aural geography, while imprecision inspires illustrators to fill the gap left by Carroll and Lear. Thirdly, the sea voyages discussed here tend to be episodic in structure, and display inconsequentiality, a lack of purpose, and a parodic undercurrent. Last but not least, although typically devoid of emotional involvement, nonsense may steer towards melancholy in which the seascapes evoke a sense of detachment and isolation. This is captured by the Peakian crag in the middle of the sea as well as Gorey's morose shoreline with endless chains of indeterminate mountains. Paradoxically, it is the blank map that seems to color one's perception of nonsense geography. *The Snark* "imposes on the design of the voyage a new and sinister pattern; it presents Nothing, not as an obstacle to be eluded or a test to be passed, but as a predatory potential of the goal itself" (Adams 1966: 96). Sinister or not, the point of literary nonsense is to tamper with the readers' expectations, and this is certainly what nonsense geography does "with the utmost delight and apathy."[3]

References

Primary sources

Carroll, Lewis. 1876. *The Hunting of the Snark: An Agony, in Eight Fits*, illus. Henry Holiday. London: Macmillan.

Carroll, Lewis. 1893. *Sylvie and Bruno Concluded*. London: Macmillan.

3. I would like to thank the editors, the reviewer, Michael Heyman and Agata Hołobut for their constructive comments on an earlier draft of this chapter.

Carroll, Lewis. 1976. *The Hunting of the Snark: An Agony in Eight Fits*, illus. Quentin Blake. London: Folio Society.
Carroll, Lewis. 2011. *The Hunting of the Snark*, illus. Tove Jansson. London: Tate.
Lear, Edward. 1846. *A Book of Nonsense*. London: Thomas McLean.
Lear, Edward. 1828–1887. *Landscape Drawings*, (MS Typ 55.11, MS Typ 55.26, TypDr 805.L513). Houghton Library, Harvard University. <http://id.lib.harvard.edu/aleph/000602418/catalog>
Lear, Edward. 1871. *Nonsense Songs, Stories, Botany, and Alphabets*. Boston MA: Osgood.
Lear, Edward. 1983. *Edward Lear's Gromboolian Poems*, illus. Jenny Thorne. London: Macmillan.
Lear, Edward. 2006. *The Complete Nonsense and Other Verse*, ed. Vivienne Noakes. London: Penguin.
Moers, Walter. 2001. *The 13 ½ Lives of Captain Bluebear*, trans. James Brownjohn. London: Vintage. (Original work published 1999).
Peake, Mervyn. 1981. *Peake's Progress: Selected Writings and Drawings of Mervyn Peake*, ed. Maeve Gilmore. Harmondsworth: Penguin.
Peake, Mervyn. 2011. *Complete Nonsense*, eds. Robert W. Maslen & G. Peter Winnington. Manchester: Fyfield Books/Carcanet.

Secondary sources

Adams, Robert Martin. 1966. *Nil: Episodes in the Literary Conquest of Void during the Nineteenth Century*. Oxford: OUP.
Anderson, Celia Catlett, & Apseloff, Marilyn. 1989. *Nonsense Literature for Children: Aesop to Seuss*. Hamden CN: Library Professional Publications.
Beckett, Sandra L. 2009. *Crossover Fiction: Global and Historical Perspectives*. London: Routledge.
Borges, Luis. 1964. On rigour in science. In *Dreamtigers*, by Luis Borges, 90. Austin TX: University of Texas Press.
Brotton, Jerry. 2012. *A History of the World in Twelve Maps*. London: Allen Lane.
Carroll, Lewis. 1876. *The Hunting of the Snark: An Agony, in Eight Fits*. illus. Henry Holiday.
Daly, Niki. 2005. *A Wanderer in Og: An Amphigory Devised for Your Amusement*. Cape Town: Double Storey.
Dodge, Martin, Kitchin, Rob & Perkins, Chris R. 2009. *Rethinking Maps: New Frontiers in Cartographic Theory*. Abingdon: Routledge.
Druker, Elina. 2006. Picture book as conceptual space: Spatial transformation in Tove Jansson's Book about Moomin, Mymble and Little My. In *From Colonialism to the Contemporary: Intertextual Transformation in World Children's and Youth Literature*, Lance Weldy (ed.), 114–125. Newcastle-upon-Tyne: Cambridge Scholars.
Eco, Umberto. 1995. On the impossibility of drawing a map of the empire on a scale of 1 to 1. In *How to Travel with a Salmon & Other Essays*, Umberto Eco, 99–106. San Diego CA: Harcourt Brace (first published 1982).
Ede, Lisa S. 1975. *The Nonsense Literature of Edward Lear and Lewis Carroll*. PhD dissertation, Ohio State University. <https://etd.ohiolink.edu/rws_etd/document/get/osu1260276849/inline> (12 March 2016).
Ede, Lisa S. 1987. Edward Lear's limericks and their illustrations. In *Explorations in the Field of Nonsense*, Wim Tigges (ed.), 103–116. Amsterdam: Rodopi.

Fisher, Crispin. 1974. A load of old nonsense, Edward Lear resurrected by four publishers. In *Children and Literature: Views and Reviews*, Virginia Haviland (ed.), 198–201. London: Bodley Head.

Goodacre, Selwyn Hugh. 2006. *All the Snarks: The Illustrated Editions of The Hunting of the Snark*. Church Hanborough: Inky Parrot Press.

Heyman, Michael. 1999. *Isles of Boshen: Edward Lear's Literary Nonsense in Context*. PhD dissertation, University of Glasgow. <http://theses.gla.ac.uk/2822> (12 March 2016).

Heyman, Michael. 2003. The decline and rise of literary nonsense in the twentieth century. In *Children's Literature and the Fin de Siècle*, Roger McGillis (ed.), 13–21. Westport CN: Praeger.

Hildebrandt, Rolf. 1970. *Nonsense-Aspekte der englischen Kinderliteratur*: Weinheim: Julius Beltz.

Kelen, Christopher, & Sundmark, Björn. 2013. Postscript: Where children rule? In *The Nation in Children's Literature: Nations of Childhood*, Christopher Kelen & Björn Sundmark (eds), 263–272. New York NY: Routledge.

Lecercle, Jean-Jacques. 1994. *Philosophy of Nonsense: The Intuitions of Victorian Nonsense Literature*. London: Routledge. doi: 10.4324/9780203310618

Lembke, Gerrit. 2011. "Der Große Ompel." Kartographie und Topographie in den Romanen Walter Moers. In *Walter Moers' Zamonien-Romane: Vermessungen eines fiktionalen Kontinents*, Gerrit Lembke (ed.), 87–120. Göttingen: V & R unipress. doi: 10.14220/9783737097925.87

McGillis, Roderick. 2002. Nonsense. In *A Companion to Victorian Poetry*, Richard Cronin, Alison Chapman & Anthony H. Harrison (eds), 155–170. Malden MA: Blackwell.

Manguel, Alberto & Guadalupi, Gianni. 1999. *The Dictionary of Imaginary Places*. London: Bloomsbury.

Maxwell, Richard. 2010. Palms and temples: Edward Lear's topographies. *Victorian Poetry* 48.1: 73–94. doi: 10.1353/vp.0.0096

Oppermann, Eva. 2011. Der deutsche Carroll. Walter Moers' zamonische Romane im Vergleich mit klassischem englischen Nonsense. In *Walter Moers' Zamonien-Romane: Vermessungen eines fiktionalen Kontinents*, Gerrit Lemke (ed.), 121–138. Göttingen: V & R unipress. doi: 10.14220/9783737097925.121

Reynolds, Kimberley. 2007. *Radical Children's Literature: Future Visions and Aesthetic Transformations in Juvenile Fiction*. Basingstoke: Palgrave Macmillan. doi: 10.1057/9780230206205

Sewell, Elizabeth. 1952. *The Field of Nonsense*. London: Chatto & Windus.

Shortsleeve, Kevin. 2002. Edward Gorey, children's literature, and nonsense verse. *Children's Literature Association Quarterly* 27(1): 27–39. doi: 10.1353/chq.0.1442

Sonstroem, David. 1967. Making earnest of game. G. M. Hopkins and nonsense poetry. *Modern Language Quarterly* 28: 192–206. doi: 10.1215/00267929-28-2-192

Stewart, Susan. 1979. *Nonsense: Aspects of Intertextuality in Folklore and Literature*. Baltimore MD: The Johns Hopkins University Press.

Stockhammer, Robert. 2007. *Die Kartierung der Erde: Macht und Lust in Karten und Literatur*. Munich: Fink.

Tigges, Wim. 1987. *Explorations in the Field of Nonsense*. Amsterdam: Rodopi.

Tigges, Wim. 1988. *An Anatomy of Literary Nonsense*. Amsterdam: Rodopi.

Wolf, Mark J. P. 2013. *Building Imaginary Worlds: The Theory and History of Subcreation*. New York NY: Routledge.

CHAPTER 10

Connecting worlds

Mapping space-time in three fictional islands

Maria Nikolajeva and Liz Taylor

This chapter, based on a crossdisciplinary framework of cultural geography and children's literature theory, discusses three children's novels set on islands, all of which operate within ambiguous fictional worlds and use ambiguous narrative perspective. The issues of belonging/not belonging, time/space connections and interactions, mythical and contemporary world, nature/culture, displacement and spatial marginalisation are emphasised through the maps that are substantially more prominent than in most conventional children's novels. Rather than an embellishment appearing outside the narrative they are in a subtle way incorporated into it, which also creates a fascinating tension between the visual map and its verbal ekphrasis.

This chapter explores three children's novels set on islands: *Kensuke's Kingdom* (1999) by Michael Morpurgo, *Gullstruck Island* (2009) by Frances Hardinge, and *Midwinterblood* (2011) by Marcus Sedgwick. These texts operate within ambiguous fictional worlds and use ambiguous narrative perspective; they illustrate different approaches to the employment and function of maps.

Islands and islandness

The field of island studies spans disciplines of science, geography, history, economics, and anthropology, and has a (somewhat uncomfortable) relationship with literary and cultural studies (Beer 1989; Fletcher 2011; Hay 2006; Royle 2001). This tension revolves round the weight and role given to representation and its relationship to the 'real world.' In the literary output of the island studies field, various characteristics of islands are repeatedly rehearsed and the relationships between them examined and critiqued. These characteristics include isolation, remoteness, boundedness, connection, disconnection, community, and idiosyncrasy

DOI 10.1075/clcc.7.11nik

(Baldacchino 2006; Conkling 2007; Conrad 2009; King 1993). Islands seem to evoke strong feelings, in particular a fascination with the miniature or with diversity within a small area. There is a particular association of islands with nature, although islands encompass a wide range of environments. The manageable size of islands and their apparently clear boundaries seem to fit with people's wish for power and control, whether the rich seeking an exclusive environment, or scientists seeking an apparently pristine one. Frequently rehearsed binaries in the islands literature include insider/outsider, utopia/dystopia, bounded/porous, belonging/entrapment. Some writers question such easy oppositions as obscuring complexity (Fletcher 2011; Savory 2011) and it is likely that most of these oppositions resolve into 'both and' depending on one's aim and perspective. In particular, there are some helpful discussions of interlinkage and connection (Dodds & Royle 2003; Fog Olwig 2007) which question assumptions of boundedness and isolation. As might be expected, the discourses of islands, and the discourses of the field of island studies, are interlaced with issues of power, control, agency, and territory, which are all tangibly present in our selected texts.

Islands, cartography, and literature

Various characteristics of islands have a particular synergy with the wish to map: fascination with the miniature, interest in diversity within, wish to control and understand. The island's apparent boundedness and initial simplicity may facilitate mapping. On a map, an island is set out, named, divided and labelled, fixed and controlled. Constructions of any previous human occupants and diversity of natural life forms may be suppressed and simplified by the act of mapping. Mapping often accompanies colonisation of territory, though it can also be used to counter hegemonic views of land (Massey 1995, 2005).

The form of maps is never neutral and objective, although 'traditional' cartography constructs and promotes this myth (Harley 1992). Mark Monmonier comments that "Not only is it easy to lie with maps, it's essential. [...] a map must distort reality" (1996: 1). Critical cartography deconstructs the powerful decisions made when constructing a map: "selection, omission, simplification, classification, the creation of hierarchies, and 'symbolization'" (Harley 1992: 243). It pays attention to the historical and social contexts of their production by deconstructing maps as texts. More recently, post-representational cartography gives greater emphasis to the performative and practised nature of maps and mapping (Rossetto 2014). From this perspective, "maps are viewed and researched as contingent, relational, embodied, fluid entities that are performed and manipulated by users in their meanings as well as in their concrete material consistency" (514).

Christina Ljungberg and Tania Rossetto draw on critical and post-representational perspectives to engage with maps and mapping in contemporary fiction. Ljungberg points out that including maps "allows writers to develop additional meaning by means of a non-sequential two-dimensional semiotic system, different from the linear, one-dimensional system of writing" (2003: 173, see also Rossetto 2014). In the three island stories we consider, the three cartographic perspectives described above are useful as epistemic reference points for exploring maps and mapping as artefact and process. Each book includes maps (whether reproduced for the reader or not) and acts of mapping. Some of these maps are external to the narrative, or extradiegetic, while others appear as artefacts within the narrative. In several cases, the extradiegetic/intradiegetic function is shifted as the narrative progresses, and their status becomes ambiguous. The tension between the reproduced map and its ekphrasis – verbal description in the text – also varies. The chosen texts, thus, offer a range of possibilities to consider the role of maps in island narratives.

Islands in children's literature

Islands have been a particularly popular topos in children's literature, not least in the adventure mode; some famous and less famous examples are *Robinson Crusoe* (1719), *Gulliver's Travels* (1726), *The Coral Island* (1858), *The Mysterious Island* (1874), *Treasure Island* (1883), *Peter Pan* (1911), *Island of the Blue Dolphins* (1960), and *Moominpappa at Sea* (1965), all of which feature maps. From a cognitive-affective perspective, an island is a highly stimulating fictional setting since in order to understand how it works, readers are expected to use their imagination, employing life-to-text projection, that is, transposing their knowledge of the actual world to explore the fictional world. While this is true of any fictional world, the island offers additional challenges because of its physical limitations and isolation. The attraction of the island as a setting for children's literature is its carnivalesque potential: the protagonist, an outsider, is temporarily placed – or rather displaced – in a space that is unfamiliar, probably hostile. As with all carnivalesque narratives, the island setting empowers the protagonist who is liberated not only from parental protection, but also from familiar societal constraints, only to find themselves in a new social framework that needs negotiation. Although in *Gullstruck Island* the arrival on the island lies beyond the plot, the spatial isolation creates the carnivalesque framework of the narrative. Our three texts are part of a long tradition, which they, however, develop in a variety of manners. Further, the non-mimetic nature of these texts allows liberties in representation of spatiality that amplify, again in a carnivalesque manner, characteristics of islandness, as well as social and interpersonal conflicts portrayed.

Thus, the reason we have chosen texts set on islands is the particular characteristics of simultaneously delineated and yet blurred spatiality, where elements such as belonging/not belonging, time/space connections and interactions, mythical and contemporary world, nature/culture, displacement and spatial marginalisation are prominent. Islands are common topoi in fiction because they allow both a metaphorical and a metonymic depiction of society. Since they are isolated from the rest of the world, it is plausible to create a world with its own rules, untouched by the outside environment or deliberately having detached itself from it.

In Hardinge's *Gullstruck Island*, metonymy is conspicuous: the island is a simplified model of a complex, multicultural society which, although depicted as pre-modern and containing supernatural elements, is otherwise a reflection of modern Western civilization. There is a world outside Gullstruck; thus, it is not a detached universe. The tropical island was colonized two centuries ago by invaders from colder climates with a highly peculiar ancestor cult which has formed the social and partly physical structure of this fictional world. Since then, the invaders lost touch with their home country, and the map reinforces this change by not showing any indication of anything outside Gullstruck, though a primitive compass rose pointing to the North hints at the world beyond. The links to the outside world have, in practice, been severed, and the island is now a self-contained world. It is not clear from the text whether the island is a remote part of the actual world or an imaginary, alternative world.

In Sedgwick's *Midwinterblood*, the island represents a part of a larger society that has deliberately isolated itself from the rest of the world – a persistent motif in myth and literature, connected with the idea of the land of immortality. The outside world exists, and although the first and the last parts are projected into the future, the fictional world represents the actual world geographically, historically and culturally: the United Kingdom and Germany are explicitly mentioned, and some historical events, such as the Second World War, play an important role.

In Morpurgo's *Kensuke's Kingdom*, two characters stranded on an island represent a clash of cultures, generations and ideologies. For Kensuke, a Japanese military officer shipwrecked on a Pacific island during the Second World War, the involuntary isolation successively develops into deliberate decision. In a way, he chooses symbolic immortality by rejecting the flow of time: he is not even aware that the war is over. Michael, on the contrary, perceives his isolation as captivity and longs to return to civilization and his own world. The outside world, again, is an accurate reflection of the actual world, and, unlike the two other texts, some of the action takes place in a concrete geographical location in the United Kingdom. Moreover, at the end of the novel, the protagonist returns to his initial location, in the conventional circular, carnivalesque movement of children's literature: home – away – home. Our three islands, then, represent a continuum from a totally isolated, self-contained world, to a world that is isolated, but with the outside world existing in the periphery, to an actual world containing a fictional island.

In all three novels, maps play a central and, we would argue, highly original role. The texts are obviously fictional, but fictional texts can, and often do, offer maps of real places. In our texts, maps represent purely imaginary places, non-signifiers in relationship to actual, observable reality. There is a more authentic map in *Kensuke's Kingdom*, to which we will return; yet the map portraying the place of action and the main conflict is imaginary. The maps both contribute to and question fictionality. Generally, maps have authority; they create a sense, albeit potentially misleading, of "reality", especially for young readers who may lack the knowledge of the actual world and therefore rely on the status of maps as an "authentic" representation. However, for an informed reader, a fictional map subverts authenticity and alerts the reader to fictionality. This tension between the purported authenticity of a map as an accurate representation of the actual world and the ambiguity of a deliberately fictional representation creates a challenging cognitive-affective situation, in which attention, imagination, memory and other cognitive activity is stimulated. Maps, therefore, contribute to the dialogics and hybridity, in Bakhtin's sense, of the text.

Within the novels that, except for *Kensuke's Kingdom*, have no illustrations apart from covers, maps carry the only visual information available to the reader. The presence of visual elements immediately creates tension between the verbal and the visual, typically focused on in picturebook, comics, and graphic novel research, but also in studies of illustrated texts. Let us remember that visual elements in a narrative can be merely decorative, or they can be an integral part of the text, where their removal would affect readers' understanding and engagement. Further, the integral visual elements can be more or less symmetrical with the verbal, that is, provide identical or similar information; they can be complementary or enhancing; and they can also be contradictory or counterpointing (see Nikolajeva & Scott 2001). From the point of view of text/image interaction, our three texts demonstrate a wide range of options.

Gullstruck Island

The map in *Gullstruck Island* appears, as in many conventional map-featuring novels, at the beginning of the book (Figure 1). It would seem that its primary function is to assist the reader's orientation in the fictional world. As demonstrated by neuroscience, visual information affects our brains quicker and more immediately than verbal (see Evans 2001: 25ff.); thus the map, preceding the verbal narrative in *Gullstruck Island*, provides an instant anchorage in the fictional world. Following the tradition of maps in children's fiction, readers may assume that, while the map is doubtless useful to consult as the story progresses, it is not indispensable for the narrative and external to it; that it is extradiegetic in the sense that it does not appear within the narrative. This will eventually prove incorrect; yet let us first consider what the map, perceived as extradiegetic, offers to the reader.

Figure 1. Map from Frances Hardinge: *Gullstruck Island*. London: Macmillan, 2009. Reproduced with author's permission.

The map is symbolic rather than iconic, and as such demands cartographic literacy. The text/image interaction is complementary: the map provides additional information, for instance, featuring spaces not covered by the characters' movement, but mentioned in the verbal narrative, such as the capital, Port Suddenwind, and the island of Mother Tooth. The map gives the general idea about the shape of the island with its ragged coastline, which, apart from a very small portion, is unvisited within the narrative. But in the first place, the map is helpful to follow the characters' trajectories, in Doreen Massey's (2005) terms, in the landscape of the island, since it shows the landmarks mentioned in the text: the villages and towns, the volcanoes and other geographical features. It helps to grasp the mutual position of these landmarks and the relative distances between them. Since the map shows the features that the characters interact with in their journeys, the map has some narrative function and is thus temporal as well as spatial: every point is specific to a character's position in time and space. Further, since there are several central characters in the novel, the map shows where their trajectories intersect and diverge.

In *Gullstruck Island*, the map can be viewed as an attempt at objectivity, in stark contrast with the verbally constructed spatiality, which does not only refer to the physical environment, but to the social and interpersonal environment, laden with conflicts and power hierarchies. The initial map does not reflect the complex social structure of the fictional world, portrayed in minute details in the verbal text: the invisible boundaries between the various tribes and nations of the island; the particular type of landscape they favor; the languages they speak and the spiritual rites they practice; the stories they connect with landscape features, particularly volcanoes; the bizarre territorial struggle between the living and the dead.

Maps and mapping are a recurrent theme in *Gullstruck Island* as the underpinning of the whole plot is a struggle over land. The Cavelcaste colonial group came to the island to find more land for enshrining the ashes of their ancestors. However, land becomes short in Gullstruck, as much of it is either covered in jungle or is on the slopes of active and unpredictable volcanoes. As the Cavelcaste population grew (and their dead "population" too), the towns have enlarged and the farms been pushed further into marginal land. This farmland is also needed by the indigenous population groups, such as the Lace. Additionally, the Lace have knowledge of danger areas for the volcanoes (passed on through legends), which the Cavelcaste have ignored. This led to such a pressure on farmland that the Cavelcaste elite had been kidnapping Lace to mine on a nearby island, earning money to trade for food, as well as pruning down competitors. When the struggles came to a head, they also transported the Lace to resettlement "farms" – in plain words, labour camps – right in the path of the volcanoes.

One interesting facet of the story and the affordances of characters is the changes in scale and vantage point. These connect with mapping. For example, the opening sequence follows the Lost – a kind of shaman – Raglan Skein as his mind skims over the island checking the route his body will take on a journey to the Lace coast. Although he is not physically mapping at the time, his mind and the account takes the classic "god's-eye view" of the mapmaker. The narrator comments on how this zoomed-out perspective simplifies the island: "It was a relief to see the world plummet away from him so that everything became smaller. More manageable. Less dangerous" (Hardinge 2010: 1–2).

Zooming in and out is a feature of the book even after the majority of the Lost have died, as the reader follows the protagonist Hathin's perspective on her journey up and over three volcanoes, and later on the mapmaker Bridle's maps give the zoomed-out view. The story alternates the two for shorter or longer periods. For example, after Skein's original zoomed-out overview, the story descends to the emotional complexity of the Lace village. Whilst the Lace do not have maps in the standard sense, their stories are guides to a landscape previously unknown to the character, so Hathin knows the way through a cave system through the Legend of the Rivals (141), and the legends of the volcanoes are topographic in nature. The zooming-out perspective gives overview, clarity, pinned-down knowledge, whilst the zooming-in perspective gives complex, messy, often indigenous knowledge, wrapped up in myth, story, experience and emotion.

This complicated social world is not represented on the initial map, for instance, through indicating the names of the tribes, which is otherwise common in fictional maps (for instance, J. R. R. Tolkien, C. S. Lewis or Ursula Le Guin). Whether it is a conscious decision or simply an omission is of less consequence in the beginning of the text. What is interesting, however, is that while the reader can go back to the map to check where exactly the characters are at any given moment and where they are in relation to each other, there is no indication of their trespassing on social boundaries (something clearly emphasized on the map in *Kensuke's Kingdom* as we will show).

However, the diegetic status of the map suddenly changes halfway through the novel, since it appears as an artefact within the narrative. Moreover, it turns out that maps and map-making are well known in the fictional world of the novel. As the narrative progresses, maps acquire a more central role, not only in the material world of the novel, but also in its social world. For instance, the protagonist learns that a certain town is featured on maps with a different name than it is known by (173). Place names reflect the tribes' relationship to and ownership of the landscape. A mapmaker's shop is a meeting point where essential information is obtained by the various actors of the narrative, and while the mapmaker himself is dead, possibly murdered, his maps serve the villains and the heroes to the same degree. Maps are also used as an appeal to external and objective truth, for example the Reckoning Leader, Dance, shows a map to the former nuisance-control officer to back up her story of the Lace disappearances. Moreover, the making of the maps turns out to be the pivotal point of the whole plot:

> And then a Lost mapmaker called Bridle noticed. He'd been watching the volcanoes [...] painting a new map of them every week, because he'd seen them starting to move, changing shape. And so he spotted the new buildings on Mother Tooth. I think *that's* the reason the Lost were killed. They found out that there were secret forced mines on the volcanoes [...] and that the volcanoes were waking up. (468)

This shifts the plot onto the issues of land ownership and competition over resources. The Cavelcaste leaders did not wish the indigenous people to know about the plans for their further subjection in order that the Cavelcaste community could survive into the future.

The map at the beginning of the novel, thus, appears to be intradiegetic, an object existing within the fictional world. Moreover, the blanks on the map are not coincidental: some of the important places, including the location of several tribes and the secret camps of the revengers, the tiding huts where shamans exchange information, or the school that fosters the shamans, and not least the roads connecting these places, are not indicated. The numerous, poetically-sounding geographical places, that the characters pass through, such as Knotted Tail, Leaping Waters, and Wild Man's Cradle, are not featured either. And yet, in the later part of the novel, the characters constantly consult their maps to gain advantage over their antagonists. Map-reading becomes a key to survival. This is an unexpected turn in the narrative showing how the seemingly decorative visual element, a map at the beginning of the book, is gradually integrated into the narrative itself. For the reader, access to the map from the beginning aligns them cognitively with the heroes as well as their adversaries; the map thus supports the multiple narrative perspective of the text.

As always, mapping or other ordering of land is a powerful act. The Cavelcaste Nuisance Control Officer "reshapes the world with his pencil" (323) to pin down the Lace to particular areas (375). However, the mapmaker Bridle used his Lost powers to map the activity of the volcanoes and the topography of the mines, enabling the Lost to gain powerful knowledge of the Cavelcaste plot and the likely timescale of eruptions. The Lost were then murdered for this knowledge. The subaltern Lace lead by Hathin gain knowledge of the plots by connecting together Bridle's maps with various other clues. Their response also includes mapped knowledge, for example, they mark locations of Cavelcaste protagonists on a map for the Reckoning to capture (316). The Lace's knowledge enables them to overthrow the Cavelcaste leaders and to create seeds of a new order where the dead are no longer given precedence over land and a more sustainable future is possible for the living.

Kensuke's Kingdom

The two maps in *Kensuke's Kingdom* are seemingly also used in a conventional manner; one to support the account of the character/narrator's voyage around the world; the other to provide the visual setting of the island on which he is shipwrecked. The map of the route appears at the back of the novel, together with Glossary and Author's afterword (Figure 2). It is, therefore, natural to perceive it as another extradiegetic map, provided for the reader to follow the plot. The route is clearly marked, from the starting point in England, calling at Spain, West Africa, Brazil, Cape, rounding the Southern coast of Australia and ending abruptly among Pacific islands as Michael is washed overboard. The major ocean currents are indicated with arrows and identified through their verbal nicknames, such as Roaring Forties. The map is slightly more iconic than the one in *Gullstruck Island*, showing a whale, flying fish and sharks, and the boat in the middle of the Indian Ocean. These images possibly create a temporal mini-narrative, reflecting certain episodes in Michael's account; however, they mostly have a decorative function, echoing the images of sea monsters on authentic historical maps.

However, at a closer consideration, the map is not merely an informative tool for the reader. It looks like a blank map where Michael, as part of his

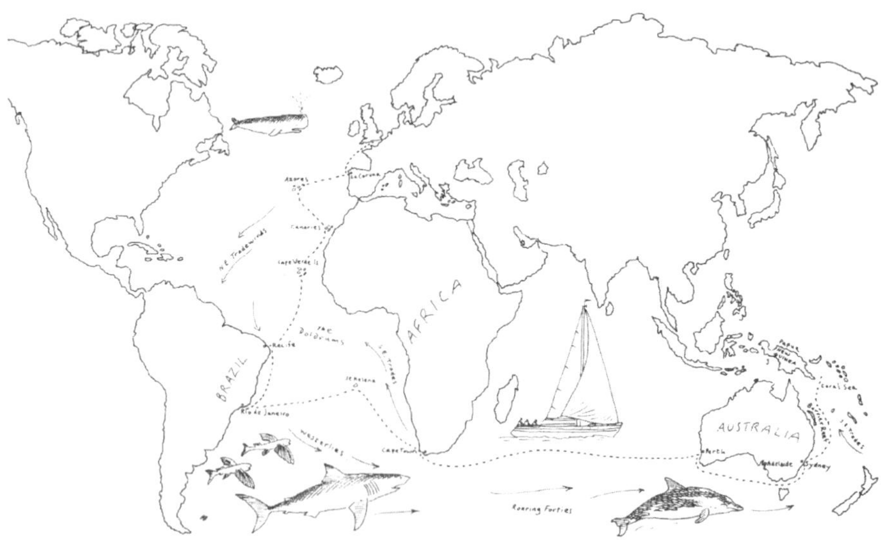

Figure 2. Map from Michael Morpurgo: *Kensuke's Kingdom*. Illustrated by Michael Foreman. London: Egmont, 2004. Illustrations copyright © 1999 Michael Foreman. Published by Egmont UK Limited and used with permission

home-schooling – or should we say boat-schooling – has filled in, lazily, the names for Brazil, Africa and Australia, while the rest of the world remains, literally, blank. This de-contextualization of the voyage reflects this stage of the protagonist's identity formation; his initial reluctance to go on the voyage and his lack of interest contrasting with the environmental, social, and interpersonal lessons he learns on the island. The final map, then, can be viewed as intradiegetic, an integral part of the narrative, created by the narrator and reflecting his subjective perception of space. Moreover, it is anticipated within the text by fragments, alongside conventional illustrations and Michael's sketches. Put together, these fragments add up to the map at the end of the book. This creates a radically different word/image tension, since the map and the fragments offer a parallel narrative, both complementing and contradicting the verbal story. Michael's diary is full of gaps, and the events and places he describes are seemingly random. Large portions of the voyage are omitted altogether, However, a map of the world in the twentieth century, even a blank one, cannot simply contain empty spaces like a historical map might; therefore the map compensates for the omissions in the narrator's verbal discourse, but, since it is also a product of his non-verbal narration, it is just as subjective, unreliable and self-contradictory.

The map of the island, appearing as the frontispiece of the novel and thus preceding the turning point of the plot, is more complex and becomes a significant counterpointing visual narrative, focused on the issues of power, inclusion/exclusion and place-related identity formation (Figure 3). This map is undoubtedly intradiegetic, drawn by the narrator who refers to himself in first person, in captions: "My end", "My first fire", as well as in legends: "My first landing place", "The cave where I spent my first night". Again, the various elements of the map are temporally and sequentially determined. It is not clear at what point during his sojourn on the island Michael draws the map; since he has lost his possessions and stopped writing his journal, it is possible that the map is created later, on his return home. In any case, the physical map is anticipated by Kensuke's drawing in sand:

> He was drawing an outline of something [...] It was a map of the island [...]. Then, very deliberately, he etched out a straight line, top to bottom, cutting the smaller end of the island off from the larger one.
> "You, boy. You here," he said [...] "Kensuke. I, Kensuke. My island". (77)

The personal claim of space and subsequent negotiations between Michael and Kensuke form the central conflict of the narrative. The map is highly iconic, reflecting not only the features of the landscape, but various events of the narrative. It is, therefore, a dynamic map, portraying the various moments of the protagonist's exploration of physical and social space in simultaneous succession.

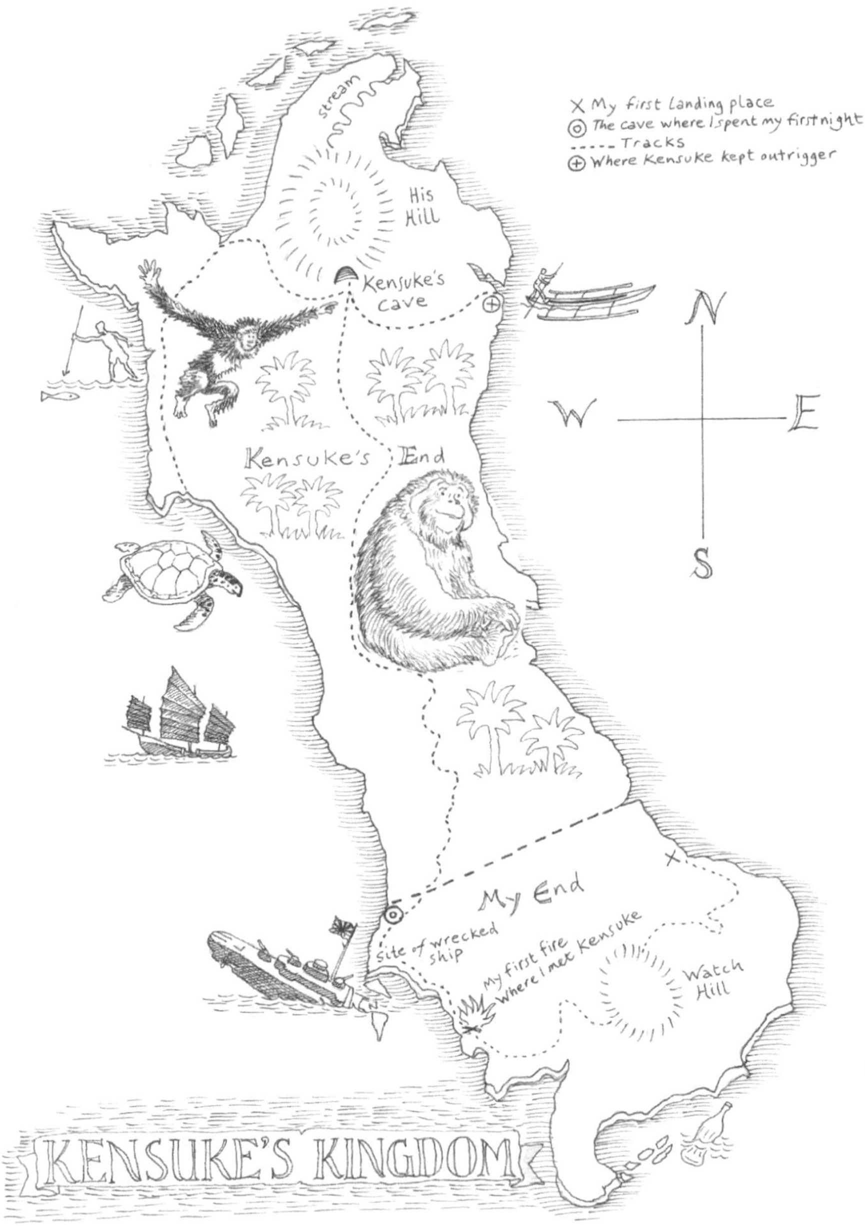

Figure 3. Map on the frontispiece of Michael Morpurgo: *Kensuke's Kingdom*. Illustrated by Michael Foreman. London: Egmont, 2004. Illustrations copyright © 1999 Michael Foreman. Published by Egmont UK Limited and used with permission

Midwinterblood

Finally, in *Midwinterblood*, the actual map is not included in the text, yet it is an indispensable part of the narrative itself. The map is an ekphrasis, a verbal representation of a visual representation, as such twice removed from the reader. It is initially presented through external and internal focalization: Eric, the protagonist of the first chapter, looks at it and contemplates it.

The lack of a map of Blessed/Blood Island is a deliberate reinforcement of the plot, as a key element is the disorientation or dislocation of a character, particularly in parts 1 and 3. Instead we share the developing understanding of the island of the outcomers (Eric in part 1, David in part 3) as they struggle to figure out where they are. This work of orientation is most pronounced and explicit in the case of the journalist, Eric, as he explores the island looking for the secret production facility of the dragon orchid, rumoured to be an elixir of life. The sense of mystery and confusion is heightened by the loss of the digital map that Eric brought with him, when his PDA battery fails and his charger has mysteriously disappeared. He requests a map from an islander, and receives one which looks official (in that "it is printed and there's a title and a price on the back of it", Sedgwick 2011: 32), but he realizes that it is incomplete and does not match his memory of the digital map. The assumption that a printed and purchased map would be complete and accurate is an interesting one, and the realisation that this assumption is incorrect adds to the reader's experience of disorientation as norms are undercut.

> He realises that the map in front of him is not the same as the one he had recorded back in the office.
> That one had two halves, a very distinct shape, like the two wings of a butterfly, though the western half slightly smaller, giving it a lopsided look. The two halves were joined by a narrow strip of land.
> Eric looks at the paper map in his hand. Only the eastern part of the island is printed. Half the island is missing.
> Now why, he thinks, would they print a map of only half of the island?
> That would be stupid. Unless, unless, unless you wanted to keep half of it secret. (32)

As it turns out, Eric's guess is correct, and the western part of the island is indeed a well-kept secret of the islanders, the part where the mysterious orchids grow, and where most of the key episodes of the novel take place.

Since the map is never made available for the reader, neither extradiegetically nor intradiegetically, the cognitive engagement it invites is extremely intense: readers need to use imagination to reproduce the map in their minds and, moreover, keep it firmly in their minds throughout the rest of the novel, since it is required for understanding the plot, the character construction and the central ideological thrust of the novel. The cognitive function of memory is therefore necessary to follow the changes of landscape, physical, social and interpersonal. The map as a material object is not present in any chapter except the first. However, it implicitly exists throughout all the historical levels, gradually revealed, as the narrative progresses in reverse chronology. Geography and landscape are essential for plot development.

In parts 1 and 3 in particular, there are many references to wayfinding, journeys, landmarks, and compass directions as the lead characters try to make sense of their surroundings. However, these are hard to join up, and the lack of a definitive map in the book does not allow the reader the luxury of being in the know, being able to pinpoint the protagonist's location even when the character is themselves unaware, as is possible in many books with maps. Instead, the shape of the island emerges particularly as Eric's mind clears and he fights physical and mental barriers to access the western half of the island.

Whilst information given in the book would allow a simple map of Blessed/Blood Island to be constructed, the two dimensions would not do justice to a story which is intricately interlinked through four dimensions. Instead, the reader is left to piece together the puzzle of a journey in space-time through the seven lifetimes of Eric and Merle, navigating through the recurring motifs such as sacrifice and figures such as hares and dragons, to recognize points of intersection in their relationship across the centuries.

The status of the setting and thus the map is ambiguous. It alludes to the various myths of Hyperborea, the happy land in the North, beyond known physical or human geography; therefore the ambiguity of the fictional map is not altogether implausible. The island may easily be one of the many small islands off Svalbard. The port of Skarpness from which Eric takes the ferry in part 1 does not match any existing place, but since the episode is set in the distant future, the place name may have been corrupted. It pretends to sound authentic, and the whole set-up suggests a realist, authentic, or at least quasi-authentic world. Although the authenticity is subverted by the futuristic backdrop, subsequent chapters mention places beyond the island that, even if not named explicitly, suggests both real geography and history. The island is consistently throughout the novel presented as an actual place, existing, apart from the futuristic chapter, in an actual time.

The setting is not merely integral for the plot, but the very engine of the plot; a meeting place and the cause of all events. The seven chapters and epilogue take place on the island in different times of history, going back from year 2073 all the way into "Time unknown", presumably Iron Age from which the midwinter sacrifice legend originates; possibly the ninth century, not long before Christianity reached Scandinavia. The fictitious map is therefore multilayered, reflecting the multiplicity of historical periods.

Temporally, then, the novel presents an unusual, although not unique pattern of moving backwards in time. This movement implies that the environment and the characters' trajectories, in Massey's terms, go in opposite directions. Although seemingly static in space, the island has its trajectory that unfolds backwards in the narrative. The church-like building that Eric sees in ruins in part 1 is whole and inhabited in part 4, but built on the ruins of a much more ancient sacred site. The enigma of the Viking grave discovered by the archaeologists in part 2 – a skeleton of an adult holding a skeleton of a child – is revealed in part 6 that takes place in the Viking era, explaining the remains of wood as the stakes used to kill the vampire. The unexploded bomb that nearly kills the archaeologists in part 2 is dropped by aeroplanes during the Second World War, described in Part 3. The whole novel is reminiscent of an archaeological excavation, digging deeper and deeper into the many cultural layers of the island. After the first two chapters, the reader is expected to recognize the setting, and it is not described in detail any more, although some significant features are repeatedly highlighted, particularly the western part of the island where the mysterious orchids bloom.

And yet, although the setting is sufficiently revealed to the reader, the material map featured through ekphrasis in the first chapter is deliberately distorted. While the island itself is formed like a butterfly, only one half of it is represented on the map. This significant absence can be viewed as a separation of space into sacred and profane, and the most important events and encounters happen in the sacred half, not represented on the map. Ultimately, the novel features a mystery plot with a clear spatial dimension: all clues are found on the missing half of the map. The reader's task becomes to keep track of the geographical features of the island as well as its history and social structures.

Significantly, the novel contains another ekphrasis, the eponymous *Midwinterblood*, more correctly, *Midvinterblot* (Midwinter Sacrifice), a 1915 painting, at present in the National Museum in Stockholm, by the Swedish artist Carl Larsson, portrayed in the novel under the transparent name Eric Carlsson. Like the map, the ekphrasis alludes to something authentic, yet makes no definite statements. This controversial piece of art depicts the central and dramatic moment of an ancient legend, in this case derived from Norse mythology, but occurring widely in various cultures: a king is sacrificed in time of famine to ensure future harvest. The painting was at the time of its creation criticized for inaccuracies and anachronisms, but it is a powerful and overwhelming piece that has fascinated generations of viewers and critics (Gunnarsson 2008). In the afterword, Sedgwick provides some background about the painting, including the fact that the Swedish word "blot" means "sacrifice" rather than "blood", even though the words undeniably are related etymologically.

The painting is introduced in the novel twice; initially in the first part, without further detail. The full ekphrasis appears in part 4, that takes place in 1902, when Eric Carlsson the painter dies in his temple-like house on the western – hidden, sacred, unmapped – half of the island, just after putting the finishing touches to his masterpiece. Finally, in part 7, in "time unknown" we witness the actual sacrifice scene that has inspired the painter. While the painting has a slightly different narrative function in the novel than the map, it is equally demanding on the reader's attention. Narratively, like the map and the island itself, it is continuous rather than static, and although seemingly portraying a single event, represents the recurrent actions, possibly interrupted by the final sacrifice. Moreover, like the map, the painting exists as a material object in the chronologically later, but narratively earlier chapters, while the very last chapter describes the event that inspired the painting, a human sacrifice. The painting thus becomes a complement and a counterpoint to the map, an unuttered visual experience shared by the reader and a number of fictional characters.

The cross-disciplinary approach to the selected text has proved fruitful as it enabled us to explore the representation and function of maps in the selected texts from a variety of mutually complementing perspectives. From a consideration of these three island narratives, we have seen that their maps, even when they may initially seem extradiegetic, are profoundly implicated in the production of the narrative. This is not surprising because maps are never neutral, objective, and external, even when they are pretending hard to be so. A map is always political, in that it is produced by a particular person at a particular time for a particular reason, within a complex web of power relations. The very act of mapping, the choices of selection and focus, is a powerful act. However, in these stories, we also see maps as sites of resistance, subversion, and transgression, as individuals or groups who are not in conventional positions of power, use them to challenge the dominant individuals or groups, with different forms of success. Thus the maps and acts of mapping in these books are deployed in subtle ways to produce complex narratives of space-time. The comparison between the three texts reveals a range of possibilities in terms of verbal/visual and extradiegetic/intradiegetic tension, which points at creative and imaginative use of this artistic device by the authors we have discussed.

References

Primary sources

Hardinge, Frances. 2010. *Gullstruck Island*. London: Macmillan (first published 2009).
Morpurgo, Michael. 2004. *Kensuke's Kingdom*. London: Egmont (first published 1999).
Sedgwick, Marcus. 2011. *Midwinterblood*. London: Orion.

Secondary sources

Baldacchino, Godfrey. 2006. Islands, island studies, island studies journal. *Island Studies Journal* 1(1): 3–18.
Beer, Gillian. 1989. Discourses of the island. In *Literature and Science as Modes of Expression*, Frederick Amrine (ed.), 1–27. Dordrecht: Kluwer. doi: 10.1007/978-94-009-2297-6_1
Conkling, P. 2007. On islanders and islandness. *The Geographical Review* 97(2): 191–201. doi: 10.1111/j.1931-0846.2007.tb00398.x
Conrad, Philip. 2009. *Islands: A Trip through Time and Space*. London: Thames and Hudson.
Dodds, Klaus & Royle, Stephen. 2003. Introduction: Rethinking islands. *Journal of Historical Geography*, 29(4): 487–498. doi: 10.1006/jhge.2002.0406
Evans, Dylan. 2001. *Emotions. A Very Short Introduction*. Oxford: OUP.
Fletcher, Lisa. 2011. "...some distance to go": A critical survey of island studies. *New Literatures Review, Islands Special Issue* 17–34. <http://www.islandstudies.ca/NLR2011> (15 June 2016).
Fog Olwig, Karen. 2007. Islands as places of being and belonging. *The Geographical Review* 97(2): 260–273. doi: 10.1111/j.1931-0846.2007.tb00402.x
Gunnarsson, Torsten. 2008. *Carl Larsson*, translated by Mora Naylor. Stockholm: Nationalmuseum.
Harley, J. Brian. 1992. Deconstructing the map. Reprinted in *Writing Worlds: Discourse, Text and Metaphor in the Representation of Landscape*, Trevor Barnes & James Duncan (eds), 231–247. London: Routledge (first published 1989).
Hay, Pete. 2006. A phenomenology of islands. *Island Studies Journal* 1(1): 19–42.
King, Russell. 1993. The geographical fascination of islands. In *The Development Process in Small Island States*, Douglas Lockhardt, David Drakakis-Smith & John Schembri (eds), 13–37. London: Routledge.
Ljungberg, Christina. 2003. Constructing new "realities": The performative function of maps in contemporary fiction. In *Representing Realities: Essays on American Literature, Art and Culture*, Beverly Maeder (ed.), 159–176. Tübingen: Gunter Narr.
Massey, Doreen. 1995. Imagining the world. In *Geographical Worlds*, John Allen & Doreen Massey (eds), 5–52. Oxford: Open University/OUP.
Massey, Doreen. 2005. *For Space*. London: Sage.
Monmonier, Mark. 1996. *How to Lie with Maps*. Chicago IL: University of Chicago Press. doi: 10.7208/chicago/9780226029009.001.0001
Nikolajeva, Maria & Scott, Carole. 2001. *How Picturebooks Work*. New York NY: Garland.
Rossetto, Tania. 2014. Theorizing maps with literature. *Progress in Human Geography* 38(4): 513–530. doi: 10.1177/0309132513510587
Royle, Stephen. 2001. *A geography of islands: Small island insularity*. London: Routledge.
Savory, Elaine. 2011. Utopia, Dystopia, and Caribbean Heterotopia: Writing/reading the small island. *New Literatures Review, Islands special issue* 35–56. <http://www.islandstudies.ca/NLR2011>

CHAPTER 11

Mapping illusions

Between the child's fantasy world of Lev Kassil's *Schwambrania* and the geography of a fledgling Soviet state

Olga Mikhaylova

This chapter examines the artistic functions of the visual and verbal depiction of a child's fantasy country in Lev Kassil's novel *Schwambrania* (1933) against the background of the state's interest in geography and cartography. After a short overview of the political circumstances that accompanied the reforms in Soviet cartography, this chapter applies Harley's approach to the interpretation of the two maps of the child's fantasy world of Schwambrania, considering the graphic and linguistic components of these maps and their description in the text, and, in addition, reconstructing the different types of context relevant to Kassil's book.

It can hardly be said that maps in the Soviet literature for children and young adults of the 1930s have been extensively studied in previous research. This seems unusual for an era that was marked by the proclaimed geographical predominance of the fledgling Soviet state and hence an era in which increased attention was devoted to geography and cartography. Much of the difficulty of interpreting the role of maps (be they textually described or visual) in Lev Kassil's *Shvambraniia* (Schwambrania, 1933) lies in the tendency to label the work as exclusively satirical and humorous and thus lacking any inherent sociological or ideological components. For instance, some Soviet critics explored the origin of toponyms in the map of Schwambrania in relation to their humorous and satirical possibilities and intentions (Loiter 1979; Zubareva 1968). Loiter also provided a detailed analysis of the fictional sources that provided names for Schwambranian settings, characters, and events (1979: 189–203). However, according to John Brian Harley, the analysis of a map (its caption, the chapter of which it is a part, and its individual signs, symbols, or decorative emblems) cannot divorce the map from its context (Harley

DOI 10.1075/clcc.7.12mik

2001: 47). I will consider the close correlation of the historical, social, and political contexts with aesthetic issues in Kassil's creative world, and with his mapmaking in particular. This approach makes Harley's tripartite model of contextualization an appropriate theoretical and methodological starting point for this chapter.

Harley states that "maps are text in the same senses that other nonverbal sign systems – paintings, prints, theatre, films, television, music – are texts. [...] Maps are a graphic language to be decoded. They are a construction of reality, images laden with intentions and consequences that can be studied in the societies of their time" (2001: 36). In interpreting maps as texts, Harley assigns a special value to context, since a map is not an isolated object. He goes on to delineate three aspects of context that intersect with the reading of maps as texts: "the context of the cartographer, the context of other maps, and the context of society" (38). The first type establishes the mapmaker's intention and "the relationship between the facts of map-makers' lives and what appears on the map" (38). The context of other maps can be revealed through reference to the wider cartographic output of an age, since "maps are often representations of time as much as space" (44). The third type of context – that of society – presupposes an exploration of maps within the framework of specific historical circumstances and conditions. The present chapter, taking Harley's model into account, explores the artistic functions of the verbal and visual geographical and cartographical material of Kassil's book with reference to these three types of context.

Contextualizing Kassil's mapping

Before introducing "the context of the cartographer" for Kassil, it is important to place his mapping within the social context "provided by contemporaneous attitudes towards mapping, map-reading and map-making" (Cooper 2012: 34). According to the title page of the first edition, *Schwambrania* was first published in 1933, though the dust jacket indicates 1932. Kassil started writing this novel at the end of 1930, as he informed his parents in a letter dated December 1, 1930. Kassil's letters to his parents are published in Taratuta (1979). It was the beginning of the 1930s when the status of geography and cartography was fundamentally changed due to incipient reforms. Galina Orlova has collected a multitude of resources concerning these reforms and synthesized her work in several essays (2006, 2008). The main points of her research help to crystallize the context of *Schwambrania*'s publication.

As Orlova states, geography in the 1930s was transformed from a marginal discipline into a powerful tool of political propaganda. It was allotted a central position in school curricula of the time. The reform of school geography was marked by a turn towards physical geography, with its focus on visualization. Schools enthusiastically started to use globes, pictures, photos, films, and models as possible media for overcoming "visual poverty" (2008: 88). The principle of generalization in Soviet school cartography meant that all insignificant details had to be deleted from the map (Orlova 2006: 91). Generalization presented in this way revealed and imposed a hierarchical principal of space arrangement: the most important things should be highlighted, and the least important obscured. Maps that did not meet this requirement were criticized as being "monotonous" (96–97). As Orlova encapsulates it, cartographic reality and the ways in which it was perceived were severely controlled and even falsified. A young map reader was expected to see objects that did not exist. For example, some objects that had only been planned for construction were automatically represented as already completed on the maps, in accordance with the policy of the five-year-plan (91). The social context of mapping unveiled by Orlova clearly reflects the idea that "behind the map maker lies a set of power relations, creating its own specification" (Harley 2001: 63). And this specification is addressed primarily to children.

It was not only the maps in schoolchildren's textbooks that labored in the service of the state and started to "perform the state" (Wood 2012: 284); maps in popular magazines for adults and children also had political agendas. For example, the *Vokrug Sveta* (Around the World) magazine, starting in 1927, mostly included maps that glorify Soviet achievements in discovering new lands in the Arctic region or in testing ways of territorial control, such as aviation. In 1925 the first issue of *Vsemirnyi Sledopyt* (The Worldwide Pathfinder) was published; it featured various "adventurous" stories including maps. This journal often expressed the concept of oppression in colonial countries through pictures of maps. The same idea was also rather popular in some journals for children. The "Map of World Slavery" (Figure 1) was printed in the first issue of *Pioner* (The Pioneer) magazine in 1931.

The main idea of this map was to demonstrate that different types of slavery existed in the majority of the world's countries. Only "one sixth of the world" – the USSR – is not labeled as having slavery. The USSR is proclaimed a "country of free labor" in a bold-print caption below the map. The map leaves out Antarctica, as a territory where there are no slaves, but it thus expands the "presence" of the USSR on the map through the distortion of the northern polar region, which is vastly enlarged beyond its actual dimensions. Orlova notes that the project of exploring the polar regions in the 1930s was perceived as "embodying the spirit of Soviet utopia" (2006: 82). She observes that the authorities appropriated the methods of distorting cartographical images in order to "naturalize" the main ideological constructions of the era. A map such as this one embraces deliberate distortions of the map's content for political purposes and co-opts all the relevant ideas being disseminated in other parts of the official press. In spite of its conventionality, this

Figure 1. "Map of World Slavery". In *Pioner* (The Pioneer) 1931: 4

map exemplifies the thesis that maps in textbooks were not the only tools of visual politics. Significantly, extracts from *Schwambrania* were also printed in the same issue of *Pioner* that contained the "Map of World Slavery." This was the first publication of any part of the novel that was intended for children. As the cartographer of his fictitious Schwambrania, Kassil linked his verbal and visual maps within the book to the social and political order of a particular period and place. Thus, voluntarily or not, Kassil reflected in his story the idea that a map can be more than just a representation of a geographical space, and demonstrated the power of maps to express ideological values.

Authorial mapping in *Schwambrania*: The first map of an imaginary state

An examination of Kassil's representations of Schwambrania requires comparatively little comment on the content of the novel itself. The story's action is set in two dimensions. The realistic dimension takes place in the provincial Russian town of Pokrovsk and encompasses the period from the eve of World War I, the Bolshevik Revolution, through the subsequent years up to 1932, when the novel was published; these last years are depicted in the epilogue. The main characters of the novel, Lev and Osip, who are to some extent based on Kassil's autobiographical data, are the sons of a doctor. They cannot see justice in the world that surrounded them, and escape their reality by inventing the land of Schwambrania. Thus, a second dimension appears in the story. The boys crowd their land with characters and situations from beloved books that reveal the era of the "golden" childhood experienced by these brothers. They invent a history, geography, and an original form of statehood in accordance with their own perceptions of good and evil. The events in Schwambrania to some extent duplicate events in Pokrovsk: war, revolution, and political meetings. However, the darker the brothers' lives become in reality – with hunger, deaths, a typhoid epidemic, and social and administrative chaos – the more prosperous and attractive Schwambrania becomes, although the brothers confess that they gradually have less time for this game. Nonetheless, at almost the very beginning of the novel Kassil notifies the reader that Schwambrania will be destroyed by the better reality of Communism. The main narrative does not include any positive changes in the reality of Soviet Pokrovsk; however, the epilogue reveals that Pokrovsk has become Engels, in which the old locales have been replaced by a new Soviet infrastructure that arose from real activity, not fantasy.

There are two maps of Schwambrania in the book, each of which embodies a different idea. According to Harley, in order to properly understand the "evidence" of maps, it is absolutely essential to "know more than we commonly do about the intention and circumstances of those who drew them" (2001: 38). The origin of the first map of Schwambrania was a domestic episode in the author's life. Kassil claims that the first map, in the form of a big tooth accompanied by the Schwambranian coat of arms, was taken from his and his brother's childish pictures (Figure 2), which partly explains the use of prerevolutionary orthography in the captions. Thus, the first map of Schwambrania appears to be a real piece of documentary evidence of a specific time, since the book was published after the orthographic reforms. The continent's shape, which is described as tooth-like, when turned upside-down resembles a crown. This image hints at the early royal mythology of Schwambrania, because "the disappearance of the queen brought everything to a head," as the beginning of the story states (Kassil 1978: 6). Drawn by the younger brother, the first map reflects the idea of justice, as is made explicit by its description in the text. The boys mapped this utopia of childhood with a visual emphasis on justice. Maria Nikolajeva states that "Schwambrania is the land of complete justice, balance, and harmony. Even its map is perfectly symmetrical" (2000: 65) and the landscape is totally "fair":

> Schwambrania was a truly symmetrical land. [...] To the West were mountains, a city and the sea. To the East were mountains, a city and the sea. There was a bay on the left and a bay on the right. This symmetry reflected the true justice which governed Schwambrania and the rules of our game. [...] Symmetry is a balance of

> lines, a linear system of justice. Schwambrania was a land of true justice, where all the good things in life and even the terrain were fairly distributed. There was a bay on the left and a bay on the right, the city of Drandzonsk in the West and the city of Argonsk in the East. Justice reigned. (17)

However, justice in Schwambrania is intended in its sociological, not ethical, meaning, which is emphasized both visually and verbally. First, the boys include social injustices that they encountered in real life, for example, child labor and the impunity enjoyed by the director of a factory at which hundreds of people had been seriously injured. Finally, as they report, "We ended our list of the world's injustices by drawing a long line along the margin and printing a stern and angry word along its entire length. The word was: Injustices" (40). In addition, the children's residence in Schwambrania is textually represented as a geographical

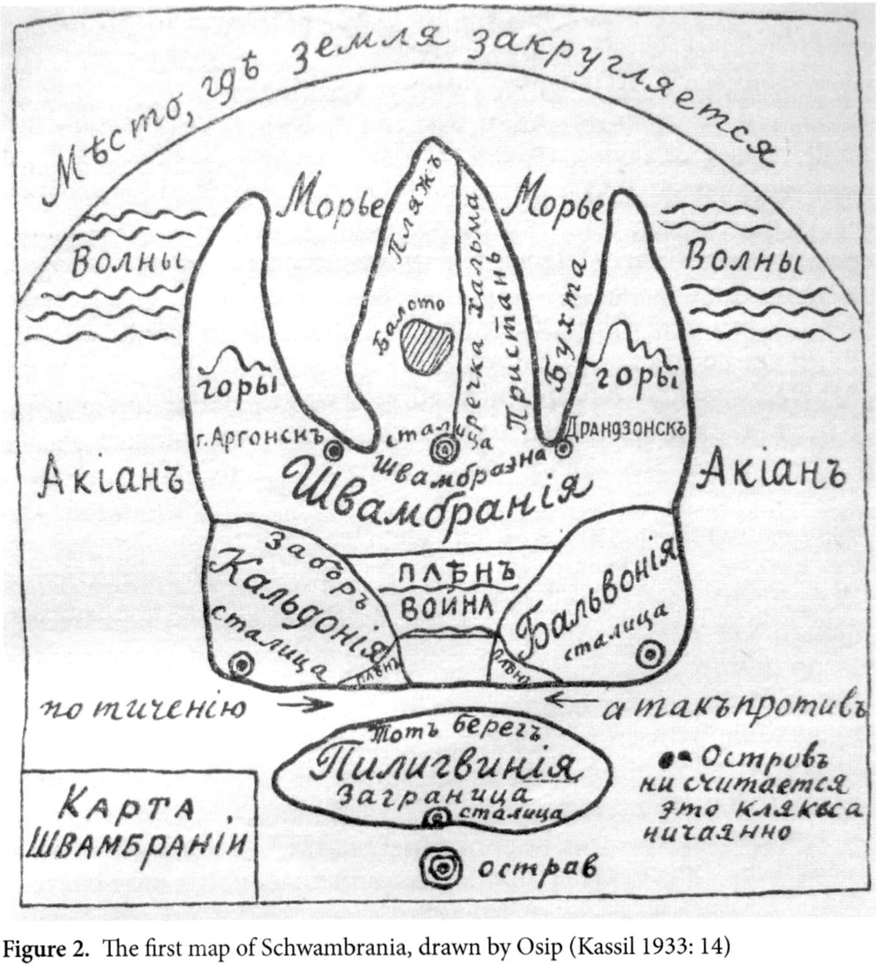

Figure 2. The first map of Schwambrania, drawn by Osip (Kassil 1933: 14)

"height," as opposed to the one in the real Pokrovsk, where the brothers live and invent their fictional country. Here Kassil follows the tradition of children's literature in which natural heights are associated with outstanding moral and ethical achievements:

> When in Schwambrania, we lived on the main street of Drandzonsk, on the 1,001st floor of a diamond house. When in Russia we lived in the town of Pokrovsk on the Volga River, opposite the city of Saratov. We lived on the first floor of a house on Market Square. (22)

The author depicts an anti-picturesque space of a provincial town, which offers the reader a kind of tour through the dirty and culturally marginalized topographies of Pokrovsk. However, after the Revolution, these relative positions were changed: the final place for Schwambrania, rather symbolically, was found on the basement level of a "dead" house. Kassil's description of the first map of Schwambrania draws attention to a borderline area of this country. Schwambrania ended in the place "where the earth curves" (15). This phrase, emphasized typographically where it first occurs, is transformed into a leitmotif. Through the entire narrative, Osip strives to find the place "where the earth curves" in the real Pokrovsk. The functional role of this liminal place seems to have a multiple meaning. First, it can be interpreted with reference to a characteristic tradition of children's literature: as Pauline Dewan notes, "The single dominant theme of children's literature is that of growing up and moving out of childhood into adulthood" (2010: 270). The borderline disappears when adult undertakings, such as war or revolution, are described: "We imagined that all real battles took place in a special hard-packed, cleanly-swept square area like a parade ground. The earth never curved here" (Kassil 1978: 18). Marina Balina observes that the first map of Schwambrania explicitly reflects the idea of childhood with its accorded right as a time in which mistakes can be made. She notes that almost all geographical objects are rendered with childish spellings that do not follow orthographic rules (2012: 49). The childish misspellings underscore the naiveté of the fantasy. The lettering itself, however, is quite perfect, adult-like. The "place where the earth curves," where Schwambrania also ends, can be interpreted as a symbolic representation of the threshold of the childhood world.

Another interpretation of the foregrounding of this phrase within the text brings it into the "context of society," with an eye to the changes taking place in the territory of the Volga German Autonomous Soviet Socialist Republic (hereinafter referred to as VGASSR), where the novel's action is set. By the time of *Schwambrania*'s publication, Kassil had witnessed two geographical shifts – the emergence of the Soviet state in 1922 and the establishment of the VGASSR, with its capital in the town of Pokrovsk, in 1924. The latter event was of great territorial importance for people living in the area of Saratov and in the Samara Volga region: the area, which was mostly populated by Volga Germans, had been recognized in 1918 in accordance with its national identity. Nonetheless, it was little more than several disjoint territories to which it was impossible to provide administrative resources and communication. In the beginning of the 1920s the process of "rounding" or "curving" these German lands began. These terms meant that the various German areas were integrated with the lands located between them, which were inhabited by Russians, Ukrainians, Tatars, Estonians, and others. Edgar Gross (1926), an active statesperson and communist party member, published his research on the cultural and administrative life of the Volga Germans. The main goal of his research, according to the author's preface, was to provide a full and true picture of the VGASSR in 1926. The description of the Republic's geography matches the chapter "A Place on the Map" in *Schwambrania* almost literally. Gross attached a map of the Republic after the land's "curving" in 1922, highlighting the "rounded-off territories." One can assume that Kassil used the notion of "curving" deliberately when he delimited Schwambrania by this area, which emphasized Osip's interest in where the world curves; no doubt, he had in mind the process of the land's "curving" that started in the VGASSR in the 1920s. This Republic ended where the earth was rounded off, or, in other words, "curved." Schwambrania, according to its first map, also ended where the earth curved. Historically, as Denis Wood notes, "the map was an artefact that constructed the state, that literally helped to bring the state into being" (2012: 297). Maps were "a graphic performance of statehood [that] conjured the state as such into existence" (ibid.). For Edgar Gross, it was important to attach a map: the map confirmed that there could be a national union in 1926 between these disjoint regions. His map is a good example of an "existent thing" that "obscures the origins of the state in history" (298). The description of the Schwambranian maps fulfills the same function. The juxtaposition of fictional and real geopolitical methods of delimiting areas could easily be challenged except for several arguments.

As a contributor to *Novyi LEF* (The New Left Front), Kassil presumably followed one of the main principles of this journal, namely, that narration should have a documentary basis. An extract from "The Black Book," the first part of *Schwambrania*, was published in *Novyi LEF* in 1928, and the journal's editors informed the readers that it was an example of factual narration based only on documents. As he provided extracts from his novel for printing in *Novyi LEF*, and also admired the creator of the journal, Vladimir Mayakovsky, Kassil could not have escaped the main artistic principles proclaimed by the editors. Thus, besides the theme of maps and real documents within the text, the inclusion of letters both in the real dimension (a student's love letter) and in the country of the children's fantasy (a letter to Mr. King of Schwambrania), Kassil referred to a collection of official decrees that were imposed upon the territory of the VGASSR (*Sbornik Uzakonenii*1926). This local constitution was in force long after the Revolution. It included decrees concerning all aspects of a citizen's life, including general ones regarding matters such as healthcare, education, insurance, and labor, and specific decrees concerning measures against dog bites, typhoid epidemics, and others. Kassil depicted most of these decrees as an ordinary part of the social life of Pokrovsk citizens. Decree No. 15, for example, specifies regulations for keeping streets and market squares clean (*Sbornik Uzakonenii*1926: 69). It was a relevant point for Pokrovsk citizens, as Kassil notes, describing Breshka Street with its "dry, staccato sound of roasted sunflower seeds being cracked floating above the crowd. The sidewalks were black from discarded sunflower shells" (Kassil 1978: 23). Or decree No. 8, clause 3, which prohibited young people from attending amusement venues including theatres, cinemas, or clubs. Citizens were fined for disobeying (*Sbornik Uzakonenii*1926: 80–81). Kassil writes, "Pupils are not allowed to attend the theatre, cinematograph or other places of amusement [...] Pupils are strictly forbidden to frequent confectionaries, cafes, restaurants, public gardens, etc." (Kassil 1978: 84). In this passage, the usual metaphorically abundant language of *Schwambrania* is replaced by an official style (passive voice, the inclusion of "etc."), highlighting the allusion to its nonfictional source. These examples indicate that Kassil was not simply describing an old world order that had to be severely criticized and destroyed by the new and better life of Communism. Even though he depicted the real, ordinary life of Pokrovsk, the ways of representing similar events in Schwambrania and Pokrovsk cannot be reduced to simple "mirroring." It is the map that provides the most important parallels. Significant geographical events of Kassil's homeland, such as land "curving," were embedded in the map of the imaginary state. Observation of this artistic device facilitates thinking about a new role of maps in Kassil's novel: the authorial map becomes a form of the writer's reflection upon the historical events of his childhood.

A borderline of the imagined Schwambrania is mapped visually, while the borderline of real Pokrovsk – that is, the Volga river – is emphasized verbally. River symbolism plays an important part in various genres; rivers are especially important as boundary markers. A river brings life to the routine of a little town and defines the characters that live in it. The Volga has a symbolic significance in Russian folklore and literature, and in Kassil's story, the Volga entirely determines the life of Pokrovsk and Schwambrania and of the inhabitants of these two places. Neither the landscape nor the view of the Volga (both traditional in Russian literature) is presented to the reader through the text. Nonetheless, it is in accordance with Russian literary tradition that the other bank of the river is whence the news about the beginning of the Revolution arrived. The Volga divides the routine life of Pokrovsk from the new life that revolution brings. Thus the role of the Volga is functional, not descriptive. Kassil seems to follow the literary trends concerning descriptions of nature declared in *Novyi LEF*. Authors in the journal appealed to other writers to get rid of all descriptions of nature, as they found them unnecessary and lacking in the documentary value that was of supreme importance to the principles of *Novyi LEF*. For example, V. Pertsov in his article "What Was the Weather like During the Civil War?", printed in *Novyi LEF* in 1927, deprecates the literary cliché of nature descriptions when they play no functional role in the narrative (1927: 36–45). Thus, both liminal places stimulate mediation between opposing states of being and experiences. On the map of Schwambrania, the place "where the earth curves" and where Schwambrania also ends stands for the boundary between childhood and adulthood. At the same time, it also refers to the author's own geographical experience, as he had witnessed a significant shift of his homeland on the map.

The second map of Schwambrania

The boys drew a new map of Schwambrania when they realized that "all of life was ruled by some sort of struggle" (Kassil 1978: 141):

> Now that we were a bit older we became convinced that there was very little symmetry in the world. [...] The time had come for us to review the borders of Schwambrania. Thus, a new map was drawn up. (141)

The fact that a new map appears in the text, this time with the formerly symmetrical borders "distorted," points to another possible interpretation of Osip's interest in "where the earth curves" – a place where distortion takes place. Since the text mentions that the borders of Schwambrania were revised, we can see the boys themselves engaged in the practices of inventing geography (the first map) and changing it (the second map). This brings to mind Orlova's statement about the Soviet redesign of reality in tandem with reforms in geography. Toponyms on this map are spelled correctly, and the handwriting betrays a more mature author of its captions. The landscape of this map is worked out in detail (Figure 3). New states have appeared on the Big Tooth Continent, and they have been delineated from Schwambrania with the use of a state border symbol. Rivers, islands, archipelagos, and capes are now indicated. Lakes, seas, oceans, forests, and mountains are given names. Shading and double lines, respectively, serve as identification symbols for coastal zones and mountains. Thus, in obvious contrast to the first map, Schwambrania is now presented to the reader with ample topographical detail. This more complex map seems to reflect the official appeals to overcome "visual poverty" in mapmaking: its author could hardly be accused of making a visually

Figure 3. The map of Schwambrania under Brenabor IV (Kassil 1933: 83)

monotonous map. Was Kassil aware of the frustrating situation within geography and cartography in the 1920s, and did he take this into consideration when creating his map? The context of his subsequent literary works, as well as the text of *Schwambrania* itself, provides an answer to this question. An episode described in the chapter "Primary School Schwambrania" is particularly relevant to this issue. Osip, the younger brother who had begun primary school, "drew the outline of Schwambrania on the large wall map in the classroom" (365). The geography teacher was absent at the time, and the lesson was being given by the temporary principal, Kocherygin:

> "What country's this?" he said, pointing to the strange land. "Hm?"
> [...] "It's Schwambrania," Oska[1] teased.
> [...] "Never heard of it."
> "How come it's not in the book?" his classmates demanded.
> "It's not on the map yet, because it's a very new country."
> "Go on, tell us about it," Kocherygin said.
> And so Oska went over to the big map and spent the rest of the lesson talking about Schwambrania. He spoke in detail of the flora and fauna of the Big Tooth Continent. [...] Kocherygin was quite pleased with the Schwambranian geography lesson. [...] He was beaming. "We're studying about Schwambrania in school now," he said proudly. (366)

In this scene, the main question of Leo Tolstoy's essay "Who Should Learn Writing of Whom: Peasant Children of Us or We of Peasant Children?" (1862) (in which he offered a revolutionary understanding of children's thoughts, appealing to give a child "perfect freedom" in education) is raised (Tolstoy 1899, 322). Kassil portrays Osip as a brilliant teacher, who presents a new map and expounds on the geography of Schwambrania. In contrast, all the principal can do is just to ask the children to learn Schwambranian geography by heart by the next lesson. This episode exemplifies the state of ignorance of geography in the revolutionary years, the time period of the novel's setting. As Orlova states, this ignorance affected the majority of the population, including school heads and representatives of the party elite (2006: 83–87). Kassil satirizes the principal's ignorance, while at the same time he presents to the reader a geographical discovery made within a schoolroom. Orlova points out a widespread practice: any geographical phenomenon was first supposed to be mapped in order to be interpreted. For example, using maps, schoolchildren would discover an island previously unknown to them. Such schoolroom geographical discoveries were regular occurrences in school map-reading (91).

Another confirmation of Kassil's awareness of and concern about geographical ignorance comes from his short story "Istoriia s geografiei" (An Incident with Geography), first published in 1937.[2] The plot correlates with the just-described episode in *Schwambrania*. The setting is a Volga region town, and the sophisticated reader can surmise that the author's hometown is Pokrovsk. The geography teacher, Peter, recalls an incident from his Revolution-era youth when, as a twenty-year-old (and not yet a teacher), he had to hide in a school from the tsar's officers. Taking advantage of an opportunity presented by a real teacher's absence that day, he poses as a geography teacher. During his improvised geography lesson,

1. "Oska" is a nickname for Osip.

2. This story was published in 1937 under the title "Stanovoi Hrebet." The new title – *An Incident with Geography* – appeared in 1948.

Peter looks at the map and notes that it is absolutely barren: nothing is written on it, not a single letter. Moreover, when he points at a mountain range somewhere in the territory of Russia, he has no idea of its geographical name. The title of this short story was "lifted" verbatim from an article printed in *Komsomol'skaia Pravda* (The Young Communist Truth) in 1934, a central party newspaper aimed mostly at young adults. The article also accuses school directors and teachers of geographical and cartographical ignorance.

Thus, Kassil resorted to the same plot at least twice – in *Schwambrania* and in his later short story – for different artistic purposes. My analysis has revealed that the episode featured in the chapter "Primary School Schwambrania" was not just a comic event that befell Osip. The fact that Osip charts a nonexistent state on the map and then presents the map as real during the lesson illustrates how maps can construct a new reality. Furthermore, the second map of Schwambrania, which followed the new cartographic principles for overcoming visual poverty, is an excellent example of a map as a social construction. There is another episode within the novel that reveals how easily Schwambrania has become part of real life. The boys are taken to the Cheka office after a bureaucrat (actually, a representative of the secret police) finds documents entitled "Battle map," "A guide to the city of P.," "Secret instructions," and a "List of conspirators" (406), which are only subsequently revealed to derive from the boys' game. The fact that the Cheka Commissar initially takes the Schwambranian artefacts very seriously reveals the rather dangerous stakes of the boys' entertainment. A confrontation with a Cheka Commissar could understandably be considered a frightening encounter with the authorities; after all, one of the boys' aunts "was used to uttering these words [the Cheka] in a fierce stage whisper" (405). However, the boys perceive their visit to the Cheka office as a regular adventure of their Schwambranian life, without suspecting any danger. This episode notably reveals the duality of address of the story to both children and adults, who would read this scene very differently.

However, the imaginary visual map of Schwambrania is balanced by a globe, another form of "control over the image of the world" (Harley 2001: 49). A globe is depicted on the cover of the first edition of *Schwambrania* (Figure 4).

Symbolizing reality, the globe is displayed in the foreground, obstructing the part of the Schwambranian coat of arms where the Big Tooth Continent is depicted and anticipating the end of the story. Kassil, who was concerned about possible accusations of political apathy, created the cover himself, which was supposed to deal with a struggle between two principles: a decrepit world order (like Schwambrania, ruined at the end of the story) and a youthful revolutionary confidence (see Taratuta 1979: 228). However, closer attention to the book cover reveals the following components in it: the photo of the globe and the "real" coat of arms, upon which the images of a ship and a car have been superimposed, serve as a

Figure 4. Cover of Lev Kassil: *Shvambraniia*. Moscow: Federatsiia, 1933

documentary part of the image; the only original elements of the Schwambranian coat of arms shown here are the checker pattern and the chess queen, which stand for the symbolic representation of a game. The use of collage technique that combines documentary elements with stylized imagery gives the latter a different status, since the pictorial fragments have become part of reality. The globe on the cover looks unstable, and at the same time only a partial image is shown, including dark "unknown" areas. The part of the globe that presumably depicts the definite location of Schwambrania on it, according to the description in the text, is turned away from the viewer:

> Schwambrania had to be given a definite place on the map [note that in the English translation the original word 'globe' in this passage was substituted by 'map']. We found a good spot for it in the Southern Hemisphere, in the middle of the ocean. [...] The Big Tooth Continent was situated in the Pacific Ocean to the east of Australia, having absorbed some of the islands of Oceania. Its northern borders, reaching as far as the equator, had a flourishing tropical flora, while its southern borders were frozen wastelands, lying in close proximity to the Antarctic. (139)

This opens up the possibility that the lack of a visible location not mean that "there is no Schwambrania," as the epilogue states. According to Harley, maps can also be interpreted by what they ignore. In such an interpretation, the globe labors in the service of the educational process, offering a specific way of seeing geography. The statements about the globe near the end of the text seem to reflect the author's sorrow about its new role: "As for the globe, we have long since learned its true use and purpose: it is not a revelation, it is simply a visual aid" (Kassil 1978: 476). The opposition between visual aid and revelation unveils another antithesis: childhood and pedagogy. A globe that could be the source of a child's fantasy – a revelation – and the place with imaginary lands on its surface was transformed into a visual model for educational purposes, presenting adulthood with its complete mapping of the world and thus eradicating revelation. The globe is deemed to be a form of realistic interpretation of the world; therefore, when "the globe has spun full circle" (482), the narrator concedes, "there is no Schwambrania" (482). Such a statement refers to the actual meaning of "utopia" as "no place." Kassil seemingly shows acceptance of the fact that Schwambrania does not exist at all. Indeed, the progression of the story moves from cartographic sketching of the imaginary country, filling in its details, putting it on the globe, presenting Schwambrania at school, and thus putting it into the minds of others, to replacing it with the children's library, dismantling Schwambrania for firewood, and then eliminating it. The novel thus provides the idea of a geographical elimination of fantasy. At the end of the story, the image of the world presented by the globe provides no place for the children's fantasy. However, the body of the story shows how captivating the fantasy is for the boys, and how it amuses others (even the head of the Cheka); it influences Lev in his desire to become a sailor, as he mentions at the end of the story (480). Furthermore, in the epilogue Lev reads *Schwambrania* to his family in the presence of his niece – a representative of the new Soviet generation. This scene can be interpreted as a symbolic continuation of the fantasy world that is codified through the gift that Lev gives his infant niece – a globe-rattle. Thus, the fantasy is shared with others and has not been replaced entirely by the new, real world.

Maps of Schwambrania: Leaving aside child's fantasy

The geographical material that is represented by the real world of the author's hometown (Pokrovsk) and the fantasy world of Schwambrania in the two maps included in Kassil's novel reflect the changes in the official views of geography and cartography during the time in which the novel is set and during the period of the book's creation and first publication (1928–1933). The two maps of Schwambrania not only represent the children's fantasy world but also embody ideas that fit well into the political agenda of the era. Visual material – the first map of Schwambrania – is the element that uncovers an issue of the highest justice. However, the verbal description of this map clarifies that justice is understood in its sociological, not ethical, meaning. Thus, justice and injustice could be mapped in the children's fantasy. The second map is what proclaims the impossibility of a totally fair, symmetrical world. The "review" of the Schwambranian map – with its revision of boundaries, distortions, and the change in map orthography – is totally in keeping with the redesign of reality according to the new cartographic principles. This depiction of the children's fantasy world conformed well to the discursive practice of map representation in 1920s and 1930s Soviet magazines, including those intended for children.

However, according to Kassil's main idea, which is articulated in his letters to his parents, the nonexistent land – the "soap bubble" of Schwambrania – is destined to destruction. The author used geographical devices for this purpose as well. He noted that Pokrovsk no longer existed, having become Engels, and described the geography of the new Soviet town in detail. He introduced the globe as a symbol of reality and at the same time as a tool representing a one-sided view of the world, in contrast to the maps that were used in visualizing Schwambrania. Kassil witnessed changes to the maps of the whole country and, on a smaller scale, of his homeland, the territory of the Volga Germans. He was not only a mapmaker but also a map-reader. His personal geography in this first novel embodied this geographical experience and his aesthetic interpretation of the official cartographical representation of space.

References

Primary sources

Istoriia s geografiei. 1934. *Komsomol'skaia Pravda*, 204.

Kassil, Lev. 1933. *Shvambraniia*. Moscow: Federatsiia.

Kassil, Lev. 1937. Stanovoi khrebet. *Murzilka* 10: 16–18.

Kassil, Lev. 1978. *The Black Book and Schwambrania*, trans. by Fainna Glagoleva. Moscow: Progress.

Secondary sources

Balina, Marina. 2012. "Voobrazhaemaia geografiia" v detskikh povestiakh L. Kassilia. *RSUH/RGGU Bulletin: Cultural Studies. Art Studies. Museology* 11(91): 46–53.

Cooper, David. 2012. Critical literary cartography: Text, maps and a Coleridge notebook. In *Mapping Cultures*, Les Roberts (ed.), 29–52. Basingstoke: Palgrave Macmillan. doi: 10.1057/9781137025050.0007

Crampton, Jeremy. 2001. Maps as social constructions: Power, communication and visualization. *Progress in Human Geography* 25(2): 235–252. doi: 10.1191/030913201678580494

Dewan, Pauline. 2010. *The Art of Place in Literature for Children and Young Adults: How Locale Shapes a Story*. Lewiston NY: Mellen.

Galereia kolonial'nykh narodov mira. 1929. *Vsemirnyi Sledopyt* 8: 628.

Gross, Edgar. 1926. *Avtonomnaia Sotsialisticheskaia Sovetskaia Respublika Nemtsev Povolzh'ia*. Pokrovsk: Nemgosizdat.

Harley, John Brian. 2001. *The New Nature of Maps: Essays in the History of Cartography*. Baltimore MD: The Johns Hopkins University Press.

Karta mirovogo rabstva. 1931. *Pioner* 1: 4.

Loiter, Sof'ia. 1979. Iumor "Konduita i Shvambranii" L. Kassilia i detskii fol'klor. In *Zhizn' i tvorchestvo L'va Kassilia*, Lev Razgon (ed.), 189–203. Moscow: Detskaia literatura.

Nikolajeva, Maria. 2000. *From Mythic to Linear: Time in Children's Literature*. Lanham MD & London: Scarecrow Press.

Orlova, Galina. 2006. Kartograficheskii povorot: Shkol'naia geografiia i vizual'naia politika v epokhu bol'shikh utopii. *Voprosy Obrazovaniia* 3: 81–102.

Orlova, Galina. 2008. Sovetskaia kartografiia v stalinskuiu epokhu: Detskaia versiia. *Neprikosnovennyi zapas* 58(2): 85–101.

Pertsov, Viktor. 1927. Kakaia byla pogoda v epochu Grazhdanskoi voiny? *Novyi LEF* 7: 36–45.

Sbornik uzakonenii rasporiazhenii raboche-krest'ianskogo Pravitel'stva Avtonomnoi Sotsialisticheskoi Sovetskoi Respubliki Nemtsev Povolzhia i obiazatel'nykh Postanovlenii Pokrovskikh Gorsoveta i Kantispolkoma, deistvuiushchikh k 1-mu avgusta 1926 goda. 1926. Pokrovsk: Izdanie TSIKa ASSRNP.

Taratuta, Evgenia. 1979. Da zdravstvuet "Schwambrania!" ili sorok let spustia. Istoriia sozdaniia, izdaniia "Schwambranii i sporov vokrug nee, rasskazannaia samim L'vom Kassilem v pis'makh k roditeliam. In *Zhizn' i tvorchestvo L'va Kassilia*, Lev Razgon (ed.), 204–265. Moscow: Detskaia literatura.

Tolstoy, Leo. 1899. *The Complete Works of Lyof N. Tolstoï*; [v. 10], trans. by Nathan Haskell Dole. New York NY: T.Y. Crowell.

Velikiie perelioty 1926 goda. 1927. *Vokrug sveta* 2 (1927): 24–26.
Wood, Denis. 2012. The anthropology of cartography. In *Mapping Cultures*, Les Roberts (ed.), 280–303. Basingstoke: Palgrave Macmillan. doi: 10.1057/9781137025050.0022
Zubareva, Evgenia. 1968. Problemy iumora v khudozhestvennoi literature dlia detei i podrostkov. PhD dissertation, Moskovskii Pedagogicheskii Gosudarstvennyi Institut imeni V. I. Lenina, Moscow.

CHAPTER 12

Mapping Middle Earth

A Tolkienian legacy

Björn Sundmark

In this chapter, J. R. R. Tolkien's fantasy maps in *The Hobbit* (1937) and *The Lord of the Rings* (1954–55) are assessed and analyzed. The analysis shows that the five maps – two in *The Hobbit* and three in *The Lord of the Rings* – are less uniform than one would assume. It is also clear that the maps in *The Hobbit* represent a more child-oriented aesthetics than in the latter work. A few examples are then given of how Tolkien's maps have influenced subsequent writers of fantasy. Finally, it is demonstrated how the Tolkienian fantasy map is transformed when it is moved from the printed page to the screen.

The Maps. I am stumped. Indeed in a panic. They are essential; and urgent; but I just cannot get them done.
Tolkien quoted in Carpenter (2011: 171)

Maps are worrying me
Tolkien quoted in Carpenter (2011: 168)

Introduction

In critical discourse about fantasy maps J. R. R. Tolkien's *The Hobbit* (1937) and *The Lord of the Rings* (1954–55) are indispensable. To be sure, fantasy-inspired narratives, fantastic elements, and literary fairy tales are as old and widespread as literature itself. Similarly, maps can be found in fantastic narratives, such as Jonathan Swift's *Gulliver's Travels* (1726), which predate Tolkien's works by hundreds of years. There is, however, widespread critical consensus that fantasy as a *genre* rather than as a mode of writing is largely a result of Tolkien's achievement, and that his maps are part and parcel of this generic construction. Tolkien's Middle Earth is a fully realized and believable secondary world, and the published maps in *The Hobbit* and *The Lord of the Rings* contribute to this effect in significant

DOI 10.1075/clcc.7.13sun

ways.[1] Hence, the focus in this chapter will be on Tolkien's maps of Middle Earth. Moreover, it is clear that Tolkien's maps have exerted a lasting influence on subsequent fantasy writing (see Ekman 2010). In the concluding section of this chapter I will therefore touch on the changing role of the Tolkienian fantasy map as it is moved from the printed page to the screen (my examples in this section will mainly be taken from Peter Jackson's *The Fellowship of the Ring*, 2001–2003), and, finally, to the use of maps in George R. R. Martin's book series "A Song of Ice and Fire" (1996ff) as well as the corresponding TV series *Game of Thrones* (Benioff and Weiss, 2011ff.).

Here, at the outset, I also wish to clarify that when I discuss the influence of Tolkien's maps on the map conventions of fantasy I do not generally differentiate between fantasy for children and adults. The main reason is that fantasy is a typical crossover genre, something that is quintessentially true of Tolkien's works too. Over the years, millions of children and teenagers have read *The Lord of the Rings* trilogy, and just as many adults have read *The Hobbit*. The second reason is that Tolkien's influence on maps in children's fantasy books stems from both his more child-oriented *The Hobbit* and his more adult-oriented trilogy. Thus it would make little sense to discuss Tolkien's influence on (children's) fantasy based on only the two maps in the earlier work. Having said this I acknowledge that there are differences in the conceptualization of the maps in *The Hobbit* and *The Lord of the Rings*, and that these differences may also be discussed in terms of child/adult adaptation. I will briefly touch on this aspect too, but it is not part of my main line of argument.

The map iconotext

Although maps are rich iconotexts in their combination of cartographic symbols, writing (for instance, names, places), and pictorial content, they are not usually identified as such. It is likely that their position on the threshold of the 'real' text signaled by words, as 'endpapers' or a 'frontispiece,' is partly to blame for this misconception. Following the lead of Gerard Genette (1997) this has led critics to see maps as paratexts (or peritexts), not really integral to the narrative (Honeyman 2001; Mendlesohn 2008; Meissner 2011). But as Anthony Pavlik (2010) has shown, recognizing maps as paratexts does not necessarily mean that they are unimportant or do not fulfill important narratological functions. Another reason that maps

1. For copyright reasons Tolkien's maps may not be reproduced. I therefore refer the reader to the published texts. The five maps can also be found online by combining the search terms "Tolkien" and "map" with, respectively, "Wilderland," "Thror," "Shire," "Middle Earth," and "Gondor."

have tended to be overlooked by critics could be that the cartographic content tends to muddle the neat image-text binary as it was originally developed by Kristin Hallberg (1982) and later on by Maria Nikolajeva and Carole Scott (2001). However, as I have argued elsewhere and at more length, maps are in fact integral to the narrative and can be fruitfully analyzed precisely as iconotexts by broadening the concept to include the cartographic symbols (Sundmark 2014b).

The map iconotext can be identified as a composite of verbal text, cartography, and illustration. The verbal signifiers contained within the map typically refer to place names or objects in the map, or instructions on how to read and use the map. But it is the cartographic symbols that most obviously mark this kind of iconotext as a "map." The cartographic signs are in themselves halfway between the verbal and the visual, and include such elements as compass symbols, scale, longitude and latitude indicators, political borders, plot itineraries, elevation, battlegrounds, the X for "hidden treasure," and symbolic monsters.

The pictorial element can vary greatly and is of course impossible to separate entirely from artistically conceived cartographic symbols. However, a map drawn from a vertical perspective reduces the pictorial content automatically by flattening the landscape features. The panorama or bird's-eye view, by contrast, makes it possible to represent mountains and trees in relief. A combination is also possible, as in J. R. R. Tolkien's maps of Middle Earth, where the vertical perspective is combined with mountains and other landscape features in relief, as if seen from a high altitude. As a rule maps on a large scale also reduce the pictorial; a world map has less room for flamboyant illustration than a map of, say, the Hundred Acre Wood of Milne's *Winnie-the-Pooh* (1926). Finally, in maps where the referential function is more important than the poetic, the pictorial elements tend to be minimalized or even distorted with regard to position and scale. The London Tube map is an example of such a (topological) map.

As for the concepts of "place" and "space," they are complex and contested terms. There is on the one hand the established, everyday usage of the terms, but there are also specialized applications of the terms, sometimes conflicting, not least in the fields of cultural geography and literary studies. In this chapter I draw on Michel de Certeau's (2002) and Henri Lefebvre's (1991) work in which place and space are distinctly conceptualized. Thus when I refer to place I limit my analysis to the referential capacity of the iconotext. As I see it, analyses of place focus on how referentiality is systematized through language and aesthetics. Thus, place is intimately connected to the ways in which "setting" is constructed in literature according to literary, rhetorical, and aesthetic conventions. "Space," as I use it in the context of this chapter, goes deeper. It can be understood as the situated, re-presented and re-imagined experience of place. Accordingly, maps not only systematize place; as Henri Lefebvre has noted, they also produce an imaginative "social space" (68–169). In other words, maps not only operate on the level of place and setting, but have the affective and creative potentiality of producing an imagined space.

The inherent world-making potential is the most important aspect of the map-iconotext. It also explains why maps are particularly common in fantasy fiction. World-making, or secondary world creation as Tolkien calls it, strives towards fantasy and verisimilitude at the same time. The effect of the fantastic is all the greater the better we can suspend disbelief. Maps anchor the fantasy to the real. They make the secondary world consistent and believable. Realistic stories do not have the same need for maps to create place and setting, although they may want maps for the story itself (treasure map) or referencing (keeping track of events and places).

Other than the referencing (place) function and the aesthetic (space) function (both of which are extradiegetic), there is, however, a third possibility: the map can be part of the story (the diegetic function), as in the case of the map in Robert Louis Stevenson's *Treasure Island* (1883). Thus, maps in fantasy books have three basic functions (see also Sundmark 2014a, 2014b). First, they produce a fictional space for the reader, creating a vista of the secondary world in which the story is set. Second, maps can have a referencing and indexing function, enabling the reader to keep track of the main events of the storyline as well as the places in which they occur. Third, maps can be used diegetically – in other words, be part of the fictional universe itself.

Maps in travel tales and adventure stories

Tolkien may have had a huge influence on later fantasy writing, but his own inspirations are obscure. The genealogy of the fictional map harks back to the travel tales of the 18th century; there is much to suggest that maps in travel accounts, whether real or fictional, were customary and expected by the readers. The classic example is *Gulliver's Travels* (1726) by Jonathan Swift, which shows the location of imaginary places such as Brobdingnag and Lilliput grafted onto copies of real maps by the cartographer Herman Moll (see Bracher 1944). From Gulliver, the step to including maps in boys' adventure stories, especially ones that involve travel, such as Robert Louis Stevenson's map of *Treasure Island*, is not great. A possible inspiration for Tolkien may have been adventure stories and travel tales such as these; for *The Hobbit* is that too – a travel book and a boy's adventure story. Today we anachronistically think of it as fantasy, simply, but on publication it was a ground-breaking, hard-to-define children's book, in which Tolkien idiosyncratically blended humor and horror, fairy tale and epic, children's adventure story and the travel tale (see Anderson 1988; Sundmark 2014c).

A major reason why travel narratives have maps is to enable the reader (and the author!) to keep track of the characters and places. This is what I have elsewhere called the "referencing and indexing function of maps" (Sundmark 2014a). To Tolkien this "keeping track"-function was important. In a letter to Naomi Mitchison, who at the time was proof-reading *The Lord of the Rings*, Tolkien writes: "I am sorry about the Geography. It must have been dreadfully difficult without a map or maps" (Carpenter 2011: 177). In the same letter he acknowledges how important maps are to the author too:

> I wisely started with a map, and made the story fit (generally with meticulous care for distances). The other way about lands one in confusion and impossibilities and in any case it is weary work to compose a map from a story – as I fear you have found. (177)

However, Tolkien is well aware that maps are not only about creating order. In a letter to the publisher Allen & Unwin he writes, "there should be picturesque maps, providing more than a mere index to what is said in the text" (Carpenter 2011: 171). As I see it, the word "picturesque" here points to the aesthetic dimension of maps that can help the reader imagine another reality, the secondary world; for maps not only systematize place, but, as I have argued above, produce an imagined "space."

Tolkien does not mention any particular source of inspiration when it comes to maps, but he has acknowledged the influence of, for instance, Rider Haggard on his work (Nelson 2006: 368–369). Arguably, the "Sherd of Amenartas" represented in Haggard's *She* (1887) could, although it is not a map, be seen as a counterpart to Thror's map in *The Hobbit*. Both of these artifacts are heirlooms as well as guides to a treasure. Moreover, as Wayne Hammond and Christina Scull note, Thror's map is "a painstakingly crafted 'facsimile' meant to give verisimilitude to Tolkien's fiction" (2000: 95). This too makes it similar in function to Haggard's "Sherd of Amenartas." Verisimilitude and suspension of disbelief can be brought about not only by the idea of the facsimile (elsewhere Tolkien considers inserting fragments of "burned manuscripts" for the same reason) but by employing maps that look as much like maps of the real world as possible, and where distance and scale are plausible.

The Hobbit: The map of Wilderland and Thror's map

Beginning with the two published maps in *The Hobbit*, the map of Wilderland (frontispiece) and Thror's map (endpaper), the three map functions outlined above will be examined. The maps will be analyzed as a particular kind of "iconotext," that is, as a "text" consisting of verbal and pictorial components, where the object of scrutiny can either be limited to a page (or spread) or be extended to include a whole illustrated book. The "map iconotext" differs from other iconotexts in that it is made up of a third component besides the verbal and the pictorial-decorative – the cartographic (map symbols).

In pictorial terms, the map of Wilderland may be described as a landscape seen from an extreme altitude. The perspective is not vertical, but shows mountains and trees in relief. Rivers and marshes and houses are depicted as well. The reader can also see several spiders and a dragon. Many of these pictorial features can of course also be regarded as cartographic symbols (of forests, habitations, monsters, and so on). Other more obvious cartographic details are the dotted lines representing paths, the double lines showing roads, the compass rose indicating north, and the arrows pointing towards "Hobbiton," "Goblin Gate & Eyrie," and the "Iron Hills."

A curious aspect of this map is the double vertical line to the left called "Edge of the Wild," and above that an arrow pointing to the left saying "Western lands." This hypothetical line is absent from the map of Middle Earth in *Lord of the Rings*. According to *The Tolkien Encyclopedia*, the prosaic reason for this line was that Tolkien's first map of Middle Earth "was drawn on three-hole school paper with a printed margin" (Campbell 2006: 407); the line (and the placing of the compass rose on the original drawing) would have hidden the holes. But this does not explain why Tolkien did not simply make the line coincide with the border of the map. Instead, what lies west of the line, the almost empty margin, is still part of the map.

Plausibly, this border represents the passage from the Shire, something closely related to the primary world – as Tolkien understood it and conceived it – into the secondary world, Wilderland (Carpenter 2011: 235, 250). The map models readily available to Tolkien, like the one in *Treasure Island*, do not portray the domestic starting point either, but rather the locus of action and heightened imagination. By not including the Shire on the map, the risk is of course that readers do not perceive this region as part of the same secondary world creation, and that Bilbo and Co. seem to pass from a primary world to a secondary world. This must be avoided. Tolkien does not want to suggest that Bilbo and the others arrive in Wilderland by some magic means, such as going through a wardrobe. Tolkien's views on the nature of the fairy tale (and thus of fantasy) prevent that approach. The entire narrative should play out in the secondary world.[2] By drawing a hypothetical line across the landscape of Middle Earth, Tolkien shows that the lands to the west

2. For an exposition of Tolkien's views on secondary world creation, see his essay "On Fairy Stories" (1934).

are part of the same world as "Wilderland," yet different, domestic, and for that reason, unmapped. It also suggests that Tolkien at this stage had not yet perfected his theory of fantasy; for the edge reminds the reader of the primary-secondary world divide, which Tolkien otherwise aims to suspend in his fiction. The edge is interesting too, since fantasy maps (and real ones!) often locate the dangerous unknown in the uncharted white spaces of the margins (Ekman 2010). I will come back to this, but my point here is that Tolkien in the map of Wilderland inverts this logic by letting Bilbo's home be the unknown and uncontrolled space, whereas the dangerous Wilderland is revealed in rich and sumptuous detail.

In an interesting discussion of the function of the Wilderland border, Patrick Brückner (2008) argues that although Tolkien's intention with it was no doubt to mark the transition from "the real" to "the fantastic," the demarcation line fails to serve as an essential divide. Brückner's main argument is that dragons, such as Smaug, are grounded in an "epic-historical" context rather than in the fantastic. However, while I agree that the border is dubious, and a contestable point of departure for fantasy (or a secondary world), Brückner's argumentation about dragons as signifiers of the real is not convincing. Rather, it is in the nature of fantasy to make the secondary world as believable and identifiable as possible (despite the fantastic premise), in this case by referencing epic uses of dragons.

Except that the map of Wilderland does not show the entire extent of the quest (the "There and Back Again" of the subtitle), it amply fulfills the referencing function maps usually have. As I have already pointed out, most of the important sites of action are marked in the map, and one can quite easily follow the company on their way towards Erebor Mountain. In fact, the map references places that are not mentioned at all or only parenthetically in the text, such as "woodmen," "old ford," "Mountains of Mirkwood," and "Mount Gundabad." This surplus or redundancy indicates a larger backstory, and can therefore act as a stimulus on the imagination of the reader. The "picturesque" element is also well developed in everything from lettering to the individually drawn (symbolic) trees. The choice of old-fashioned map symbols, such as the obliquely depicted mountains and the mythological creatures, evokes a feeling of mythological time. Thus, this is indeed a map that can help produce space, in this case "Wilderland."

When it comes to Thror's map Tolkien originally wished to have it printed either when it is first displayed at Bag End or when Elrond finds the moon runes on it (Hammond and Scull 1995: 91–94). But technical (and economic) reasons prevented this, and instead the map appears as an endpaper. Its status is different from the map of Wilderland since it is used in the narrative itself. As for the other two functions, I would argue that the referential function is limited. The reader is not much helped by it when following Bilbo and the dwarves in their endeavors. On the other hand its status as an artifact and facsimile makes it very powerful when it comes to evoking a sense of place, and not only of Erebor and environs, but equally as much of the fictitious world of *The Hobbit* as a whole. Again the perspective is a bird's-eye view, but the map has a more medieval aura than the map of Wilderland. The stylized mountain, the different variants of runes, the calligraphic lettering, the symbolic dragon, the lapidary fragments ("here was Girion, lord in Dale"), the hand pointing to the mountain (similar to what one can see in medieval manuscripts and so-called *Mappa Mundi*), even the medieval orientation of the map, with east at the top – all of these traits are suggestive of great age and mystery (see Hammond & Scull 1995: 94).

The three maps of *The Lord of the Rings*

The maps in *The Lord of the Rings* are different in many ways from the ones in *The Hobbit*. None of them are used in the story itself, like Thror's map; nor do they tend towards facsimile or archaic artifact. The "picturesque" is toned down too. Gone are the symbolic dragons and spiders (and their webs!) and other quaint details of the map of Wilderland and Thror's map. I would argue that this marks a difference between a more child-oriented aesthetics in *The Hobbit* and a more adult-oriented and "realistic" mode of mapmaking in *The Lord of the Rings*. This is in line with the findings of other critics. Nina Goga has for instance shown that the pictorial element tends to be more dominant in children's maps than in maps for adults (2015). This is something that can be supported by making a comparison between the maps in *The Hobbit* and those in *The Lord of the Rings*. Spiderwebs and dragons and other decorative elements are notably absent from the latter. In this context it is interesting to note that Pauline Baynes's reworking of the map of Middle Earth – published as a poster and as a large postcard, and not meant to be used as a book endpaper – is again much more "picturesque" and childish, with its symbolic ships and animals, leaf-sprouting compass, and superimposed illustrations – and all of it in color, of course! In addition, one could add that the emphasis on the pictorial (and corresponding liberty vis à vis modern cartographic conventions) often lends these maps a humorous aspect.

The map of Middle Earth comes either first in the book as a large foldout map, or as a page-sized reference map followed by four separate, enlarged map sections, distributed over the three books (Campbell 2006: 407). In contrast to the map of Wilderland, this map shows the entire fictitious world in which the action takes place. The map is bordered by "water margins" – to the west by a coastline, and to the north, east and south by white, uncharted spaces, referred to with obscure place indicators such as "Northern Waste," "Forodwaith," "Rhûn," "Khand," and "Haradwaith," if at all. Thus Middle Earth is represented as a separate whole, similar to an island (hence the cartographic term "water margin"). This is different from the map of Wilderland, which appears as a slice of a secondary world with no water margins (wet or otherwise). The map of Wilderland, by contrast, is closely cropped to the Mountains in the north and west; it cuts across Mirkwood and leaves out the Shire, the Iron Hills, and the Necromancer's stronghold. It has almost no empty spaces.

In the map of Middle Earth it is not the domestic space, the Shire, that is unplottable and outside the map. Instead it is what lies beyond the sea to the west, home of the High Elves (Valinor), that is left out –part of another order altogether in the Tolkienian mythos. But a reading of the map does not hint at what is beyond the sea, and its significance. As for what lies in the other directions, neither the map nor the book provide the reader with any clues.

Without being conspicuously archaic (like Thror's map) or picturesque, the map of Middle Earth suggests a real, believable, and self-contained world, rather than a fantastic place of the imagination. Conceivably, it may even be our own world in a remote past (as Tolkien preferred to think of it). The map picture shows Middle Earth from an extreme altitude. Mountains, hills, marshes, and forests (trees) are shown in relief, being more cartographic symbol than true pictorial representation, but otherwise it is a vertical view of the land that is presented, of coastlines, rivers, and lakes. The cartographic elements are many, such as the square compass rose, the scale, the dotted lines indicating roads, and the town and fortress symbols, and many of the pictorially appealing elements do double work as cartographic symbols. It is essentially a natural landscape that is presented, not a political map. No political or administrative borders are shown, nor are there any symbols pertaining to agriculture, natural resources, or commerce. There are also a great deal of verbal text fragments, pointing to frequently mentioned places, such as Gondor, Mordor, Rivendell, and Mirkwood. The map works as an index to the place and plot of the story. To read *The Lord of the Rings* without this map would indeed be frustrating, as we saw in the letter referred to above.

But the map does a great deal more than reference the story. It evokes a fictional space. The realism in terms of scale and cartographic detail are aimed at suspending disbelief. Providing names of places that are only mentioned in passing or not at all is another strategy. Places like Tharbad, Harlond, Isle Bay of Forochel, Ettenmoor, Rhudaur, and the Hills of Evendim suggest that there is much more to the story and to this world than meets the reading eye, providing food for thought and imagination. Moreover, such surplus naming is something that characterizes real maps too. Real maps do not come with a predetermined story and a set of perfectly matching place names; they carry names for all eventualities and situations.

It is easy to misread fictional maps as snapshots of reality, for instance neutrally representing the lay of the land at the moment the story starts (if it is a frontispiece map). Yet, more often than not the maps are more complex than that, either pointing to the prehistory and backstory that led up to the story present, or pointing forward to events that will take place during the unfolding of the narrative. The former type are "past tense" maps (Ekman 2010: 72); the latter is a future tense map. A map in the future tense reveals at a glance the movements and incidents that will take place, almost providing a plot summary. One example would be the numbered and commented map in *Watership Down* (1972) by Richard Adams. The map of Middle Earth, by contrast, does not project what is coming, the future. It does, however, provide a sense of the past by the inclusion of battle field symbols (crossed swords) at "Dagorlad or battle plain" and "Field of Celebrant." The "past tense"-orientation of the map is also sustained by explanatory notes on the map saying "Here was of old the Witch-Realm of Angmar" and "The Lost Realm of Arnor."

The map of Middle Earth could be labeled "the mother of all fantasy maps." The other published maps by Tolkien are important too, but the way the map of Middle Earth conceptualizes and encapsulates an entire fantasy world has become the model for how fantasy maps should be made. The success of *The Lord of the Rings* and the tight connection in that work between world creation and map-making has made the fantasy map a generic convention. Indeed, it has been endlessly copied by authors creating their own secondary worlds. The importance of the map of Middle Earth can for instance be shown by looking at versions to be found in fanfiction and parody. Nick Perumov's *Alvklingan* (Elven Blade 1993) set 300 years after the events recounted in *The Lord of the Rings* come with a map which provides an extension of Tolkien's original. My second example is the map-pastiche in Henry N. Beard and Douglas Kenney's *Bored of the Rings* (1969). Both Perumov and Beard and Kenney make use of Tolkien's mapping conventions: the former lovingly and faithfully, the latter playfully and mockingly. Clearly, it is the map of Middle Earth that is the template in both cases. We recognize the pictorial and cartographic representation of landscape (for example, panorama, and oblique representation of mountains) and the naming conventions and characteristics (invented languages, and so on). Unlike the map of Wilderland there are no mythological beasts and other decorative or archaizing traits.

The two other maps found in *The Lord of the Rings* depart in significant ways from the map of Middle Earth. In fact, each of the five published maps in *The Hobbit* and *The Lord of the Rings* are different from the other, an indication, perhaps, that the fantasy map conventions that Tolkien himself would be instrumental in establishing were still in flux at the time of publication. One could also argue that Tolkien very consciously employs different map strategies, because he pursues different purposes with them. Thus, the map of the Shire approximates the common British ordnance map in its representation of roads, bridges, borders, forests, and major habitations. Tolkien thus connects the Shire symbolically with Britain through his choice of map template. There is nothing "fantastic" about the map, not even the place names, with their rural English connotations (for instance, "Woody End," "Willowbottom," "Little Delving"). It shows the central part of the Shire with nature formations (hills, rivers, and forests), major habitations, and roads. Unlike the map of Middle Earth it also shows the borders between the four farthings that make up the Shire. Whereas the Shire is completely left out of the picture in *The Hobbit*, it is doubly represented in *The Lord of the Rings* – separately, with the realistic map described above, and also at the heart of the map of Middle Earth. It is as if Tolkien is saying that home and hearth and the real world are actually located in the faerie realm, that fantasy is grounded in reality.

The third map in *The Lord of the Rings* is different in its own way. It centers on the action in the third book: Frodo and Sam's quest into Mordor, and the scene of war between Gondor and Mordor. The most striking thing about this map is the use of height contours to show mountain elevations. This is a much more recent cartographic technique than Tolkien's usual reliefs (with hachures), and the historicizing effect is therefore reduced. According to Ekman it is a rather rare feature in fantasy to use elevation contours (2010: 60–64). From a pictorial and aesthetic point of view, however, the bold double lines are dramatic and expressive. It is almost as if the lands of Gondor and Mordor have been animated into conflict themselves. It is also worth noting that the vertical perspective is not entirely consistent; the forests of Firien and Druadan are viewed obliquely here, as in all of the other published maps by Tolkien. Finally, as with the map of the Shire, the third map shows an administrative and political border, the one between Rohan and Gondor.

So far I have ventured to show that the two maps in *The Hobbit* and the three in *The Lord of the Rings* are quite heterogeneous in design and conceptualization; it is, for instance clear that the maps in *The Hobbit* represent a more child-oriented aesthetics than in the latter work. Moreover, it seems likely that the variation between the five maps partly at least has to do with for whom Tolkien addressed his books, that is, if he had a child or adult audience in mind. But the differences are probably also due to the pioneering nature of Tolkien's work, both in terms of fantasy writing in general, and of using maps in fantasy in particular.

Let us now examine the Tolkienian legacy, by looking at one particular example, and then follow the ways in which the fantasy map is transformed and given renewed meaning when it is moved from the printed page to the screen.

In the Tolkien tradition: A Song of Ice and Fire

To chart the Tolkien tradition until today, even with regard to such a limited topic as maps, would require a book-length study. In this chapter I will limit my investigation to one late example, George R. R. Martin's series of books *A Song of Ice and Fire* (1996–2011). The series is often referred to as *Game of Thrones*, which is the title of the first book in the series and also, more importantly, the title of the TV series based on the novels. All of the books in the series come with maps, mainly of the land of Westeros, the locus of most of the action. This body of land is surrounded by the sea on three sides and disappears into the white spaces (as in "unknown" and "snow-covered") of the north. There are also a few maps of adjacent lands, as well as a city map of the capital of Westeros, King's Landing. The maps are fairly conventional as fantasy maps go. They strive for realism and verisimilitude, while appearing as a medieval fantasy. As is to be expected there are many similarities with Tolkien's map of Middle Earth. A similar perspective is evoked: vertical, yet representing forests and mountains in relief. Towns and fortresses are indicated and named, roads are given as dotted lines. No political borders are given, which is curious given the importance of the borders between the seven kingdoms of Westeros. A difference between the map of Middle Earth and the maps of Westeros can be found in the naming practice. Whereas Tolkien excels in inventing names in different languages, and often providing two names for the same place (Rhovanion, or Wilderland; Baranduin, or the Brandywine river), Martin uses English sounding names for most places in Westeros (Winterfell, Ashford, The Reach). "Dorne" has an exotic ring to it, perhaps, but even in that southern part of Westeros most places carry names like "Sandstone" and "Sunspear," all safely English. Outside of Westeros, however, more exotic-sounding places and languages can be found (Valyria, Braavos, Quarth, Volantis). Thus, in a sense Westeros is a savage version of The Shire/England, with magic pressing in from the margins, threatening the wall in the north, which is there to keep the wildlings and "white walkers" and magical creatures at bay, and from over the sea where magic still appears to be a possibility (and a threat).

The Chamber of the Painted Table

So far I have only discussed the frontispiece maps of Martin's series. Although inferior to Tolkien's maps, they fulfill their functions by helping produce a fictional space and keep track of events and places (functions one and two). Interestingly, however, Martin also describes a map that has a function in the narrative itself in two of the books; here is the description in *A Storm of Swords* (2000):

> At the very top of the Stone Drum, within the great round room called the Chamber of the Painted Table, they found Stannis Baratheon standing behind the artifact that gave the hall its name, a massive slab of wood carved and painted in the shape of Westeros as it had been in the time of Aegon the Conqueror. An iron brazier stood beside the king, its coals glowing a ruddy orange. Four tall pointed windows looked out to north, south, east, and west. Beyond was the night and the starry sky. (491)

The location is important: high up in Dragonstone Castle, commanding a view in all directions, the reader of the map merges into the reader of the land itself, map and land becoming one. This process becomes even clearer when Stannis in the next quotation confuses the "message" he reads into the map with the world outside.

> Stannis touched the Painted Table. "Look at it, Onion knight. My realm, by rights. My Westeros." He swept a hand across it. "This talk of Seven Kingdoms is a folly. Aegon saw that three hundred years ago when he stood where we are standing. They painted this table at his command. River and bays they painted, hills, mountains, castles and cities and market towns, lakes and swamps and forests… but no borders. It is all one. One realm, for one king to rule alone." (498)

The map provides the illusion that Westeros can be reduced to a map. Always a false presumption, in this case it becomes particularly ironic since Stannis Baratheon's power at this point in the narrative does not extend much beyond the Chamber of the Painted Table and Dragonstone. But power and political realities are not Stannis's forte. Instead he sees in the map a mystical connection between the land (the "hills, mountains, castles, cities,"etc.) and his claim to it ("My realm").

Dynamic maps: From Middle Earth to Westeros

The idea of a metonymic relationship between land and map is raised by the presence of the "painted table." But such a metonymic relationship is even further accentuated if we switch medium, from verbal text (books) to moving images (film and TV). I have argued that Tolkien's maps have been instrumental in establishing the conventions of fantasy maps, and that the map has become a standard prop in fantasy fiction. So much so, that when *The Lord of the Rings* was filmed the opening sequence shows a version of the map of Middle Earth (Figure 1). The camera first shows the whole map and then, when Galadriel's voice-over talks about the creation of the one ring, zooms in on Mordor and Mt Doom. In the final map clip the parchment turns brown and starts to burn, the scene fading over into that of a village being sacked and burnt. The map in this sequence is interchangeable with the land. Middle Earth is burning, the map is burning – it is the same thing.

Figure 1. Detail of the map of Middle Earth used in the opening of the 2001 *The Fellowship of the Ring* (the first in Peter Jackson's film trilogy of *The Lord of the Rings*. At this moment the map is seemingly catching fire (a fire that starts in Mordor).

The film medium also allows the map to be dynamic rather than static. In the example above the map catches fire. Films of other books have explored the dynamic possibilities of maps even further. In J. K. Rowling's *Harry Potter and the Prisoner of Azkaban* (1999, chapter three), for example, the Marauder's map displays the movements and whereabouts of everyone in Hogwarts. This magical property of the map is of course described in the Harry Potter books, but only film can visualize it. Needless to say, a static illustration of the Marauder's map would be quite pointless.

This takes us to the map opening of the TV series *Game of Thrones*. Angus Wall, who created the opening credits, says in an interview that HBO asked him to do something "like the map that begins books like *The Lord of the Rings*" yet "different from the standard tropes for fantasy maps" (Appelo 2011). It should look "nonfuturistic" and "evoke the Middle Earth-ish setting of George R. R. Martin's book." Wall also comments on the machinery and moving parts of the map trailer: "It had to look like it was made in that time, so we immediately referenced Leonardo da Vinci's machines [...] We wanted it to look like a real place" (Figure 2).

Figure 2. Screen capture from the opening "map" credits of the Game of Thrones TV series: King's Landing emerging from the landscape

The interview shows the filmmakers' indebtedness to fantasy maps in general and to Tolkien's maps in particular. Although the interview does not bring this up, it is highly likely that the "painted table" of Dragonstone also served as inspiration. Like Stannis Baratheon at the map table, the viewer can survey all of Westeros at a glance. The interview mentions how the camera "swoops from kingdom to kingdom," the effect being that of a bird or a dragon scanning the land. But the

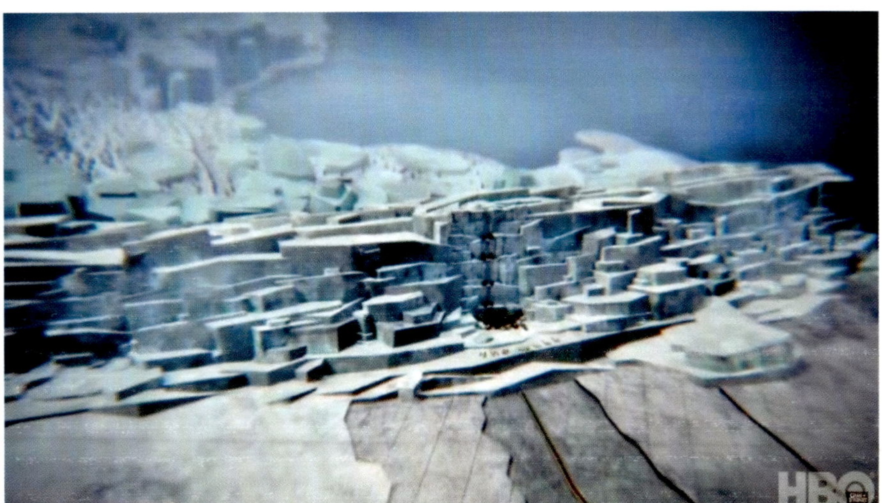

Figure 3. Screen capture from the opening "map" credits of the Game of Thrones TV series: the wall in the north

dynamism is not only built into the viewing; the land itself is animated. When the camera eye comes to rest on a sigil or family crest, the "sigil becomes the main cog that triggers the animation" (Appelo 2011). Wall concludes, "so the model of the place emerges out of the floor of the map and comes to life."

These dynamic and metonymic qualities of the map featured in the opening credits of the *Game of Thrones* TV series contribute to how viewers imagine this fictional world. This map is not a static representation of geographical features of the land, but a living and symbolically charged thing, like the land itself (Figure 3). The use of the map sequence also reminds the viewer of the general lay of the land, some of the place names, and the main sites featured in the episode (since the opening points to the locations which will be focused in each episode by swooping down on those places). Finally, the intertextual references to the fantasy map tradition also make it clear to viewers what genre to expect. In these ways, the opening map sequence of *Game of Thrones* testifies to the importance and strength of the fantasy map tradition, as initiated by Tolkien, while at the same time showing how maps can be made to mean more in a new media context.

References

Primary sources

Adams, Richard. 1972. *Watership Down*. London: Rex Collings.
Beard, Henry N. & Kenney, Douglas. 1969. *Bored of the Rings*. New York NY: Signet.
Benioff, David & Weiss, D.B. (producers). 2011ff. *Game of Thrones* (TV series). USA: HBO.
Haggard, H. Rider. 2008. *She*. London: OUP (first published 1887).
Jackson, Peter (director). 2001. *The Fellowship of the Ring*. New Zealand: Wingnut.
Martin, George R. R. 1996. *A Game of Thrones*. New York NY: Bantam.
Martin, George R. R. 2011. *A Storm of Swords*. New York NY: Bantam (first published 2000).
Milne. A. A. 2005. *Winnie-the-Pooh*. London: Penguin (first published 1926).
Perumov, Nick. 2010. *Alvklingan*. Stockholm: Coltso (first published 1993).
Rowling, Joanne K. 1999. *Harry Potter and the Prisoner of Azkaban*. London: Bloomsbury.
Stevenson, Robert Louis. 2011. *Treasure Island*. Oxford: OUP (first published 1883).
Swift, Jonathan. 1992. *Gulliver's Travels*. London: Wordsworth (first published 1726).
Tolkien, John R. R. 1968. *The Lord of the Rings*. London: Allen & Unwin (first published 1954–1955).
Tolkien, John R. R. 2002. *The Hobbit*. New York: Harper Collins (first published 1937).

Secondary sources

Anderson, Douglas. 1988. *The Annotated Hobbit*. London: Unwin.
Appelo, Tim. 2011. Secrets behind "Game of thrones" opening credits. *Hollywood Reporter*. 19 April 2011. <http://www.hollywoodreporter.com/race/secrets-game-thrones-opening-credits-179656> (21 February 2015).

Bracher, Frederick. 1944. The maps in "Gulliver's Travels". *Huntington Library Quarterly* 8.1: 59–74. <http://www.jstor.org/stable/3815865> (21 February 2015).

Brückner, Patrick. 2008. "Until the dragon comes": Tolkien's dragon-motif as a poetological concept. In *Tolkien's Shorter Works: Essays of the Jena Conference 2007*, Margaret Hiley & Frank Weinreich (eds), 101–135. Zurich: Walking Tree.

Campbell, Alice. 2006. Maps. In *J. R. R. Tolkien Encyclopedia: Scholarship and Critical Assessment*, Michael D. C. Drout (ed.), 405–408. New York NY: Routledge.

Carpenter, Humphrey. 2011. *The Letters of J. R. R. Tolkien*. Boston MA: Houghton Mifflin.

De Certeau, Michel. 2002. *The Practice of Everyday Life*. Berkeley CA: University of California Press (first published 1984).

Ekman, Stefan. 2010. *Writing Worlds, Reading Landscapes: An Exploration of Settings in Fantasy*. PhD dissertation, Lund University.

Genette, Gerard. 1997. *Paratexts: Thresholds of Interpretation*, trans. J. E. Lewin. Cambridge: CUP. doi: 10.1017/CBO9780511549373

Goga, Nina. 2015. *Kart i barnelitteraturen*. Kristiansand: Portal Akademisk.

Hallberg, Kristin. 1982. Litteraturvetenskapen och bilderboksforskningen. *Tidskrift för litteraturvetenskap* 3–4: 163–168.

Hammond, Wayne G. & Scull, Christina. 1995. *J. R. R. Tolkien – Artist and Illustrator*. Boston MA: Houghton Mifflin.

Honeyman, Susan E. 2001. Childhood bound: In gardens, maps, and pictures. *Mosaic: A Journal for the Interdisciplinary Study of Literature* 34(2): 117–132.

Lefebvre, Henri. 1991. *The Production of Space*, trans. Donald Nicholson-Smith. Oxford: Basil Blackwell (first published 1974).

Meissner, Corey. 2011. *"Reading is meant for training": Maps, Nation and Empire in British Children's Literature, 1800–1940*. MA thesis, University of South Carolina.

Mendlesohn, Farah. 2008. *Rhetorics of Fantasy*. Middletown CT: Wesleyan University Press.

Nelson, Dale. 2006. Literary influences, nineteenth and twentieth centuries. In *J. R. R. Tolkien Encyclopedia: Scholarship and Critical Assessment*, Michael D. C. Drout (ed.), 366–377. New York NY: Routledge.

Nikolajeva, Maria & Scott, Carole 2001. *How Picturebooks Work*. New York NY: Garland.

Pavlik, Anthony. 2010. "A special kind of reading game": Maps in children's literature. *International Research in Children's Literature* 3: 28–43. doi: 10.3366/ircl.2010.0004

Sundmark, Björn. 2014a. "Dragons be here": Teaching children's literature and creative writing with the help of maps. In *Thinking through Children's Literature in the Classroom*, Agustín Reyes-Torres, Luis S. Villacañas-de-Castro & Betlem Soler-Pardo (eds), 64–77. Newcastle-upon-Tyne: Cambridge Scholars.

Sundmark, Björn. 2014b. "A serious game": Mapping Moominland. *The Lion and the Unicorn* 38: 162–181. doi: 10.1353/uni.2014.0022

Sundmark, Björn. 2014c. "En hobbit och ett mumintroll skulle kunna mötas i bästa sämja": Receptionen av Bilbo, en hobbits äventyr (1962). *Barnboken* 37(2): 1–17.

Tolkien, J. R. R. 2001. On fairy stories. In *Tree and Leaf*, by J. R. R. Tolkien. London: Harper Collins. 11–70 (first published 1934).

CHAPTER 13

Landscapes of growth, faith, and doubt

Mixing and mapping fantasy geography and contemporary political issues

Nina Goga

The research literature on the hallmarks and history of fantasy has become quite comprehensive, and includes analyses of specific works or series in the genre. A large number of fantasy studies examine typical themes, motifs, and characteristics of the genre such as the struggle between good and evil, the chosen child, and the passage between the primary and secondary worlds. Although several research studies on fantasy have pointed out that maps are provided in many books to help readers find their way to the various places and navigate the depicted landscapes, fewer explore the mystical, fantastic, and magic places displayed in the maps.

In the wake of J. K. Rowling's *Harry Potter* books (1997–2007) and Lene Kaaberbøl's *Skammerens børn* (The Shamer's child) series (2000–2003), there has been a growing interest on the part of publishers in Norwegian fantasy for children and young adults. One example is the award-winning fantasy novel *Landet under isen* (The Land beneath the Ice, 2009) by Lars Mæhle. The book has been described as being willing to put religious beliefs on the agenda, more explicitly, to question the conflicts and similarities between Judaism, Christianity, and Islam (Emanuelsen 2010). This agenda seems very much in accordance with the notion that "it's in fantasy that we come closest to religion, to philosophy, in children's literature" (Baker 2006: 238). The Danish researcher of children's literature Anna Karlskov Skyggebjerg seems to be of the same opinion when she states that: "it is common in fantastic literature for children to transmit ideological and/or religious messages" (2005: 280, all translations from this book are mine).

In addition to the generally accepted description of the book, I would add that *The Land beneath the Ice* consists of a mix of fantasy and crime stories. I would also claim that this mix is particularly explicit in the two maps presented on the endpapers of the book: a city map and a larger secondary world map (see Figures 1 and

DOI 10.1075/clcc.7.14goa

2). The city map corresponds with the crime story and the secondary world map corresponds with the fantasy story. More specifically, the city map underscores the detail-oriented focus on the crime scene, and the fantasy map depicts the unfamiliar landscapes of fantasy geography.

According to Deirdre Baker (2006), maps in fantasy for children are often based upon recognizable geographical patterns associated with predictable and conventional worldviews. The most striking geographical patterns identified by Baker are mountain barriers in the distant north, sea on the western or eastern borders, and deserts and wastelands or plains in the middle. In addition to these patterns or cartographical features, Stefan Ekman (2013) notes that most fantasy maps "follow the modern convention of placing north at the top" (31) and that fantasy maps seldom are provided with legends and scales (36). He also points out that one of the functions "all the roads that crawl all over the maps have" is that of "possible travel routes, […] telling the reader that journeying through this fictional world is possible, even mandatory – the map is a traveling aid, a tool for exploration" (42). Like Baker and Ekman, Björn Sundmark (2014a; 2014b; 2017) has examined maps in fantasy. In addition to mandatory remarks on the influence of J. R. R. Tolkien's maps in *The Hobbit* (1937), Sundmark (2014a) claims that one of the reasons for providing maps in fantasy novels is to

> anchor the fantasy to the real. They make the secondary world consistent and believable. Realistic stories do not have the same need for maps to create place and setting. Although they may want maps for the story itself (treasure map) or referencing (keeping track of events and place). (68)

However, the maps in *The Land beneath the Ice*, which are not an explicit part of the plot, seem to serve not only as "a reference guide to plot and place" (Sundmark 2014b: 166), but also as visual expressions of the faith and doubt-directed identity development of the protagonist.

Sixteen-year-old Leo Rubin is the protagonist of *The Land beneath the Ice*. He moves between the landscape of crime and the landscape of fantasy. In addition to Leo, the crime investigator Magne Jerstad also plays an important role in the crime story part of the book. Leo lives in Smalvik (Narrow Bay), a village that, without the fish factory, "would have been a dark spot on the map" (Mæhle 2009: 18, all translations from this book are mine). Because of the increasing darkness that has threatened Narrow Bay in recent years, nothing grows and all life will soon disappear. Foreshadowing indicates that Leo is the one who is to end the darkness. In order to fulfill this quest, Leo has to find and read seven protocols that, in conjunction, will reveal the legend of the Land beneath the Ice. In addition to the quest, Leo is facing the familiar challenges of contemporary youth related to maturation and identity. He is caught in-between his cultural heritage and his own ideas and beliefs. He has to cope with both external danger and inner uncertainty. The external danger relates to his ability to orient himself in the city maze. His inner uncertainty relates to his capacity to recognize his own identity and to believe there is a place for everyone in the world.

Referring to Roberta Trites' (2014) research on the prevalence of various metaphors of growth in many young adult novels, I would claim that the process of maturation and *Bildung* (formation) that Leo experiences is expressed not only in his journey through the Land beneath the Ice, but also in the ongoing organic processes associated with the relationship between light and dark and life and death. The view that growth is a result of a process expressed through a journey is also linked to other metaphors. The protagonist is a traveler, and the task he has to carry out implies the need to reach a goal by following a marked route, passing a number of landmarks or milestones. On his journey, a guide accompanies the traveler, who becomes particularly important when the traveler faces challenges, often described as crossroads (Trites 2014: 21f.). As we shall see, the metaphors of growth, journey, and traveler are highly significant and at work in both the fantasy and the crime stories in *The Land beneath the Ice*.

By focusing on what I consider the landscapes of growth, faith, and doubt, and by focusing in detail on the way the protagonist moves in these landscapes, I shall explore the ways in which the maps in *The Land beneath the Ice* reflect and strengthen, or elaborate, both the bodily and the personal inner struggles of the protagonist, struggles which may be linked to the overall message of the book. That is, we are all humans struggling to fit into our own life, as well as into the local and global society we are all part of. In addition, I will clarify how and why the book is both a fantasy novel and a contemporary political and ideological crime novel. I seek to establish the connection between the cartographic expression, the bodily movements, and the questions regarding growth, faith, and doubt addressed in the novel.

The fantasy world

In her dissertation, *Den fantastiske fortælling i dansk børnelitteratur 1967–2003* (The Fantastic Story in Danish Children's Literature 1967–2003, 2005), Skyggebjerg points out that the fantasy genre is rooted in two different traditions: "One continental and original Germanic tradition [...] in opposition to an Anglo-Saxon tradition," and claims that Nordic fantastic stories are "positioned at an interesting intersection between the two traditions" (9). Skyggebjerg explains the distinction between the Germanic tradition (fantastic stories) and the Anglo-Saxon tradition (fantasy) as having cultural and historical roots. The genre entitled *fantastic stories* stems from the experimental and (German) gothic tradition of the nineteenth century, which developed when also ideas of Bildung were flourishing, while the fantasy genre developed later and reached its peak in twentieth-century English literature. The idea of two separated worlds is a defining hallmark of the latter (25). E. T. A. Hoffmann's "Das fremde Kind" (The Strange Child, 1817) is an example of the German tradition, while J. M. Barrie's *Peter Pan and Wendy* (1911) and J. R. R. Tolkien's *The Hobbit or There and Back Again* (1937) are examples of the Anglo-Saxon tradition.

Although Skyggebjerg primarily employs the term 'fantastic story' and only secondarily terms such as 'fantastic literature' and 'fantasy,' I have chosen to employ the term 'fantasy' in my discussion. I consider this justified since in the last 10–15 years the term 'fantasy' has been accepted by Norwegian publishers and adopted by the young fantasy readers themselves. To exemplify this, it is worth mentioning that *The Land beneath the Ice* is subtitled "en fantasy roman" (a fantasy novel).

Another scholar of fantasy who has contributed to the definition and categorization of the fantasy genre is Farah Mendlesohn. In her seminal work *Rhetorics of Fantasy* (2008), she lists four categories within the fantastic: the portal-quest fantasy, the immersive fantasy, the intrusion fantasy, and the liminal fantasy. If *The Land beneath the Ice* is to be placed in one of these categories, it best fits the portal-quest fantasy. According to Mendlesohn, it is most likely in both portal and quest fantasies that "a character leaves her familiar surroundings and passes through a portal into an unknown world" (2008: 1). She also notes that "[t]he position of the reader in the quest and portal fantasy is one of companion-audience" (1), and that the protagonist often provides the reader "with a guided tour of the landscapes" (xix).

I have chosen to focus on Skyggebjerg's deliniation for a number of reasons. First, Skyggebjerg makes an important observation regarding the confrontation between the real and the supernatural: the confrontation becomes evident in the adult-child contrast or conflict, in which the child is open to an expansion of the concept of normality while the adult retains a rational conception of reality (2005: 17). This observation is also valid for *The Land beneath the Ice*. While Leo is the one sent through the fantasy landscape, crime investigator Magne Jerstad struggles to understand the rationality of the crime scene and the community in which it has been committed.

Second, based on previous attempts to define fantasy as a genre, Skyggebjerg creates her own analytic tool (62–65). In her analysis, she studies motifs such as the chosen or unfamiliar (alien) child, the secondary world, and the metamorphosis. She examines how the fantastic story for children has a special preference for taboo themes (illness, sorrow, and death) and for philosophical, religious, and ethical questions. Her analytical approach is useful when discussing the genre categorization of the novel *The Land beneath the Ice*, but since Skyggebjerg only briefly mentions fantasy geography, I will draw on Göte Klingberg's (1980) characterization of "the unfamiliar worlds", Maria Nikolajeva's (1988) analysis of "the Magic Space," Catherine Butler's (2012) notes on Ursula Le Guin's Earthsea landscape, and Levy & Mendlesohn's (2016) characterization of medievalism and mythopoeic fantasy to add other crucial perspectives to my reading of the novel. It should be noted that, like most researchers on fantasy, Klingberg, Nikolajeva, Butler, and Levy & Mendlesohn base their examination on English and American fantasy novels written between 1900 and 2010.

Klingberg's examinations of the 'unfamiliar worlds' are based on an understanding of these worlds as phenomena which "appear in or opposed to the everyday reality" (1980: 12, all translations from this book are mine). This means "that the world in which the unfamiliar world appears is well known and everyday-like [...] that it is an everyday world for the people, who live at the same time as the author. However the surroundings may be historical" (12). It is crucial to Klingberg that the depiction of the unfamiliar world, and what happens there, is as credible as the depiction of the everyday world; it should be consistent, coherent, and constructed in a logical way. According to Klingberg, an unfamiliar world may also be described without any connection to our own world. In addition to references to Tolkien's Middle Earth, Lewis' Narnia, and Lloyd Alexander's Prydain in the chapter on the mythical land, Klingberg takes a closer look at Ursula K. Le Guin's Earthsea series. The geography of the Earthsea universe and other similar universes is described by Klingberg as a "detailed depiction with place names in foreign languages. Typically one draws maps of this universe" (13). According to Butler (2012), the landscape of the Earthsea universe is part of "a world (complete with endpaper map) in which medival technology, co-exists with wizardly magic" (229). She also notes that Le Guin's prose is "supple and poetic" and "shares with Tolkien's an archaic quality of cadence and word choice" (229). The maps of the mythic landscapes may help in the construction of a consistent, logical, and lucid world. The naming and the linguistic resemblance of the place names may have the same function. As with the maps of Earthsea, the place names on the map of the Land beneath the Ice have the ring of a foreign world or distant time, for example, Roselunden (the Rose Grove), Speglsalen (the Mirror Hall), and Blånebb (Blue Beak).

This is a feature Klingberg also observed, noting that there is often a clear connection between the archaic language and the fact that a great many mythical and unfamiliar worlds are medieval-like. When describing the land of Alan Garner's *Elidor* (1965), Klingberg claims that this is "a mythical land of the medieval type" (1980: 69). This characteristic seems to apply to the fantasy geography of *The Land beneath the Ice*, since the various towns Leo has to pass through are described as being narrow and maze-like.

In 1988, Nikolajeva pointed out Tolkien's distinction between a primary and a secondary world and claims that "[t]he secondary world is the most important narrative element in fantasy" (43). Nikolajeva has devoted a whole chapter to the various forms the magical places take in secondary worlds. These places can be closed, open, or implicit, and are identified as being either lands beyond our known geography, distinct planets or islands, or lands beneath the earth or sea (or ice I would add). They are accessible through a picture, a wardrobe, or an object, or are located behind a mirror or in a parallel world. In addition, Nikolajeva explores the most characteristic descriptions of the magic places, focusing in particular on Lewis' books about Narnia since "not many secondary worlds are described as minutely as Narnia" (53). A curious detail worth mentioning in relation to this is the implied reference to Lewis' Narnia when one of Leo's many transitions takes place in a wardrobe. Lewis' Narnia books pushed British children's fantasy "towards portals, myth-magic and destinarianism" (Levy & Mendlesohn 2016: 133). Lars Mæhle's novel is openly indebted to the books by Lewis.

In addition to her analysis of the magic places of fantasy novels, it is also interesting to note the way Nikolajeva relates her study to Mikhail Bakhtin's concept of the chronotope and refers to "[t]he complicated temporal relationship between the primary and the secondary chronotopes" (1988: 62). Most important to Nikolajeva is Bakhtin's idea that "each literary mode possesses its own chronotope, its own comprehension of time and space" (133). And although she is not very specific about her understanding of Bakhtin and does not actively use chronotope thinking, she returns to it in her conclusion and presents what she calls the fantasy chronotope: "a unique combination of temporal and spatial relations with one common denomination: magic, that is, non-rational presentation of extraordinary events, beings and objects" (114). The concept 'fantasy chronotope' is very much in accordance with Bakhtin's (1981) statement regarding the intrinsic generic significance of the chronotope: it "can even be said that it is precisely the chronotope that defines genre and generic distinctions" (120). According to Bakhtin, adventure time belongs to the unfamiliar world and several chronotopes may be identified as characteristic of adventure time. One of these is the road chronotope. People escape or chase along routes and roads in the landscape. Following an escape or chase, the hero or heroine often arrives at a new place and meets new people. In these plot elements, there is evidence of what Bakhtin calls the meeting and the threshold chronotopes. One specific kind of meeting takes place in public places or market places.

It seems relevant to discuss maps in fantasy novels in light of Bakhtin's characterization of the relation between time and space in what he calls adventure time. When studing *The Land beneath the Ice*, it is relevant to examine how the various chronotopes contribute to the shaping and development of the protagonist's/

protagonists' character; that is, how they are depicted as they move through the various landscapes and how these movements may be traced in the maps.

Traveling between crime and fantasy

The relation between the real and the unknown and unfamiliar is clearly expressed in *The Land beneath the Ice*, primarily in the way the chapters of the book are structured and in the landscapes displayed in the two maps in the book. The first map, located at the beginning, depicts the village of Narrow Bay; the second, at the end, depicts the Land beneath the Ice. The map depicting Narrow Bay links to the story about crime investigator Magne Jerstad's efforts to solve a criminal case in which four young people's corpses have been discovered in the cellar of a prestigious estate in Narrow Bay. The map depicting the Land beneath the Ice relates to the story of Leo Rubin and his mission in an unfamiliar landscape. However, the maps and the stories become interwoven, as elements from one story are illuminated by elements from the other.

The two stories are separated in time, which is indicated by the time markers of each chapter. Every chapter heading in the crime story is dated very precisely, for example, "Now, day 1:10 a.m." The chapter headings in the fantasy story, although less precise, follow their own pattern throughout the book, for example, "One year earlier." Throughout the book, the reader moves between the two stories. Then, in the end, in the final battle (in the estate library), the two stories merge.

The crime story in *The Land beneath the Ice* shares some of the hallmarks of both the hard-boiled crime novel and the police novel (Bergman & Kärrholm 2011; Goga 2015). Although Narrow Bay is only a small village, it is possible to detect a parallel between the dark, twisting forest path and the urban maze geography that is a well-known characteristic of hard-boiled crime stories. Investigator Jerstad is a mix of the lonely, melancholic, and physically vulnerable detective. His view of the world is critical, rational, and ironic. He describes Leo Rubin's story as "the most fantastic" he has ever heard, but he tells himself, "I won't doubt this story – however fantasizing and crazy it may sound. It is better to see if there is something to be learned from this story, whether it is true or false" (Mæhle 2009: 540). As he is leaving Narrow Bay in a helicopter at the end of the book, Jerstad's thoughts about the criminal case swing between two explanations, one rational and the other irrational or inexplicable.

The disposition of the secondary world of the fantasy story is explained with reference to a mix of legends and history of religion. Referring to the typology developed by Nikolajeva, the Land beneath the Ice could be defined as an open secondary world with recognizable medieval characteristics. It is linked to the real world, Narrow Bay, by a tunnel, but there are also several other passages that access and extend the tunnel. Access can be gained via Ulveporten (the entrance to the estate) or the dungeon of the estate, and after the tunnel, there is a suspension bridge, a solid door (at least five meters tall), a gate, and the Grenselandsbyen (Border Village). In addition, the various villages and towns in the Land beneath the Ice have city gates and alleys that have to be negotiated.

When describing the secondary worlds in fantasy novels, words like medieval and the Middle Ages are, as already mentioned, often used (see Klingberg (1980: 69), Nikolajeva (1988: 70), Immel, Knoepflmacher & Briggs (2009: 226), Ekman (2013: 45), Mostue (2014: 48), and Levy & Mendlesohn (2016: 133–159)). In many respects, the maps in fantasy novels resemble medieval maps, but the cartographic medievalness is rarely consistent. Medieval maps were usually oriented towards the east (the direction from Europe to Jerusalem); only at the beginning of the nineteenth century did north become the prevailing cartographic point of orientation (Reinhartz 2012: 2). This praxis is also the dominant one in fantasy maps. While many medieval maps had empty white spots, often in the inland area, fantasy maps seldom have such a terra incognita. Although, as Baker (2006) observes, fantasy maps have wastelands or plains in the middle, these areas are usually named and the topography is known. By mixing cartographic features of medieval maps and a modern north-south orientation, fantasy maps convey and support the purpose of the fantasy genre: to understand our own life situation through staging another time and world.

The medieval features of the secondary world in *The Land beneath the Ice* are most clearly expressed in the almost formulaic descriptions of the towns Leo travels through. In the Border Village, the streets are all paved with stones and the "stone houses are connected to each other like bunches of grapes [...] and there are alleys and tall stonewalls wherever you turn" (Mæhle 2009: 216). When Leo has to sneak out of Sørbyen (Southern Town) together with the mysterious Elyar, who serves as a guide, he describes the cityscape as dense and maze-like:

> Back in the streets again. Back in the misty dark. Back again between stalls, shops and pubs. Back in the buzz of voices. Back again between carriages, fluttering hens, wagging stray dogs and cats that slip around the corners. Back between enormous but decaying stone buildings. (302)

The traveler's, or Leo's, struggle to negotiate the mazy towns, to orient himself, and to pass through could be interpreted as the protagonist's struggle to understand what is going on in the labyrinth of his own mind.

The legend of the Land beneath the Ice states that the chosen one's role is to stifle the darkness. Leo does not understand why he has to be the chosen one. His doubts about his own ability to fill this role are continuously trickling through his mind. When Leo gets to know Elyar, who turns out to be the leader of the liberation army in the Land beneath the Ice, he learns that he has qualities that are going to be crucial to their battle: "That is what the prophecy tells. Besides, you have an important advantage: the Black Monk may underestimate you. You know the story of David and Goliath?" (249f.). The advantages Elyar refers to are the fact that Leo is unknown, bashful, and insecure, and that he does not consider himself important and unbeatable. This humble attitude means that he resembles other chosen ones, like Jesus and Mohammed, but also chosen ones familiar from children's literature, like Jonatan (and Rusky) in Astrid Lindgren's *The Brothers Lionheart* (1973), like Peter, Susan, and Lucy (and Edmund) in Lewis' *The Lion, the Witch and the Wardrobe* (1950), and like Harry Potter. They all fight in organized resistance or liberation groups, and they all have to deal with traitors.

Leo himself is not sure what it is that qualifies him to be a chosen one. He knows it has to do with *the innermost*, with "something different furthest inside" (184), but he has no clear idea what and where *the innermost* is. Is it to be sought within himself or in the inner reaches of the Mirror Hall, where the Black Monk resides? Leo's search for *the innermost* can be investigated as a crucial element in the book's central problem of *Bildung* and as a characteristic feature of the young adult novel. The search is a sort of journey. He searches for the innermost within himself at the same time as he moves deeper and deeper into the Land beneath the Ice, where the Mirror Hall could be interpreted as *the innermost* of the fantasy landscape.

Similarly, plant metaphors are often highly significant metaphors for *Bildung* in young adult literature. These metaphors coincide and connect in the image of growth and cultivation. In *The Land beneath the Ice*, it is stressed that Leo is not as tall as one would expect for his age. In order to win the struggle against the darkness and the Black Monk, he, like a plant, needs nourishment; this takes the form of knowledge about the content of the protocols, and of people with whom he can become friends. In other words, he has to be nourished by humaneness. The darkness that covers Narrow Bay, which is spread by the Black Monk, hinders and destroys nature's growth. When Leo, in the end, stifles the darkness, light returns and the landscape becomes "Fertile. Green. Full of life" (541).

The most striking difference between the two maps of the book is the tension between light and dark. The Narrow Bay map is dominated by the black fill color that is used between the depicted buildings, streets, woods, and bodies of water (Figure 1). The map design highlights the creepy and dark atmosphere in the village. The atmosphere is due to the black smoke that is pouring out of the nearby glacier. On the map depicting the Land beneath the Ice, the color black appears like a wall behind Mount Blue Beak in the north. It can be deduced that this is located to the north of Southern Town. In contrast, it is difficult to decide what is

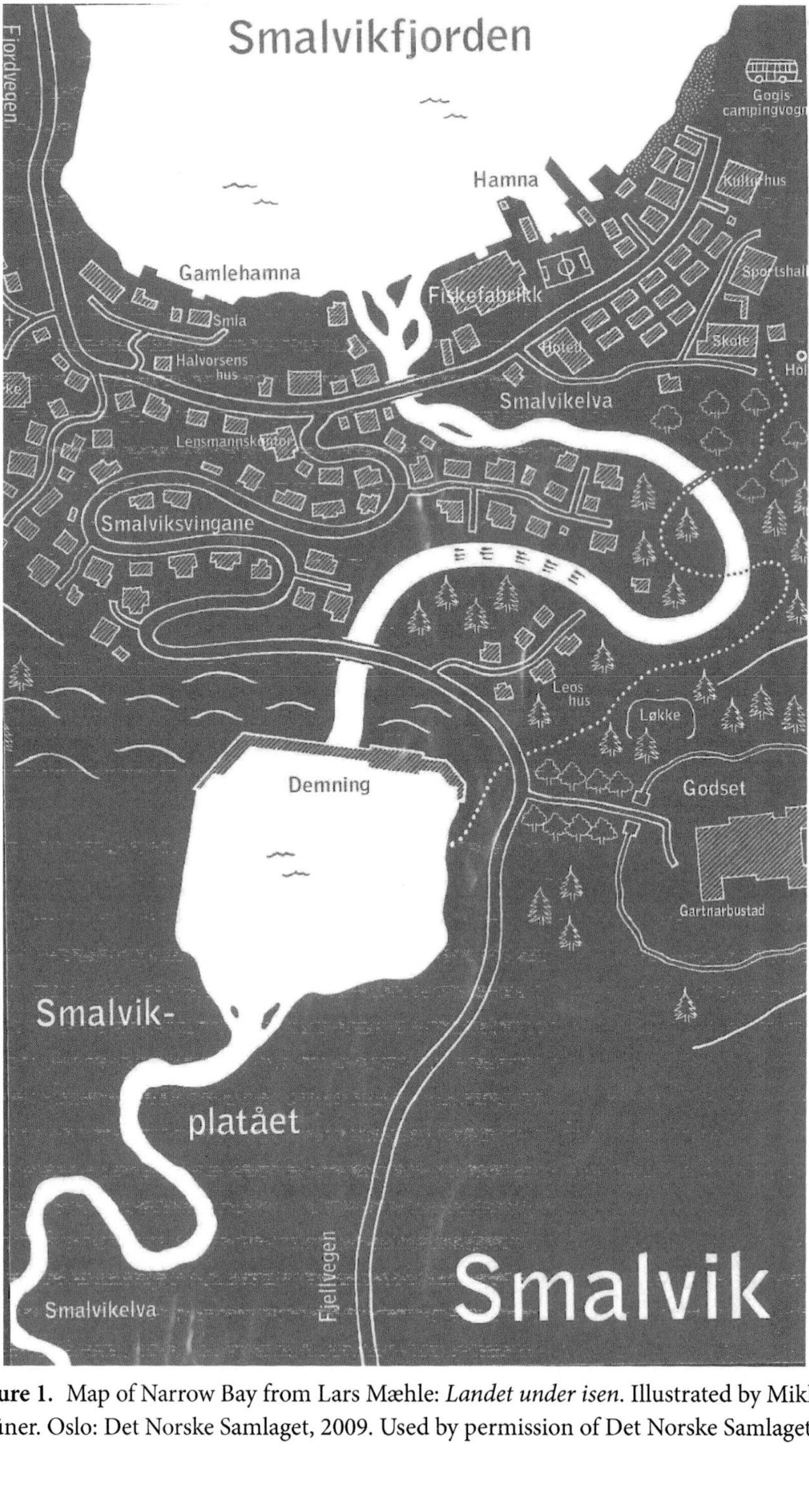

Figure 1. Map of Narrow Bay from Lars Mæhle: *Landet under isen*. Illustrated by Mikkel Grüner. Oslo: Det Norske Samlaget, 2009. Used by permission of Det Norske Samlaget

north on the Narrow Bay map, and to decide exactly where the passage between the two worlds is positioned. The tunnel is in the estate cellar, but it is very long and there is no indication of what direction it takes. It is possible to deduce that north on the Narrow Bay map lies where the base of the mountain plateau is depicted, based on the position of Blue Beak and the investigator's reflections on the mountain when he arrives in the village: "the mountain towers above the inner part of the glacier" (9). Thus, the bottom of the Narrow Bay map covers or is close to the bottom of the Land beneath the Ice map.

By tracing on the map the description of the place given by the investigator when he arrives by helicopter, the reader can gain quite a clear survey of the village and how it is "squeezed between mountains at the end of a fjord arm" (8). The name Narrow Bay suits the topography of the place. The Narrow Bay map is provided with few of the features that Dennis Reinhartz (2012) lists as typical of the anatomy of maps; it lacks features such as scale, a compass rose, and abstract symbols. The stamped text, "Smalvik," signals only the map's theme. All the buildings and the soccer field are drawn with the precision of a city planner. The perspective is close to vertical, but some details give the impression of the landscape being viewed from an oblique angle. In contrast, the trees and "Gogi's caravan" are viewed from the side. This mix of perspectives coincides with the prevailing atmosphere of the place. The on-going investigation involves a detailed mapping of possible suspects' movements at the time of the crime. While this mapping can create a feeling of a degree of security and faith in a rational explanation, the village and the investigator are troubled by a sensation of being under surveillance. The viewpoint in the oblique perspective seems to be located somewhere on the mountain plateau, which is close to the residence of the Black Monk.

Mapped movement

As with other maps in crime novels, crucial buildings and places – such as the estate, the winding path, and the meandering river – are marked on the Narrow Bay map. The winding path serves as the supporting axis of the crime story's topography. Thus, the map works as an index of the investigator's movements during the twenty-four hours from his arrival until his meeting with Leo in the estate library, where he gives Leo the powerful amulet that permits him to defeat the darkness. Although the crime story does not function as a whodunit crime (in Norwegian, and Swedish, often termed puslespillkrim/pusseldecakar [puzzle crime]), the investigator applies a puzzle metaphor when he solves the case and reveals the Black Monk's identity: "All the pieces fell into place" (Mæhle 2009: 502). We may imagine the Narrow Bay map as the board on which the pieces are intended to fall into place, and the pieces are those that the investigator and the reader have collected by pacing out the village house by house. While the map lacks an indication of scale, the time spent by the investigator moving between the various places and the detailed descriptions of these movements make it possible for the reader to gain an impression of the distances between places and buildings. Each chapter in the crime story is linked to a visit the investigator pays to one of the characters involved in the case. Immediately after his arrival, Jerstad visits the crime scene, and then he moves to the police station, the school, Leo's grandparents' house, Narrow Bay hotel, the church, the blacksmith's workshop, and so on.

Jerstad is constantly moving, and at a great pace. His restlessness also establishes a complex picture of the investigator as systematic, intuitive, analytical, and sensuous. The description of his movements and of the places he calls at serves to increase the suspense. This is particularly evident in the depiction of his walks on the steep and winding forest path. The detailed description of these passages almost invites the reader to trace his progress on the map. The detective's wanderings along the path simulate his thought processes; following the path "clear[s] his thoughts" (453). He walks, reflects, doubts – afraid of overlooking something of importance. In the midst of this, his thoughts also turn to religious and philosophical speculation. Several times during his investigation, Jerstad returns to the path. Finally, at the end, he understands that he will find the answer to the puzzle on the estate and in the dungeon and the tunnel there. When the pieces fall into place and the last battle is about to be fought, the library maze replaces the winding path. Once again, he has to find his way through it. His way of moving along the forest path has been stored as an embodied experience and a cognitive map that he activates in the final moments. In addition, the amulet he is holding in his hand leads him "faster and faster between bookshelves and books criss-crossing the corridors as in a maze of streets and dead-end roads" (522).

Like the Narrow Bay map, the map depicting the Land beneath the Ice provides few traditional cartographic features (Figure 2). The scale is only understandable in the light of the verbal specification of the time spent moving from one place to another. Otherwise, the map has several features characteristic of fantasy maps, such as a mountain in the north, and wasteland and desert in the middle; but there are no rivers, coastlines, or water. In addition, medieval features are detectable in the oblique perspective and the way the various towns are depicted. The printed text at the bottom signals the theme of the map, and scattered on the map are some features that may symbolize that which sparkles as a "bright grain of dust." As mentioned, the name Southern Town may indicate the way the map is oriented: "In the Land beneath the Ice there are three tribes, each one settled in their own town. The youngest tribe lives in the south, the middle tribe in the Mid-empire and the oldest tribe in the far north" (140). Hence the presumed north-south

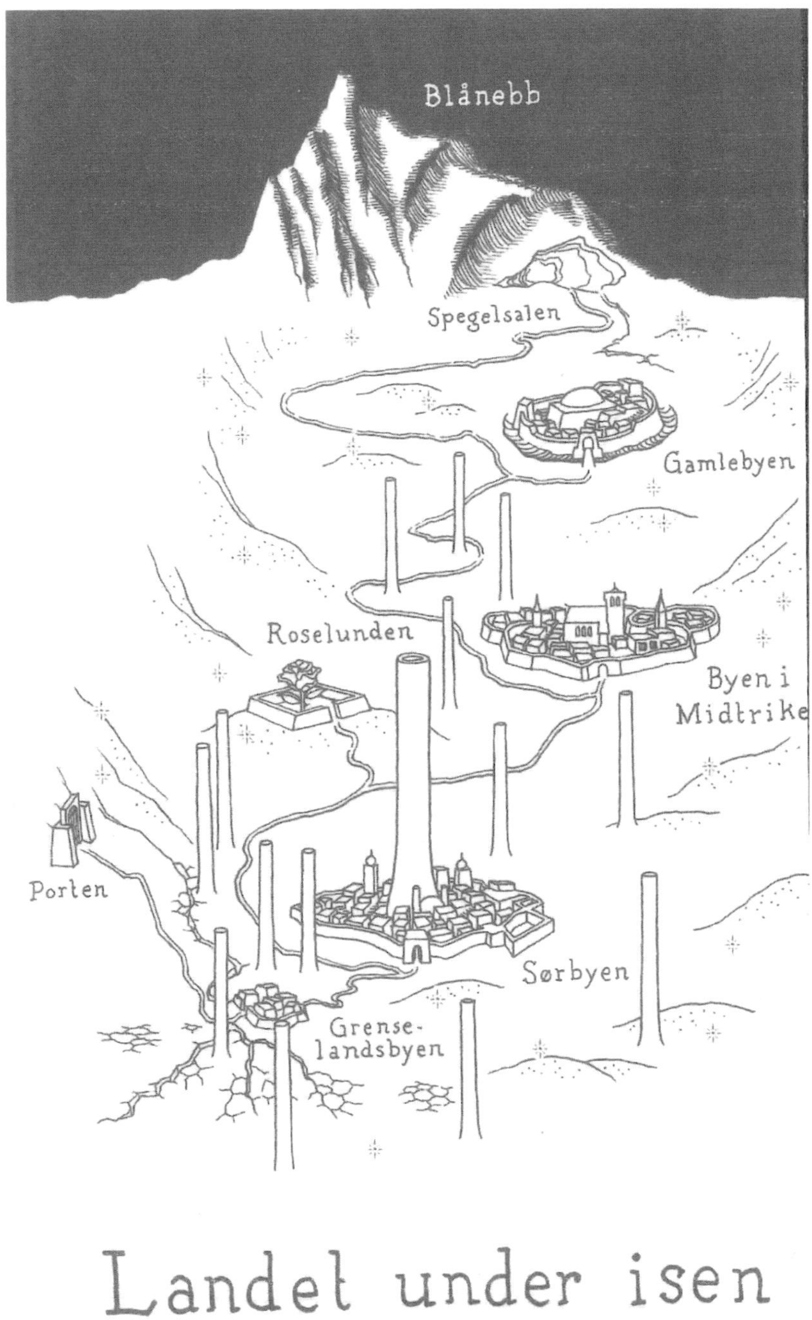

Figure 2. Map of the Land beneath the Ice from Lars Mæhle: *Landet under isen*. Illustrated by Mikkel Grüner. Oslo: Det Norske Samlaget, 2009. Used by permission of Det Norske Samlaget

orientation is supported by the description of the Land beneath the Ice presented to Leo on his way through the tunnel.

Leo's first encounter with this landscape is not necessarily the reader's first encounter. An observant reader has already discovered the map at the back, and in the light of this, has already imagined how the landscape features and the various towns are distributed and connected. At first the Land beneath the Ice fascinates Leo. The landscape is bathed in a blue light that creates a peculiar atmosphere. However, his gaze is soon directed away from the heavenly light to the earth he is to walk upon.

As Leo enters the various towns, the reader who studies the map will not only recognize the medieval looking town arrangement, but also the various religious buildings characteristic of the tribe: the minaret of Southern Town, the church of Midtriket (Mid Empire), and the synagogue of Gamlebyen (Old Town). Another remarkable building on the map is the ziggurat, explained verbally as "old temple towers" (215) and "sepulchres" (216). Leo learns that "the tallest and holiest ziggurat is found in Southern Town, in the middle of the enormous temple square" (216). Later, when he enters the ziggurat, he describes the building as a landmark and the "center of the compass needle" (253). This is in accordance with the history of architecture, which views the ziggurat as the "center of the world" and as "the earthly throne of the gods, a ladder to heaven, a monumental sacrificial altar" (Tuan 1974: 91).

Although the reader may already have studied the maps depicting the Land beneath the Ice long before Leo arrives there halfway through the book, the interaction between the text and map only fully comes into play when Leo's wanderings begin. While the investigator's movements are characterized by criss-crossing, Leo's movements have a more decisive direction. This decisiveness is evident in the roads included on the map. In contrast to the investigator, who constantly has to allow for possible route shifts, Leo's challenge is to reach a specific goal. Part of this challenge has to do with his physical limitations. Already at the beginning of his journey, he breaks his ankle. This hampers his movements and plays a crucial role not only in the construction of suspense, but also in his fulfillment of the quest. The quest is not only related to the battle of good versus evil and dark forces, but also about achieving self-knowledge (and knowledge about his parents), and about maturation and growth – about *Bildung*.

There are numerous examples of travel metaphors (referring to Trites 2014) in the novel. Already in Border Village, the liberation soldier Omar tells Leo that "the route to freedom goes through the chosen one" (227); and in the second protocol, he reads, "the real journey, the route to the real route, passes through the journey of the soul. It passes through the heart" (281). In other words, Leo's journey from Narrow Bay through the Land beneath the Ice is a religious journey of liberation for those who inhabit the Land beneath the Ice, and a personal journey of *Bildung* from child to adult for Leo himself.

As mentioned, Leo cannot move freely and the implications of this warrant closer examination. The text offers evidence of his pain on several occasions:

> We are walking. The solid soil bumps against the soles of our feet. Every bump against the sole hurts. The pain in my ankle is worse than ever. Red shadows dance in front of me, merging with the dark blue ahead of me. (228)

At the beginning of his journey, various guides accompany Leo, but eventually he has to find his own way, and in Old Town, he has to hide. When he decides to continue, he is exhausted: "My body is hollowed, weak; I can hardly manage to drag myself forward. Despite this, I force my feet to go on through the streets, through the smoke, through the terrible smell and through the soundlessness" (427). The way his movements are described becomes increasingly physical and near-sighted, and at the same time more distant: "My shoes move mechanically. One in front of the other. I observe them. They appear to be strangers. My body. My feet. Those who are walking in front of me on the cold, solid desert sand, this burned, desolated landscape" (429). When finally he reaches his goal, his pace becomes gentler although it still "smarts" (429). He also tries to rally his wits: "Focus on the quest. That is the most important thing. I have to gather the threads, pick out the important elements in the protocols" (430). As in the case of the investigator, there is a connection between the movements of Leo's body and the flow of his thoughts. Hence, his physical disorder reflects a psychic disorder. The battle between good and evil, light and dark is also a battle between love and hate, and an attempt to understand "those strange gusts of mind" (382). Thus, the journey and the fight for liberation take place as much in the human mind as in the maze-like, medieval towns and on the winding roads of the Land beneath the Ice.

In the innermost part of the Land beneath the Ice, the Mirror Hall at the foot of Mount Blue Beak, Leo kills the traitor Julian and his father, and then stifles the last piece of light. Darkness and black smoke pour out over the landscape. These killings mark the turning point of the journey. Leo now heads back to Narrow Bay, but he is not walking. Instead, he glides through the landscape and is out of contact with himself: "You know nothing. That is what is unbearable. You can only glide and glide upon the landscape [...]" (463). This absence of the senses lasts until Leo is back in Narrow Bay and once again feels pain and exhaustion. The last stage of his progress up to the estate is out of his control: "my feet run driven by fever" (488). The fever directs his movements and guides him to and through the library maze to where the Black Monk is revealed together with the content of the last protocol. The protocol explains the relationship between love and hate or anger and gives no final answer as to which one of these is the main human force, which one "propels us" (514). The Black Monk, who believed Leo had been stiffened by death rage after killing Julian and his father, asks Leo "Are you not able to proceed?" (517), and this is true until the investigator arrives and gives him the amulet. In possession of the amulet, Leo is able to move on, to "see the right route" and thereby become "a true traveler" (285). The aim of the quest is twofold: to enable light, seasons, and the natural order to return to Narrow Bay, and to initiate Leo as a true traveler, one who knows the mazes of the human mind.

The true traveler

Trites' study of growth metaphors in young adult novels reveals that the growth and maturation of literary characters is often expressed in comparisons with processes found in cycles in nature. Becoming a true traveler means undergoing an organic and mental transformation. In *The Land beneath the Ice*, this is depicted as winding one's way "like the snake out of its skin" (528), and thereby casting off one's old skin and changing character. The process by which Leo casts off his skin may be interpreted as a ritual passage from childhood to adulthood, as a crucial moment in the process of maturation.

The Land beneath the Ice is a fantasy novel in which the battle between good and evil is fought in the light of reflections upon the possibilities for peaceful coexistence between people of different religious beliefs. Nevertheless, the major religious questions regarding the inner truth of man are epitomized in a young boy's search for knowledge about his own heritage and his own ethical values. Thus, *The Land beneath the Ice* is also a Bildungsroman in which the ability to find one's way in a strange and estranged landscape is of the greatest importance, providing opportunities for personal growth, intellectual as well as physical. The fact that the book has maps that may help the reader follow in the footsteps of the protagonists also gives the reader the opportunity to become a traveler, not only in the two worlds of the fiction, but perhaps also in her own inner, fantastic landscape.

Acknowledgements

This chapter is based on an extensive examination of three Nordic fantasy novels for children and young adults published in Goga (2015).

References

Primary source

Mæhle, Lars. 2009. *Landet under isen*. Oslo: Det Norske Samlaget.

Secondary sources

Baker, Deirdre F. 2006. What we found on our journey through fantasy land. *Children's Literature in Education* 3: 237–251. doi: 10.1007/s10583-006-9009-1

Bakhtin, Mikhail M. 1981. Forms of time and of the chronotope in the novel. In *The Dialogic Imagination*, Michael Holquist (ed.), 119–258. Austin TX: University of Texas Press.

Bergman, Kerstin & Kärrholm, Sara. 2011. *Kriminallitteratur. Utveckling, genrer, perspektiv*. Lund: Studentlitteratur.

Butler, Catherine. 2012. Modern children's fantasy. In *The Cambridge Companion to Fantasy Literature*, Edward James & Farah Mendlesohn (eds), 224–235. Cambridge: CUP. doi: 10.1017/CCOL9780521429597.021

Ekman, Stefan. 2013. *Here Be Dragons: Exploring Fantasy Maps and Settings*. Middletown CT: Wesleyan.

Emanuelsen, Marius. 2010. Hjemme best. <http://www.barnebokkritikk.no/modules.php?name=Reviews&rop=showcontent&id=714> (29 May 2014).

Goga, Nina. 2015. *Kart i barnelitteraturen*. Kristiansand: Portal Akademisk.

Immel, Andrea, Knoepflmacher, U. C. & Briggs, Julia. 2009. Fantasy's alternative geography for children. In *The Cambridge Companion to Children's Literature*, M. O. Grenby & Andrea Immel (eds), 226–241. Cambridge: CUP. doi: 10.1017/CCOL9780521868198.014

Klingberg, Göte. 1980. *De främmande världarna i barne- och ungdomslitteraturen*. Stockholm: Rabén & Sjögren.

Levy, Michael & Mendlesohn, Farah. 2016. *Children's Fantasy Literature. An Introduction*. Cambridge: CUP.

Mendlesohn, Farah. 2008. *Rhetorics of Fantasy*. Middletown CT: Wesleyan.

Mostue, Sigbjørn. 2014. Fantasy – fra uhu til aha. In *BU1405 Skriftserie for barne- og ungdomslitteratur*, Helga G. Eriksen & Hilde K. Kvalvaag (eds), 39–62. Oslo: Norske Barne- og Ungdomsbokforfattere.

Nikolajeva, Maria. 1988. *The Magic Code. The Use of Magical Patterns in Fantasy for Children*. Stockholm: Almqvist & Wiksell.

Reinhartz, Dennis. 2012. *The Art of the Map*. New York NY: Sterling.

Skyggebjerg, Anna Karlskov. 2005. *Den fantastiske fortælling i dansk børnelitteratur 1967–2003*. Fredriksberg: Roskilde Universitetsforlag.

Sundmark, Björn. 2014a. 'Dragons be here': Teaching children's literature and creative writing with the help of maps. In *Thinking through Children's Literature in the Classroom*, Agustín Reyes-Torres, Luis S. Villacañas-de-Castro & Betlem Soler-Pardo (eds), 64–78. Newcastle-upon-Tyne: Cambridge Scholars.

Sundmark, Björn. 2014b. 'A serious game': Mapping Moominland. *The Lion and the Unicorn* 38(2): 162–181. doi: 10.1353/uni.2014.0022

Sundmark, Björn. 2017. Mapping Middle Earth: A Tolkienian legacy. In *Maps and Mapping in Children's Literature. Landscapes, Seascapes, and Cityscapes* [Children's Literature,

Culture, and Cognition 6], Nina Goga & Bettina Kümmerling-Meibauer (eds), 123–139. Amsterdam: John Benjamins.

Trites, Roberta Seelinger. 2014. *Literary Conceptualizations of Growth. Metaphors and Cognition in Adolescent Literature* [Children's Literature, Culture, and Cognititon 2]. Amsterdam: John Benjamins.

Tuan, Yi-Fu. 1974. *Topophilia. A Study of Environmental Perception, Attitudes, and Values.* Princeton NJ: Prentice-Hall.

About the editors and contributors

Marnie Campagnaro got her PhD in Pedagogical and Educational Sciences, and teaches Theory and History of Children's Literature in Educational and Training Sciences at the University of Padua. For many years she has been dealing with cultural projects on children's literature, reading promotion, visual literacy, and narrative and imaginative thinking in children. In 2013 she succeeded in hosting the "Ninth International 'The Child and the Book' Conference" at the University of Padua. Three of her most recent publications are *Incanto e racconto nel labirinto delle figure. Albi illustrati e relazione educative* (Enchantment and Stories in the Maze of Pictures. Picturebooks and Education, with Marco Dallari, 2013), *Le terre della fantasia. Leggere la letteratura per l'infanzia e l'adolescenza* (Fantasy Lands. Reading Children's Literature, 2014), and a book chapter "'These books made me really curious': How visual explorations shape the young reader's taste" (2015, in *Challenging and Controversial Picturebooks*, ed. by Janet Evans, Routledge).

Anna Juan Cantavella holds a PhD in Social and Cultural Anthropology and is a specialist in children's literature. She is currently working as a visiting professor at the Universidad Autònoma de Barcelona, Spain, where she teaches children's literature, and is a member of the research group GRETEL (Barcelona), which investigates the relationship between children's literature and literacy. Her current research focuses on the analysis of city representations in picturebooks.

Nina Goga is a Professor at Western Norway University of Applied Sciences, Norway, where she is in charge of the only Norwegian MA program in children's literature. She is currently leading the research project "Nature in Children's Literature: Landscapes and Beings – Fostering Ecocitizens" at Bergen University College (http://blogg.hvl.no/nachilit/). Some of her recent publications are the monographs *Kart i barnelitteraturen* (Maps in Children's Literature, 2015) and *Gå til mauren. Om maur og danning i barnelitteraturen* (Go to the Ant. On Ants and Bildung in Children's Literature, 2013), and the book chapters "Learn to Read. Learn to Live. The Role of Books and Book Collections in Picturebooks" (2013, in *Picturebooks: Representation and Narration*, ed. by Bettina Kümmerling-Meibauer, Routledge) and "Children and Childhood in Scandinavian Children's Literature over the Last Fifty Years" (2013, in *Bologna: Fifty Years of Children's Books from around the World*, ed. by Giorgia Grilli).

Janet Grafton is a PhD candidate in the Environmental Studies Department at the University of Northern British Columbia in Canada. Her research centers on the use of farm narratives as a means of approaching issues of food security. This project has evolved from both academic and practical experience: in her Master's thesis, she applied ecocriticism to an analysis of the transformative capacity of green spaces in children's literature; she then spent three years working as an organic farmer before beginning her doctoral work. The end goal of her PhD project is to increase food literacy by developing a curriculum that incorporates narratives in environmental education programs for children. She teaches literature at Vancouver Island University, and continues to be involved with the farming community on Salt Spring Island, BC.

Anna Katrina Gutierrez is a children's literature expert from the Philippines. Following a PhD in Children's Literature at Macquarie University in Sydney, she completed fellowships at the Swedish Institute for Children's Books, the Hans Christian Andersen Centre, and the International Youth Library. Her publications include articles in *International Research in Children's Literature* and the *Journal for Graphic Novels and Comics*. Her doctoral thesis was awarded the Vice Chancellor's Commendation and is the basis of her book *Mixed Magic. Glocal-local dialogues in fairy tales for young readers* (John Benjamins, 2017). Katrina is the Communications & Project Manager of Lantana Publishing, where she pours her academic energies into producing beautiful books all children can enjoy.

Olga Holownia holds a PhD in English and Icelandic Studies and her research interests include contemporary Icelandic literature and culture, children's literature, poetry in performance, literary nonsense, and poetry translation. She has published articles and book chapters primarily on retellings and adaptations of myths and folktales, Icelandic folklore and mythology, literary nonsense, illustrations in children's books, and reception of translated literature, as well as on concrete poetry and the dramatic monologue. For the last several years she has been translating contemporary Icelandic and Polish poetry.

Bettina Kümmerling-Meibauer is a Professor in the German Department at the University of Tübingen. She has been a guest professor at the University of Växjö, Sweden, and the University of Vienna. She is the author of an international encyclopedia of international children's classics (Metzler, 1999) and a monograph on canon processes in children's literature (Metzler, 2003). Her (co-)edited books include *New Directions in Picturebook Research* (Routledge, 2010), *Emergent Literacy. Children's Books from 0 to 3* (Benjamins, 2011, Turkish translation in 2015),

Manga's Cultural Crossroads (Routledge, 2013), *Picturebooks. Representation and Narration* (Routledge, 2014), *Learning from Picturebooks. Perspectives from Child Development and Literacy Studies* (Routledge, 2015), *Children's Literature and the Avant-garde* (Benjamins, 2015 awarded the "Edited Book Award 2017" by the Children's Literature Association), and *Canon Constitution and Canon Change in Children's Literature* (Routledge, 2017). She has been the chair of the international project "Children's Literature and European Avant-garde," funded by the European Science Foundation. She is also the editor of the *Routledge Companion to Picturebooks* (Routledge, forthcoming). Her joint work with Jörg Meibauer aims at developing a cognitive theory of picturebooks.

Lynn S. Liben is a Distinguished Professor of Psychology at The Pennsylvania State University (USA), holding faculty appointments in the College of Health & Human Development and the College of Education. Her research focuses on spatial cognition, its development, and on how individual differences in spatial cognition are relevant for science education. Illustrative is her research examining children's and adults' success in identifying locations and directions on maps, and adults' success in mapping geological data. She has applied her research to educational programs for television, museums, and classrooms. A second research focus is on gender development and gender stereotypes, and how these influence children's educational and occupational goals. Liben is a past president of the Society for Research in Child Development, former president of the Piaget Society and of the Developmental Psychology Division of APA, and past editor of *Child Development* and of the *Journal of Experimental Child Psychology*. She is a fellow of the American Psychological Association, the Eastern Psychological Association, the Association for Psychological Science, and the American Educational Research Association, and a member of the National Academy of Sciences' Board of Science Education. She earned her BA at Cornell University and her PhD at the University of Michigan, both in psychology.

Corina Löwe is a Senior Lecturer in German Language and Literature in the Language Department of Linnaeus University, Sweden. In 2011 she defended her thesis *Von Jungen Pionieren und Gangstern. Der Kinder- und Jugendkriminalroman in der DDR* on East German detective novels for children at Stockholm University. She has published several articles on East German children's literature, for instance, on travel descriptions, intermedial aspects of Berlin in texts and films, Astrid Lindgren's work, and the didactics of literature teaching. She is currently working on a book-length study of the depiction of Berlin in children's literature. As a member of the Linnaeus University Centre for Intermedial and Multimodal Studies she is involved in two research projects: "The Anthropocene in Aesthetic Media" and "Transmediations in and of Trials."

Jörg Meibauer is a Professor of German Language and Linguistics at the Johannes Gutenberg University Mainz, Germany, and Affiliated Professor at the University of Stockholm, Sweden. He has written monographs on rhetorical questions, modal particles, pragmatics, and lying, and co-edited several collections, for instance, on sentence types, constructions, context, and pejoration. Currently, he is editing the *Oxford Handbook of Lying*. In particular, he is interested in the relation between linguistics and children's literature. His joint work with Bettina Kümmerling-Meibauer aims at developing a cognitive theory of picturebooks.

Nikola von Merveldt is an Associate Professor of German Studies in the Department of Literatures and Languages of the World at the University of Montréal, Canada. Following her studies in medieval and comparative literature in Strasbourg, France, Neuchâtel, Switzerland, Cambridge, UK, and Munich, Germany, she now works on children's literature and explores the ways in which knowledge is presented in informational literature. She is a founding member of the interdisciplinary research group on book history "Interacting with Print. Cultural Practices of Intermediality (1750–1850)" and an associate fellow of the International Youth Library in Munich.

Olga Mikhaylova is an Associate Professor at Moscow State Pedagogical University. She specializes in the history of Russian children's literature, focusing on the reader-response approach, genre and chronotope studies, the concept of visual literacy, and digital forms of literature. Many of her articles were published in Russian refereed journals. From 2013 to 2016 she worked on a monograph devoted to Russian children's literature of the 1960s at the International Youth Library in Munich as an independent researcher. At present she is preparing an academic edition of Victor Dragunsky's stories for children (to be published in 2017).

Maria Nikolajeva is a Professor of Children's Literature at the Faculty of Education, University of Cambridge, and the director of the Cambridge Research and Teaching Centre for Children's Literature. She is the author and editor of numerous books, including *Power, Voice and Subjectivity in Literature for Young Readers* (Routledge, 2010) and *Reading for Learning: Cognitive Approaches to Children's Literature* (Benjamins, 2014). In 2005 she received the International Grimm Award for lifetime achievement in children's literature research.

Björn Sundmark is a Professor of English Literature at Malmö University, Sweden, where he teaches "Children's Literature in a Global Perspective" and "Intercultural Perspectives on Children's Literature." He has published numerous articles on children's literature, and is the author of the study *Alice in the Oral-Literary Continuum* (Lund University Press, 1999). He is the editor (together with Christopher Kelen) of *The Nation in Children's Literature* (Routledge, 2013) and

Child Autonomy and Child Governance in Children's Literature: Where Children Rule (Routledge, 2016). In addition, he is the editor of *Bookbird – Journal of International Children's Literature* and associate editor of *Barnboken. Journal of Children's Literature Research.*

Liz Taylor is a Senior Lecturer at the Faculty of Education, University of Cambridge, UK. Her research interests focus on children's and young people's understandings of place and space, geography education, and rural schooling. Currently she is working on representations of Japan in English geography textbooks 1850–2000. She has collaborated with Maria Nikolajeva and other colleagues to explore various aspects of place and space linked to children's literature, including fictional fens, children's place-based identities, and representations of beds in picturebooks.

Name index

Subject index